T0249128

PRAISE FOR

Saint Hildegard:
Ancient Insights for Modern Seekers

"This is indeed a spiritual gem and one that will profoundly touch and inspire. I was very much taken with the sections on discernment and mysticism. The areas of discernment in St. Hildegard's writing were elucidated effectively. Such a labor of love."

—SUSAN BOWERS BAKER, spiritual guide and retired Director of the Jesuit Center for Spiritual Growth in Wernersville, PA

"Quotes from St. Hildegard became accessible through the seamless weaving of her words into the author's own narrative. They have life and are current for today's spiritual seeker. The personal sharing is interesting and humble, and thus helpful. The parts connected to the author's personal story are the most compelling. It was all quite rich."

—CATHIE GAUTHIER, spiritual director and author of *Nine-Tenths Love*

"Drawing on her vocation as a spiritual director and on her experience of prayer, Garthwaite brings St. Hildegard's writings vividly to life by connecting them to stories from her own vibrant spiritual journey. This rich account bridges the gap between the twelfth century and our own, illuminating the timelessness of Hildegard's wisdom for us today."

—CRISTINA L.H. TRAINA, Avery Cardinal Dulles, SJ, Chair in Catholic Theology, Fordham University

Saint Hildegard

SAINT HILDEGARD

Ancient Insights for
Modern Seekers

SUSAN GARTHWAITE

swp

SHE WRITES PRESS

Copyright © 2021 Susan Garthwaite

All rights reserved. No part of this publication may be reproduced, distributed, or transmitted in any form or by any means, including photocopying, recording, digital scanning, or other electronic or mechanical methods, without the prior written permission of the publisher, except in the case of brief quotations embodied in critical reviews and certain other noncommercial uses permitted by copyright law. For permission requests, please address She Writes Press.

Published 2021
Printed in the United States of America
Print ISBN: 978-1-64742-181-6
E-ISBN: 978-1-64742-182-3

Library of Congress Control Number: 2021910252
For information, address:
She Writes Press
1569 Solano Ave #546
Berkeley, CA 94707

She Writes Press is a division of SparkPoint Studio, LLC.

Book design by Stacey Aaronson

All company and/or product names may be trade names, logos, trademarks, and/or registered trademarks and are the property of their respective owners.

Names and identifying characteristics have been changed to protect the privacy of certain individuals.

PERMISSIONS

Scripture quotations contained herein are from the New Revised Standard Version, the HarperCollins Study Bible, Copyright © 1989 and 1993, by the Division of Christian Education of the National Council of the Churches of Christ in the United States of America. Used by permission. All rights reserved.

Excerpts from The Book of Divine Works (Liber Divinorum Operum) by Hildegard of Bingen, translated by Nathaniel M. Campbell, Copyright © 2018 by Catholic University of America Press, Washington, D.C., republished with permission of Catholic University Press conveyed through Copyright Clearance Center, Inc.

Excerpts from The Book of the Rewards of Life (Liber Vitae Meritorum) by Hildegard of Bingen, translated by Bruce W. Hozeski, Copyright © 1994 by Bruce W. Hozeski, Oxford University Press, Oxford/New York. Reproduced with permission of the Licensor through PLSclear, Ltd.

Excerpts from Homilies on the Gospels (Expositiones Evangeliorum) by Hildegard of Bingen, translated by Beverly Mayne Kienzle, Copyright © 2011 by Order of Saint Benedict, Collegeville, Minnesota, republished with permission of Liturgical Press, Collegeville, MN conveyed through Copyright Clearance Center, Inc.

Excerpts from The Letters of Hildegard of Bingen (Hildegardis Bingensis Epistolarium), Volume I, translated by Joseph L. Baird and Radd K. Ehrman, Copyright © 1994, Oxford University Press, Oxford/New York. Reproduced with permission of the Licensor.

Excerpts from The Letters of Hildegard of Bingen (Hildegardis Bingensis Epistolarium), Volume II, translated by Joseph L. Baird and Radd K. Ehrman, Copyright © 1998, Oxford University Press, Oxford/New York. Reproduced with permission of the Licensor.

Excerpts from The Letters of Hildegard of Bingen (Hildegardis Bingensis Epistolarium), Volume III, translated by Joseph L. Baird and Radd K. Ehrman, Copyright © 2004, Oxford University Press, Oxford/New York. Reproduced with permission of the Licensor.

Excerpts from Scivias by Hildegard of Bingen, from The Classics of Western Spirituality, translated by Mother Columba Hart and Jane Bishop, Copyright ©1990 by The Abbey of Regina Laudis: Benedictine Congregation Regina Laudis of the Strict Observance, Inc., Paulist Press, Inc., New York/Mahwah, N.J. Used with permission of Paulist Press conveyed through Copyright Clearance Center, Inc.

Excerpts from Solutions to Thirty-Eight Questions (Solutiones Triginta Octo Quaestionum) by Hildegard of Bingen, translated by Beverly Mayne Kienzle with Jenny C. Bledsoe and Stephen H. Behnke, Copyright © 2014 by Order of Saint Benedict, Collegeville, Minnesota, republished with permission of Liturgical Press, Collegeville, MN conveyed through Copyright Clearance Center, Inc.

❧

This Book is dedicated to my dear friends Susan, Ollie, and Basia, who inspire me to be my true self at my best; to my godsons, Mark and Gregory, and all my vast family, who energize my prayer; to Mom (may she rest in peace), who was my first spiritual director and who always encouraged me to write; to all who see integrity in endnotes and permissions; to St. Hildegard, my wise and steadfast collaborator, who reminds me to "never stop working for God"; and to God, the Main Character of this book.

Be a faithful friend to your soul. . . . Be the special friend of God.

—ST. HILDEGARD OF BINGEN

TABLE OF CONTENTS

preface

St. Hildegard is a fascinating spiritual guide, but her works are not easy to read. Today we have direct translations of her works, books with excerpts of her works, and books that examine her theology, her music, or her context. In the translations, St. Hildegard's gems and pearls of spiritual wisdom are tucked inside her long descriptions or exegesis of unusual visions. Three volumes of letters from St. Hildegard and a book of her homilies also contain pertinent messages for readers who work their way through them.

Each time I facilitated reflection days about St. Hildegard in past years, attendees requested an accessible book of her spiritual wisdom with which to pray. I could not find such a book.

The dilemma stayed with me. St. Hildegard was already influencing my spiritual life and my work as a spiritual director. I was struck by her contemporary relevance despite her twelfth-century context. I had grown in fondness and trust of her as a spiritual guide. Then it hit me: I had found and gathered the potent gems and pearls others wanted. I was partway to the book they were seeking.

I carefully and prayerfully discerned whether I was called to write this book. Finally, I said yes to God and St. Hildegard, and our collaboration was born.

Many fits and starts later, I went on retreat and prayed to be guided by my collaborators. Once gems and pearls are teased out of their original context and allowed to shine brightly, they still need a context. What was it? Where was this book going?

On retreat I asked, "What was St. Hildegard's relationship with

God? How did she know God?" My retreat director invited me to set my own answers next to St. Hildegard's. St. Hildegard provided insight into my spiritual stories, but she provided little spiritual autobiographical material of her own. I finally understood that my stories were her stories, her route to accessibility, her new context. And so we began to be in each paragraph together. I hope that she will come to be in the paragraphs of your spiritual stories as well.

St. Hildegard provided the main structure of this book. She says, "Be a faithful friend to your soul"[1] and "Be such that you become the friend of God."[2] One leads to the other. God draws us into friendship in a profound way. The stories reveal that the journey is not perfectly linear. Like us, St. Hildegard sometimes struggled to be the woman God called her to be. She resisted, then capitulated, and then, with grace, came through. She speaks to our journey.

St. Hildegard contributes unique insights for the spiritual direction ministry. Therefore, I decided to discuss spiritual direction in these pages as well. Perhaps you are a spiritual director or aspire to become one. Throughout this book, I offer example spiritual stories for your reflection on directing others. I also share vignettes of how I've handled my own spiritual direction of others. I encourage you to reflect and consider how you would guide people in these situations.

You will also discover reflection questions in the chapters to follow that will invite you to go deeper in your own spiritual experiences and pray about your growth in friendship with your soul and with God. May there be a "before this book" and an "after this book" in your own being.

St. Hildegard and I pray: "We hold you with joy in our hearts, being confident in God that through God's grace, you will be made God's dear friend."[3]

introduction

———•••———

S t. Hildegard of Bingen is the fourth woman to have been named a Doctor of the Church. She was born in 1098 to noble parents in what is now Germany. While she was still a child, her parents tithed her to God, and she was raised by the anchoress Jutta of Sponheim. They lived in a hermitage associated with the monastery of St. Disibod, a community of men. As a teenager, Hildegard made her vows as a Benedictine. When Jutta died, Hildegard succeeded her as the leader of the group of nuns that had come to live with them. Eventually, in 1150, Hildegard founded a new community for the nuns at Rupertsberg. By 1165 that abbey was thriving, and Hildegard founded a second one across the Rhine River at Eibingen.

From her earliest memory on, Hildegard had visions. In 1141 she experienced a call from God to write about them, for now she had a spiritual understanding of them. She confided in a monk, Volmar, who was her guide, and he assisted her as her first secretary. Through her early writings, Hildegard received affirmation and encouragement to continue from Bernard of Clairvaux (later a saint), her archbishop, and Pope Eugene III. She went on to write several books, as well as liturgical poetry and music and hundreds of letters, and to undertake preaching tours. Hildegard died September 17, 1179, at eighty-one. She has been venerated as a saint in the region since then.

Before her death St. Hildegard participated in the writing of her vita and the collection of her works into the "Riesencodex or Wiesbaden Codex." In this massive (18" x 12" and 33 lb.) volume, we have a definitive edition of her writings. For centuries it remained at the Rupertsberg Abbey, but it was moved about during the many wars that affected the area. It survived in a Dresden bank vault during the heavy bombing of that city in World War II. Since 1948, this remarkable twelfth-century parchment codex has resided in and been cared for by the Wiesbaden State Library, not far from the St. Hildegard Abbey. On the library's website[1] one can page through the digitalized codex and plainly see the differences in handwriting of the scribes who participated in the compilation. We now have English translations of the works in the codex.

The codex is the symbol and expression of St. Hildegard, the volume that tells us why she is a saint and a Doctor of the Church. In it she declares, "Everything that God made is life in God"[2] and describes "burning with love of God and not wanting anything else than what God wants."[3] She prays "that I may not work according to my own will, but may abandon it for Your sake . . . and thus become Your loving friend."[4] St. Hildegard realizes through her mystical experience that God "must not be concealed, but made manifest,"[5] and that "obedience is indeed a fire,"[6] and boldly declares, "I see as I saw and I hear as I heard."[7] We are now the beneficiaries of her vast spiritual wisdom, invited to befriend our souls and become the friends of God.

Most books about St. Hildegard focus on her theology or are direct translations of her writings. In this book, her spiritual wisdom is brought to bear on spiritual development and the ministry of spiritual direction. Her proposal that we befriend our souls and become the friends of God forms the heart of the book. This text is a true collaboration between the author and the saint, such that I often say "we" in reference to the writing. Hildegard's words appear in nearly every paragraph—taking us deeper, helping us see, affirming our experience, leading the way, and presenting unique spiritual insights.

Sometimes her contribution is a short phrase; of the two of us, she has the greater talent for putting things in a fresh and creative way.

How do we deepen spiritually and become a friend of our soul and a friend of God? Can the wisdom of St. Hildegard help us on this journey? As we grow spiritually, can we help guide others on their way? In the chapters to come, examples, stories, and reflection questions support spiritual deepening and growth in relationship with God.

St. Hildegard's early experiences of God caused her to seek God all her life. We begin our journey with Becoming a Seeker. God becomes real through personal experience. St. Hildegard's frankness on the matter is our starting point: "The question is: Is there a God or not? And the answer comes from the Holy Spirit Who dwells in the person: God is."[8]

How do we come to share her conviction? We reflect on our experience.

St. Hildegard says the soul is God's dwelling place in the person. To her, the soul is throughout the body and inseparable from it. To "become the faithful friend of your soul"[9] is to "become the faithful friend of God."[10] To know ourselves in our depths is to begin to know God. That self-knowledge is emphasized by all the women Doctors of the Church.

How do we befriend our soul? We "imbue our perception"[11] and develop "a taste for the gifts of God."[12] We need fruitful spiritual practices. Journaling, for example, is a way to "take stock" and "learn . . . about the pilgrimage we are on."[13] St. Hildegard encourages us to "look into and heed Scriptures,"[14] so several means of praying with Scripture are reviewed.

St. Hildegard describes the human being as "a house of prayer."[15] Prayer is about "a faithful heart fixing its spirit upon God."[16] We examine several approaches to prayer and provide examples of God's responses to the person of prayer. We learn to cultivate "the desire of the soul by which we can embrace God . . . and love God."[17]

Discretion and discernment open us to God's defense of "the inner spirit of the person who joins herself to God."[18] How do we sense God's guidance and know we are never "without help and service from above"?[19] St. Hildegard grounds discernment in what it is to be made in the image and likeness of God. She says it pleases God that we "understand what to do by the gifts of the Holy Spirit."[20] Several stories illustrate the means by which we "can choose which path to enter" and enjoy the freedom and peace of "the path of light."[21]

Throughout this book, the descriptor "Attending God"[22] is a signpost alerting you to discussions of spiritual direction. How does spiritual direction help friendship with soul and God develop? How can we grow as spiritual directors? "God in God's mercy wants to reveal."[23] How does spiritual direction support God's revealing and our response to it?

St. Hildegard urges, "Be the special friend of God so that you may become a living stone."[24] A "living stone" does not "trust in her powers alone,"[25] for "God gives you the best of treasures."[26] In this section, we affirm that all we are and all we do matters in growing friendship with God. How do we integrate it all? We leave nothing out of prayer and learn to see God in our "holy work."[27]

"What is born is called."[28] We are called to ever-greater intimacy in friendship with God as our birthright. The inadequacy of a prayer style in which we only ask for what we want and need becomes apparent. In this section, we discuss the shift in prayer to a focus on relationship with God. The process by which God develops us as friends requires our surrender in trust. We must change. St. Hildegard prays, "Try me . . . that I may . . . become your loving friend."[29]

The next section describes the "stripping away" of major impediments to the relationship with God. "You must resign all these things to God."[30] This stripping away exposes the relationship that has existed since we came into being. Now we are available to be personally and directly addressed by God in mystical experiences.

"How hard it is for mortal flesh to understand [mystical gifts]."[31] And how hard it is for a contemporary author to reveal and explain them. Here, we cover several mystical experiences of different types. A locution, something heard with inner spiritual ears, is a loving epiphany. "I heard and received,"[32] says St. Hildegard, and a "faithful person pays attention."[33] God speaks, and we are called to listen.[34]

The human mind is touched by the grace of God to "initiate good."[35] We are called to have the mind of Christ. How is this experienced mystically? "When a person's reason imitates God, she touches God."[36] Mystical experience occurs "as God foresees the need."[37] God gets in our heads, so to speak, and "gives words to ruminate upon."[38] What God asks us to do as a friend of God becomes "bright and clear in the mystery of the spiritual life."[39] Through the big thoughts arriving in prayer, we are compelled to "bring aid and comfort to the faithful."[40]

"God seeks you out," says St. Hildegard, and "touches and instructs."[41] The person's spirit "quickly perceives the One Who sent it."[42] What is God's touch like in actual experience? "God embraces with great love all things."[43] It is like "balm flooding the heart," giving hope to "the integral body."[44] Through God's mystical touch we know we are "in the sweet embrace of God"[45] and never abandoned in our need.

How should we understand mystical visions? St. Hildegard reminds us that Jesus is proof God desires to be seen and heard and to touch us. In the writings of the saints and in Scripture, we learn of those who "saw a vision of such mystery and power, that [they] trembled through and through."[46] What if visions should happen to you? Can you imagine saying, "For the love of God . . . that I may be assured"?[47]

Why is there mysticism? St. Hildegard says God entrusts experiences to us that we may bring our talent "back to God doubled in value"[48] because "God foresees the need,"[49] and so love may be "ordained in us."[50] We acquire a passion for God and God's agenda. God says to St. Hildegard, "I will prepare many hearts according to My Own Heart."[51] Mysticism transforms us into effective disciples and witnesses.

What are the responsibilities of mystics? To "never let Me go,"[52] says God to St. Hildegard. "Do not withdraw from God,"[53] says St. Hildegard. "Remain on the vine," says Jesus. Do not "remain ignorant of the nature of this grape,"[54] says St. Hildegard. Reflect; contemplate; authenticate; consult a spiritual director; become trustable to God; be the friend and disciple God seeks; grow in freedom, joy, and peace; and bear witness to the daunting truth of your experience. Embrace God's loving purposefulness when mystical experience ceases. Prepare to guide others who report mystical experiences.

Our wounds may affect our relationship with God, and so we explore deep healing in prayer. We ask, "Where was God" in our "tribulation and fear and grief in the tumult of life."[55] St. Hildegard encourages us to "cling faithfully"[56] to our Creator for our healing and liberation. Our brokenness must be unmasked in order to achieve deep healing through prayer. "God's grace through the soul . . . [becomes] like a medicine."[57] In prayer, God raises us to new life. "No person can fully know how the soul permeates the human body and blood to make up one life."[58] Even though we sometimes "endure tribulation and affliction," St. Hildegard says, "do not be afraid, because the Son of God endured the same things."[59] Deep healing in prayer shows us we are pearls of great price.

"Everything that God made is life in God,"[60] says St. Hildegard. "God lives in you,"[61] she says, and God experiences what you experience in intimate presence. We practice patience and acceptance that we might "bear prosperity and tribulation with equanimity."[62] God befriends us in our struggles toward acceptance, and "grace comes in great abundance and fruitfulness."[63] Our receipt of mercy inspires mercy for others. We discover that trauma is common in the lives of spiritual directees. They ask, "Where was God?" How do spiritual directors support them as they "show God their wounds"?[64]

How is union with God experienced? We are branches on the Vine. We can live as faulty grafts, losing our connection now and then, or as branches unlikely to snap off in an adverse wind. "Constancy," says St. Hildegard, "is the pillar and rampart of the virtues."[65] How do we grow in constancy? Through union with God in "deep profundity."[66] Only God can ensure that "there is nothing between us" and that "no one can separate us."[67] Union with God forms us to God's nature; so say the great saints. When we have grown to love God in all the places God is, we are united with God and can serve God in new freedom and joy. We can say with St. Paul, "It is no longer I who live, but it is Christ Who lives in me" (Gal 2:20).

Who guides the guides who journey with mystics? Those "illuminated with the clearest and brightest light,"[68] says St. Hildegard. Our teachers are the mystics who boldly wrote of their experiences and pray for us now that we may be "in God's service listening . . . never getting enough of the words of these . . . in the love of the Holy Spirit."[69]

"God . . . keeps you as God's friend, and therefore, the terrible shipwreck of this world will not overwhelm you."[70] The book ends with this promise. We become friends of God in the deeply committed, mutual friendship that is our eternal destiny. Our directee's direction regularly comes from God. Even so, we listen for what threatens the "honor and bliss of her happiness"[71] and our own. We accompany and pray with "those who zealously toil with God."[72] We pray God will gather us "into the bosom of God's grace"[73] for eternity.

Speaking of God's bosom: there was a moment in reading English translations of St. Hildegard's works when I encountered the phrase "His bosom." I checked the dictionary: only females have bosoms. I do not know how often translators have chosen masculine pronouns where St. Hildegard intended feminine imagery. In this book I use feminine pronouns more than masculine on purpose, as it seems just and consistent with St. Hildegard's frequent feminine imagery.

PART I

BECOMING A SEEKER

"The question is: Is there a God or not?
And the answer comes from the Holy Spirit Who dwells in
the person: God is."[1]

chapter one

---•◦•---

RADIANT BEAUTY

"Reflect on how you began
and how the course of your life has proceeded"[1]

W hen and how does one become a seeker? When and how does God become real in a person's life? Perhaps it happens before one even thinks about such questions. The Holy Spirit "kindles all good things, stirs up all good things, and teaches all good things."[2] I believe this kindling begins early in life.

We evolve from our earliest experiences of God to a central focus on God that pervades our lives. Everything counts on our spiritual journeys. God works with us uniquely as only God can. "None can act and none has such power as God,"[3] says St. Hildegard; and, "Whatever God planned, God accomplished."[4]

St. Hildegard strongly believed that the senses connect us to God. In my youth, before Vatican II, I dwelled in the reverence and order of the Roman Catholic faith that came down to me from my mother. I experienced incense, candles, Latin, genuflections, signing myself, devotions, holy water, rosaries, bells, oil, bread, wine, ashes, medals, colorful vestments, stained glass windows, statues, and crucifixes. I was a good memorizer and learned my prayers and catechism by heart. I knew all this was about God, but I did not know God. I was simply a little achiever who was stockpiling information and glorying in my senses, but not consciously seeking more. God, I now believe, was not so passive. As St. Hildegard says, "The Living Eye watches you, and wishes to have you."[5]

St. Hildegard presents a lively, intimate soul-body interaction as critical to knowing God. She writes, "The soul vivifies the body and conveys the breath of life to the senses; the body draws the soul to itself and opens the senses; and the senses touch the soul and draw the body."[6] It is the senses on which "the interior powers of the soul depend," she says. "The human senses manifest the reason and all the powers of the soul. . . . The soul emanates the senses. How? It vivifies a person's face and glorifies her with sight, hearing, taste, smell, and touch, so that by this touch she becomes watchful in all things. For the senses are the sign of all the powers of the soul."[7] To St. Hildegard, then, the senses touch the soul and are part of the soul's power, helping us to be "watchful" for God. In her own way, she argues for the role of the senses in religious ritual and sacramental life—but is that the only role the senses have in connecting us to God?

"Without fully flowering in them"

When has nature caused you to say, "God"?

One winter night, our farm was hit hard by a storm. The wind shook the old farmhouse and moaned and whistled through the big pine trees out front. Out of concern for their safety, the smaller children were not allowed out to help with evening chores. At bedtime, my sisters and I all cuddled in the same bed under piles of quilts to ward off the upstairs drafts.

Sometime during the night, the siege ended. When I awoke, the bedroom was still and bright with sunshine. I pulled on heavy clothes and double socks, went downstairs, and donned a jacket, hat, and scarf, plus mittens and boots. Then I went out the back door. Huge drifts of snow had formed over the cistern, along the yard fence, and at the barnyard gate. I saw a chaotic path where Dad and the boys had worked their way through deep snow to the barn. The dog's tracks went back and forth around the back door and then headed barnward. I could hear the muffled motor of the milking system coming from the barn. Branches poked out of drifts around the catalpa tree. In some spots the snow was light, blown off the ground into nearby giant drifts. I followed the shallower spots down the lane to the road that connected our farm with those south and north of it. I climbed a wooden gate at the entrance to a large, sloped field, perched there, and gazed.

Despite how bright it was, I could not lift my gaze from the vast, untouched field of deep snow, glittering as though tiny diamonds had been perfectly and evenly spread over its entire surface. With not even a rabbit track through the drifts as yet, the snow was as undisturbed as any scene I'd witnessed before, and any I've witnessed since. I became as still as the snow field before me and remained so, oblivious to cold.

I do not know why I was drawn to that place that day, but the experience remains a powerful memory. Even in my little-girl awareness, I knew I dare not set foot on the radiance before me. I felt the privilege of seeing what I saw and remained poised on that gate, receiving the beauty, quiet, simplicity, and purity of the scene. And then I thought, *God!*

I don't recall taking the thought further. I felt awe, though could not name it at that age. "The knowledge of God . . . lies in human hearts without fully flowering in them."[8] Now I understand that this was a moment in which God became real to me. "The Creator is known through the creation."[9] I was genuinely interested in God from that moment on. The moment had a before and after for God and me.

After that day my focus on anything I associated with God grew. My attention span in catechism class and for all church events improved. Something had changed within me; I couldn't articulate it, but as children do, I did act it out. If our car was headed for church, I wanted to be in it, even if it was just for cleaning the place. I was my mother's sidekick for all devotions. I coveted my own church sacramentals—prayer book, holy cards, rosary, little statues, a medal on a chain around my neck.

But of course what I really wanted was God: another glimpse, a satisfaction of something for which I did not know the word. St. Hildegard says, "Whoever goes climbing is seeking that toward which they climb,"[10] and she names this "longing," which "is free from the power of this world."[11] Longing furthers "God's provident will."[12] It leans toward "the things which are eternal in God and the life to come."[13] Longing is a leaning toward God and eternity. Through our longing, "God's tenderness sweetly instructs."[14] Was that happening to me?

Spiritual development, per St. Hildegard, begins when we sense what God is doing, for "a human is converted to God by the birth of God's grace."[15] We know when we have been converted to God by grace.

REFLECTION QUESTIONS

"Reflect on how you began and how the course of your life has proceeded." Recall a moment when God became real to you. What details do you remember? How did your senses "touch your soul"? In your life, has there been a before-and-after moment for you and God?

Looking back on it, what were the signs that God "wished to have you" and was "sweetly instructing" you? When did your longing begin?

What is your prayer about the reality of God in your life?

chapter two

———•••———

RECOGNITION

"Beginning to appear from around a cloud"

*H*ow has light entered your spiritual experience?
St. Hildegard says, "The Holy Spirit enkindled their hearts as the sun, beginning to appear from around a cloud, shows its burning heat by its shining light."[1] Her words describe my own early experience.

In summer following first grade I experienced another memorable sense of the Divine. Two of my siblings and I had the idea we needed a cave to play in, so we started carving one into a mud bank in the pasture just south of our house. The work was hard and slow. The soil there was clay—heavy, sticky, and red—and we had only toy shovels. At one point my siblings gave up and left, but I continued to dig in the earth for a time. The hole we'd made enlarged little more with my efforts. Finally, disappointed and covered with red earth, I climbed up the bank and leaned back on the grass above the nascent cave.

Looking up widens one's horizons and takes away the feeling of being stuck in clay, even for a child. As I gazed, the world above me seemed so clean, vibrant, and unbound. The sky was far lovelier than the heavy mud I'd been focused on. I realized a lot was going on up there. In the extravagant blue expanse, mountainous white clouds sailed along. For a moment I felt unsettled, like I was the one moving, and then I noticed a certain spot in the skyscape where sunlight illumined the clouds with greater brilliance. Before my eyes, a wide, towering cloud, at first more gray than white, rolled into the spot. It glowed gold up and down one side, and then the whole cloud lit up from within and without in stunning luminescence. I felt very small and transfixed with wonder before this magnificence, even pierced by it, and yet I was serene and happy in my little heart. Again, I simply thought, *God*—and I was excited to recognize the feeling and thought for the second time. Yes, God was real.

"The Light which fully lives"

What is it with human beings and light and spirituality?

Author John Cheever said, "It seems to me that [our] inclination toward light, toward brightness, is very nearly botanical—and I mean spiritual light. One not only needs it, one struggles for it."[2] St. Hildegard speaks of the "Living Light" that "blazes in my soul, just as it has from my childhood," and of the "unfailing Light" that reveals truths to her.[3] She describes God as "The Light which fully lives,"[4] and says, "[God] is also like fire, because God inflames and enkindles and illuminates all things without changing over time; for God is God."[5] She also writes, "The Majesty of God is without beginning or end and bright with incomparable glory, and the Divinity is so radiant that mortal sight cannot look on it."[6]

Now I see my little clay self innocently open to the brilliance of Mystery in nature, encountering Light. No doubt the experience fit nicely into my ideas at the time of what heaven might be like. Now I am intrigued by the "recognition," the connection of the two encounters, and the acknowledgment to myself of God's reality. How to recognize one's encounters with God was not included in first-grade catechism. The existence of God was simply a truth one was to memorize.

A little Catholic girl also recognizes the feeling inside that prompts her to kneel or genuflect. God grants the grace to recognize God even to little girls, and picks the moment with the greatest probability of success. Most persons I meet in spiritual direction describe in surprising detail similar experiences from their youth. Very many of them involve light in some way. In God's great generosity, my two earliest "God is real" experiences were preparatory for me.

REFLECTION QUESTIONS

Recall another early experience of God. Was there a sense of recognition for you?

Looking back on it, were your early experiences of God preparatory for something more? How so?

What is your prayer about encountering Mystery in nature?

chapter three

———•••———

THE EMBRACE

"The voice of a person's outpoured blood"

W hat early peril or situation caused you to pray in desperation?

In autumn of second grade I had a profound experience of God. My memory of it remains vivid. I was seriously injured while deep in the wood on our farm. My sibling ran to get help from a significant distance away. I was all alone, helpless in my peril. An immense, beautiful wood surrounded me. I couldn't rise from the bottom of it. I was flat on my back, horrified by the blood seeping through my clothes. The sun shone brightly on colorful leaves all around and above. Cool breezes stirred and rustled the leaves. Clouds sailed high overhead. A joyful bird choir sang as though nothing had happened. I felt like a tiny candle threatened with being snuffed out. In my terror, I cried out for help again and again. I believed my life was at stake. As my strength ebbed, I couldn't sustain all my crying out and sobbing, yet I feared I might fall asleep and not awaken.

Finally, it occurred to me to say the four prayers I had learned so far: Sign of the Cross, Glory Be, Hail Mary, and Our Father. With waning energy, I said them with heartfelt fervency. I did as God invites us: "Seek Me with a constant outcry and I will lift you up and receive you . . . Cry out and persevere in seeking Me; and I will help you . . . Speak to Me with a flood of inner tears."[1]

When even these simple, memorized prayers became hard to sustain, I said to God, "I'm down here! I want to live!" Then, finally, I simply let my silence, weakness, and bleeding speak to God of my peril and my desire to live. As St. Hildegard writes, "The voice of a person's outpoured blood rises up through her soul to cry out and lament that it has been driven from . . . the body in which God had placed it."[2] It "flies almost to the heavens wailing in its sorrow."[3]

St. Hildegard reinforces the Scriptural message that God "will always hear the cry of your prayers."[4] She says, "The all-surpassing goodness of Divinity . . . brings aid and comfort to the faithful."[5] In times of peril, we learn the truth of her words: "The mercy of God bends down to humans and has compassion on their miseries, and so is available to those who seek it."[6] As I waited and time passed, I felt forgotten and abandoned, but I soon discovered that God would not abandon me. "God, Who created you, does not wish to lose you,"[7] says St. Hildegard, for we are "exceedingly dear to God."[8]

The epitome of abandonment—a little girl confronting her own death all alone—became the epitome of Presence. In surprisingly concrete physicality, I felt gently lifted up and held close in an intimate, loving embrace, as if I were a little treasure to be preserved. "God was moved by great mercy . . . [and] drew the human toward Godself."[9] That is how it felt to me. "God calls you back from death . . . [and] will receive you lovingly and place you in Her bosom and clasp you in sweet embraces."[10] Perhaps God abandons subtlety for a child in peril. The greatness and tenderness of God felt firm, gentle, and feminine to me. "The embrace of God's maternal love . . . has nourished us unto life and is our help in perils, and is the deepest and sweetest charity."[11] Wisdom "caresses Her handiwork as one feels one's clothing."[12]

In God's embrace I felt solace and completely filled with the breath of Love. "God embraces with great love all things."[13] My trembling ceased. All-Love annihilated all fear. I did not convince myself to not be afraid or to let go of my fear or to tamp it down. It was truly, instantly gone. It was not the case that I no longer thought I was going to die; I now thought I would die in God's arms. I allowed myself to no longer struggle to stay alive; I simply rested in the solace, safety, and wonder of God's embrace. I wondered whether I had in fact already died. After a time, I slept or lost consciousness there "in the sweet embrace of God."[14]

"Concerning every matter that cannot be recuperated or restored," St. Hildegard says, "it is necessary that a human . . . have consolation when nothing else can be done."[15] I received that consolation that day. I live now convinced of this truth: "Since we are not forgotten before God, we will rise up."[16]

"The great clarity of the Divine Visitation"

When did you first discover that "God moments" are not ordinary?

I was pulled to ordinary consciousness by the shouts of my grandfather trying to locate me. In a sense, I was rescued right out of my youthful mystical experience. God's embrace cannot be fully captured by my impoverished description. I am grateful to St. Hildegard for describing her own experience as a child: "I have from earliest childhood seen great marvels which tongue has no power to express, but which the Spirit of God has taught me that I may believe."[17] She says, "Creatures are little but the power of God is great and incomprehensible."[18]

In relating this experience, I cannot explain how or why God acted as God did or make the story somehow more plausible. "God, Who rules every created being, imparts the power and strength of this blessedness by the great clarity of the Divine Visitation."[19] Clarity of God's visitation is my experience. God promises, "I am present to every creature and withdraw Myself from none. . . . I am present to them in true manifestation, never withdrawing My power from them but doing in them by the strength of My will whatever I please."[20] It pleased God to embrace me in my peril.

"A person's body is strengthened and sustained by the soul."[21] One's body most certainly shares in the experience of God. "The powers of the soul are very strong, for through them the soul knows and perceives God."[22] Without God's powerful, calming effect, I might well have perished in one last gasp of terror. "Indeed, the human person understands through the soul that she possesses God."[23] I understood that I had God.

St. Hildegard personifies the soul in this way: "I have a great duty. Oh, what am I? And what is the theme of my outcry? I am the living breath in a human being, placed in a tabernacle of marrow, veins, bones, and flesh, giving it vitality and supporting its every movement. . . . I was created by God."[24] I understand her to mean that it is our God-given capacity, the great duty of our soul, to perceive and be strengthened by God.

The soul "knows not only earthly but also heavenly things, since it wisely knows God; and it spreads itself through all the person's members; for it gives vitality to the marrow and veins and members of the whole body, as the tree from its root gives sap and greenness to all the branches."[25] This is a splendid way of saying the soul is the life in our being. "The spirit without the bloody material of the body is not the living person, and the bloody material of the body without the soul is not the living person."[26] A living person is the complete, inseparable integration of soul and body. The part of our being that "knows and senses God" is named "soul" by St. Hildegard, and it has a powerful, vitalizing role in the body.

"*The results of the miracles of God*"

How do you feel about miracles?

St. Hildegard likes to speak of miracles. She says, "It is impossible, however, for the human mind to understand God's miracles."[27] She describes human beings as "the miracles of God."[28] We glimpse that truth in newborn babies, do we not? She asks, "Truly who can count the numberless wonders that God does in the power of God's ability? No one. Indeed . . . none can act and none has such power as God."[29]

Am I, are you, a miracle of God?

In John's gospel, "signs" or "works"—that is, miracles—indicate God's presence and action in potent human experiences, especially of fear, risk, and death. Signs lead to deeper believing and recognition of God's revealing but also serve the cause of life. We are not asked to let go of our common sense or even our science in contemplating the miraculous. St. Hildegard was a woman of extraordinary common sense and intelligence, and yet she speaks of miracles. We are invited to be open to the possibility that God is actually present and acting in the lives of ordinary human beings, loving us in our human situations, bringing life and healing. In my peril, I think I was a locus of God's in-breaking.

St. Hildegard also mentions miracles to emphasize what occurs spiritually. She says, "Clearly there will be miracles in faith and human knowledge and human understanding."[30] We awaken to the deeply spiritual through our realizations of the miraculous. "That person is blessed who is awakened to heavenly things through a miracle of God."[31] We can and do emerge from horrific events as changed persons awakened to heavenly things. Although we lose any sense of being unscathed by the hazards of being human, we gain a new sense of God with us. "Evidently humanity lost the innocence it had in heaven, and is alive again in knowledge of God."[32] Though in one sense I lost consciousness, in another sense I gained consciousness. St. Hildegard says, "God had made her a new person, with a life in her different from what she had had before."[33]

"I will have faith and confidence in God"

How did the experiences of your youth affect your perception of prayer?

Though I was a mere child, my experience taught me about prayer. When our ordinary efforts to pray cease and we are still, prayer is taken over by God. God listens not just to our lips but to our whole being, and is palpably present in response. For those who know grace at an early age, the desire for that gift remains. New levels of intimacy with God open up as life goes on, but the initial experience is not erased. I am witness to the holy truth that God is with us in our most terrible situations; the worst thing that happens can paradoxically be the best thing that happens. In that wood God made an unforgettable, unmistakable claim on me that remains compelling and commits my heart to God forever. "Therefore I will have faith and confidence in God, and never blot out God's name from my heart."[34] I am aware of Whose I am, of my import.

Recalling such experiences brings gratitude and renewal. With St. Hildegard, I pray, "Fiery Spirit, fount of courage, life within life of all that has being. . . . O sacred breath, O blazing love . . . flooding the heart with the fragrance of good . . . mirror of God Who leads wanderers home and hunts out the lost, armor of the heart and hope of the integral body."[35] With her I say to God, "Holy are You for anointing those who have been desperately wounded."[36]

REFLECTION QUESTIONS

If you are comfortable recalling it, when have you been in peril or felt you desperately needed God's help? In this experience, how did Love conquer fear?

What prayers did you learn in your youth? How have they served you?

Are you "a miracle of God"? How so?

What is your prayer about God's presence and action in your worst experience?

chapter four

MOM'S ANSWER

"The senses touch the soul"

W hat is your earliest experience of talking about God with someone?

At first my experiences of God remained secrets between their Giver and me. I don't remember thinking about the experiences much, which may have preserved their integrity in my memory. But secrecy rarely lasted for an eight-year-old extrovert. I tended to speak privately to my mother of important matters. I sought her in the familiar and humbly ordinary moments of her part of farm life. I had never before tried out my questions about God, nor had she explicitly brought up God to me. I think God instills within children compelling questions about God that simply spill out.

One Friday afternoon I sat on one side of the massive threshing crew–size wood table in the farm kitchen. It was a pleasant, late-summer day and the windows and the door were open to breezes. On the other side of the table, Mom set briskly to work on her weekly pie and bread preparation. She crumbled yeast into a small bowl of warm water and sugar and set that aside. She mixed pie crust, slapped it onto a floured mat, and then slammed, rolled, and trimmed until she had a stack of eight crusts. Next, she turned back to the yeast, scooped flour, and created an enormous mass of bread dough—enough for loaves, biscuits, and cinnamon rolls that would last our large family a week. She leaned into the dough and, with the heels of her hands, slugged, punched, and turned it like she was teaching it to box. She grimaced and frowned in sync with her kneading.

For some internally urgent reason I chose this kneading moment to tell Mom about God and to ask her a question. Did the sights, sounds, and smells of the kitchen "open the senses," which in turn "touch the soul" as St. Hildegard proposed? Regrettably I cannot remember perfectly what I shared, though it was in my nature to be thorough and detailed. I can't say exactly how I worded my burning question—but I do know I was wondering about and looking for confirmation of how God reveals to a young girl. Somehow, what I said doesn't seem as important to me as Mom's response.

As I watched, my question hovering in the yeasty air, Mom's kneading gradually slowed. Gentleness crept back into her hands. She patted the dough lightly and looked over at me. Her face softened, a slight smile came, and she said, "Well, I think so. I think God is like that sometimes."

"A person who can bear up heaven by her knowledge"

In looking back, do you notice graces you could not name in your youth?

As I reflect on this tiny story now, I realize it was grace-filled. Now the symbols of kneading yeast into dough, of bread, and of table jump out at me, and I realize Mom was kneading yeast into dough in more ways than one. Momentarily, this was the kitchen of God, the Supernatural Presence in ordinary earthly activity. "For the grace of

God, in its strength and piety, bends down to the faithful and lifts them on high to heavenly places."[1]

My mother was a generous baker and listener and the shepherdess of the souls in her charge. We often experienced her wisdom in little moments of few words. Despite many other things on her mind, she could slip from Martha to Mary in short order. "Patience is perfected amid earthly things."[2] Mom regarded little chats with her children as her work, too, and was receptive, welcoming, and safe. I later learned that she was a watcher and reader of our faces as well. She was deeply spiritual, prayerful, faithful to her religious tradition (Roman Catholicism), and well prepared to be on that journey with us. She was "a person who can bear up heaven by her knowledge" and who "received a mighty and powerful gift from God."[3]

My mother had the openness and tenderness to give just the right response with just the right touch, despite not knowing what was coming. Or did she? What did she surmise from my new enthusiasm for all things religious? That day in the kitchen, she did not in any way convey that what I shared and asked was unusual or weird. Instead, she showed herself to be reflective, affectionate, and ready to hear. "Holy persons, in whom love dwells, lack for nothing, because their hearts are surrounded with gentleness and peace, as by the flowing aroma of balsam"[4]—or yeast, as the case may be.

Mom didn't catechize, push for a particular understanding, or interfere with the direction God seemed to be taking with me. "In the work of God wisdom and discretion are like two walls, with wisdom as the higher part and discretion as the lower. And God imbues the whole of the human mind with these, an equitable and just gift, that the mind may know God."[5] Mom had wisdom and discretion. She affirmed the reality of God, and yet she allowed me to draw my own conclusions. She responded in the way I needed and opened the door to more conversations about God. "Some people . . . know God, and so they carry the treasure of good will and the sweet spices of virtue."[6]

I needed a spiritual director, and God provided a good one in Mom. In talking to her, I was indirectly responding to God and acting on my desire to know God. Speaking aloud of my personal experience of God for the first time made it ever more real to me. I had moved from acting out to revealing. St. Hildegard says that when a daughter of God experiences grace, "she will feel the change in her mind, and . . . raise her eyes to see and her ears to hear and her mouth to speak and her hands to touch and her feet to walk . . . so that she will learn things her habits could not teach her."[7] My good news was not in any way lessened in sharing it, and its importance to me was honored by my mother. No matter how I described and asked about the ineffable, she listened, took me seriously, and understood. I felt affirmed and safe.

In her simple response, my mother might just as well have said, "Yes, this is the Way. Trust your experience. You are not alone," for I came away knowing, *Mom thinks God is real, too.* I felt satisfied that God was as I'd experienced. "Now we are satisfied, for we drink in God the saving cup, tasting Who God is in true faith; Whom we cannot see with the outer . . . vision, but Whom we have within by spiritual understanding, as strong wine shows its power in people's veins, though the people do not feel it but only know that it is within them."[8] God is real and reveals God's self. Mom said so. We two were now one in that faith, out loud.

In my freedom, relief, and affirmation, I knew I could come back with more such questions. Because my mother nurtured my relationship with God in that graced conversation, her door was open to the many future discussions we would have about God. "And so God's grace precedes and follows, touches and warms people, as was said; and those who desire to be the children of God can ardently receive and fulfill its words, despising fleeting things and embracing lasting ones. And so this . . . encourages the children of God."[9] To affirm a child's faith is to give her hope.

"A person cannot see God with the outer eyes, but touches God by faith inwardly in the soul."[10] Imagine how prayer is affected by the conviction that God is real. Imagine what would have happened had Mom been dismissive of or impatient with my questions.

"Attending God"

Can you tell a story of your earliest spiritual direction moment?

We can reflect on this story with spiritual direction in mind. Many times in my own practice, people have said, "I need someone to talk to about God." Mom illustrated several ways of wisdom for spiritual directors: a self-denying focus on the other, openness, receptivity, generous listening, use of few words, honoring the importance of and taking time to reflect on what was said, keeping God as the focus, sustaining a safe and companionable atmosphere, not catechizing or preaching, allowing the other to draw her own conclusions, sharing Mystery, and accepting the other's difficulty in describing the ineffable. "A person does not have the capacity to speak of God in the same way that she would speak of the humanness of a human being or the defining characteristic of a work made by human hands."[11]

Sometimes in spiritual direction I do nothing but affirm the other's experience. We all need affirmation. That affirmation flows with greatest ease when I've recognized spiritual realities in my own experience. A wise spiritual director invests in her own spiritual path, as my mother faithfully did. "By opening the inner eyes of the spirit . . . she may understand and love God the more."[12] The director's embrace of her own spiritual path and affirmation of the directee's help the directee continue on comfortably. In this way, "Grace comes in great abundance and fruitfulness."[13]

We are back to where we started: "Is there a God or not? And the answer comes from the Holy Spirit Who dwells in the person: God is, and created you, and also redeemed you. But as long as this question and answer are in a person, the power of God will not be absent from her."[14]

REFLECTION QUESTIONS

What characteristics of a person to whom you've spoken about God have helped you? Hindered you?

Of what benefit to others are your own conviction that God is real and your own investment in spiritual life?

What is your prayer about being "a person who can bear up heaven by her knowledge"?

PART II

BECOMING THE FAITHFUL FRIEND OF YOUR SOUL

*"Be a faithful friend to your soul,
so that you may live forever."*

chapter five

———•••———

ST. HILDEGARD'S
INVITATION

"Oh how much better it would be for you to know yourself"

*H*ow well do you know yourself?
St. Hildegard says, "Be a faithful friend to your soul, so that you may live forever."[1] The principal way we become faithful friends to our souls is through spiritual practices that open us to the presence and action of God. Spiritual practices help us do self-work; process our experiences; influence ourselves toward good; become the soil in which God's word can sprout and flourish; develop virtues; become deeply and fruitfully prayerful; address those things that threaten the health of our souls; receive and extend forgiveness; remain grounded even in adversity; grow in freedom; regain our path when we have derailed; cultivate loving relationships with self, others, and God; work out the story of God with us; and live in gratitude.

Befriending our souls changes us and prepares us to be friends of God. St. Hildegard says, "Oh how much better it would be for you to know yourself . . . rather than remaining in lukewarmness and hardly glancing at what is right. . . . A finished work is more acceptable than an empty noise."[2] Some of the spiritual practices that we engage are narrated below, but the list cannot cover all the options available for each person's unique journey. Each of us must find what best leads to friendship with our soul and with God.

REFLECTION QUESTIONS

> When you reflect on becoming a friend of your soul, what comes to mind?
>
> What keeps you from "remaining in lukewarmness"?
>
> What is your prayer about becoming the friend of your soul?

chapter six

————•••————

JOURNALING

"Prepare your souls for God"

*H*ow do you recount the marvels of your life?

The word *journal* originally denoted a book containing the appointed times of daily prayers. For many of us, a journal is still about prayer. Journaling was one of my first, and remains one of my favorite, spiritual practices. Not everyone has an affinity for journaling; some of my directees react to the idea as though allergic. Yet we need a means to express what transpires spiritually, to savor grace, to cultivate deeper relationships with self and God, to notice, to appropriate, to dwell with questions, and so on, so that we can credibly help others with these same things.

Writing responses to the reflection questions of this book provides journaling practice, but you may find poetry, art, music, or other means to express your relationship with self and God. The point is, God "will not sow an empty field."[1] St. Hildegard says, "O illustrious and wise ones, prepare your souls for God."[2]

My earliest journal dates to age fifteen. On the inside cover of the little notebook, I wrote the purpose of writing in it: "To aid me in being me." On the first page, I put stress on waiting, watching, and being open. I wrote that the contents would be "quotes, thoughts, prayers, original and non-original." I recorded many feelings, questions, experiences, and reflections there as well. All were fertile means to prepare my soul for God. The focus in that and in all my subsequent journals is on my spiritual life, the befriending of my soul.

My journals are not diaries—that is, dated records of daily experiences and events. In fact, there are entries in which I do not specify dates and events, though they often can be surmised. As I matured in my journaling, I grew more disciplined about noting dates, details, and sources of quotes. Today, I have boxes of filled journals—the story of my life, in more ways than one.

From the beginning, journaling helped me find God in difficult times. Due to the childhood injuries mentioned earlier, I required a series of surgeries in my teens. In the journals of that era, I dealt with what those experiences meant to me spiritually. For example, I sometimes rested alone in my room while the family farming went on without me. In my little notebook, I prayed that "in my aloneness I might enjoy Your company" and that I not "be without solitude before I realize what tremendous value it is for me, for I shouldn't be lonely in Your Presence." I described feeling "poured out" and I prayed for patience. St. Hildegard says, "Seek God . . . in the anxiety and anguish of your spirit, and you will live."[3] She invites us to "sigh to God, which is good."[4]

Later in the same journal, I wrote, "Things look so much better and there is hope once more." I expressed to God, "Your Presence has dissolved my loneliness, Your grace has comforted me." So, from earliest journals on I wrote about what I was experiencing, what I needed from God, and how God had responded to my prayer. Journaling helped me notice the connection between prayer and subsequent grace. My relationship with God grew through capturing spiritual matters in writing. "If you seek God's grace, it will not flee from you."[5] I needed to find meaning, purpose, and hope in my experiences.

My journals are the story of God with me and are analogous to Scriptures as the broader story of God with us. For me, journals are "sacramentals": reminders to pray and to notice God's presence and action.

"Take stock of yourself"

How do you work through your strong reactions?

Journaling is key to my self-work. St. Hildegard encourages, "Take stock of yourself."[6] Writing puts me in touch with my darker, shadowy side. Writing helps reveal a new, more graced way forward. When my first reaction to a situation isn't ideal, journaling helps me find a deeper, more mature, or even more just response. St. Hildegard quotes God as saying, "I am the Living Light, Who illuminates the darkness."[7] She also says, "The course of justice is called forth by upright thoughts [and] it turns a person aside from hearing evil and directs her toward the good."[8] To journal is to cooperate with God's illuminating of our darkness and calling us to good.

Self-work is essential when I am upset. For example, when a person gave me negative feedback, I named the feelings in my journal: "hurt, disappointment, anger, confusion, attacked, judged, and criticized." A few pages later, a little humility crept into my heart and onto the page. I began to see and accept the gift of truth in the feedback. "People may have quiet amidst the turbulent adversities."[9] I then considered my own feedback style in my work role. This, too, was a gift, and not just for me. I felt motivated to improve. "[Reflective] knowledge shines as brightly as daylight because through it people know and judge their actions, and the human mind that is carefully considering itself is radiant."[10]

St. Hildegard speaks bluntly of this process: "Straighten up your mind, O human. For you are disregarding the counsel. . . . What in the world are you thinking! Aren't you ashamed to walk in the darkness? . . . Shed some light on the feelings of your heart. . . . For the day grows dark for one who does not labor in the straight path of the journey."[11] Journaling helps me find that straight path. Self-work in journaling convinces me that St. Hildegard is correct when she says, "The grace of God shines like the sun and sends its gifts in various ways: in wisdom, in viridity, in moisture."[12]

"Obedience teaches"

Does a blank page invite or intimidate?

Journaling is an act of obedience, an attempt to hear and respond to God amid the noise of the world and one's inner conflicts. "Obedience teaches all good things; it indicates them just as the human points out with a finger what is desired."[13] A journal calls forth the patience to confront and fill a blank page. "[Patience] keeps and saves all works in proper moderation. . . . Patience is on the right path."[14] A journal helps us stay grounded on the spiritual path.

A journal is also a container for the joy of the spiritual journey, the wonder and savoring of generous grace, and the exhilaration of sudden enlightenment. Journals hold our artwork, poetry, and homemade psalms and magnificats, all creative and grateful responses to God.

"Learn . . . about the pilgrimage you are on"

What pilgrimage are you on?

As we write about finding God in our experiences, our stories become more articulate, complete, and even redeemed. St. Hildegard invites, "Learn first about the pilgrimage you are on."[15] We gain a personal understanding of Who God is and how God is involved in our pilgrimage through life. We glimpse God's desires for our lives and work, and perhaps we sense a call tugging at us. Knowledge of God seeps into our being.

St. Hildegard counsels, "Do not ignore . . . the Holy Spirit through negligence."[16] As we look back over journaled material, the individual stories of God with us begin to knit together into a whole. We begin to see the trajectory toward unity with God traced out a page at a time. As St. Hildegard says, "Who is the one who can recount these marvels?"[17]

Looking back over journaled pages prepares us for spiritual direction. Sometimes we focus on one particular situation or event. Often directees dwell on what is top of mind that day. Because the focus of spiritual direction is on the relationship with God, however, the patterns, dynamics, subtle movements, graces, deepening, new insights, responses, and growth over a longer period become truly relevant. "Reflect on how you began and how the course of your life has proceeded."[18] What is the course of your relationship with God?

We can relate to St. Hildegard's prayer, "Watch over and take care of the great and small who have written about Your Spirit, and over me . . . who, animated by the breath of Your Spirit, have labored over this writing."[19] She also relates God's promise: "I will prepare many hearts according to My Own Heart."[20] True, journaling costs us time and labor. But what is the cost of not recounting the marvels of one's pilgrimage?

REFLECTION QUESTIONS

What is your experience with journaling? If not journaling, what other spiritual practice helps you "prepare your soul for God" or "seek God ... in the anxiety and anguish of your spirit" or find "the straight path of the journey"?

How do you capture or remember the story of God with you? If a journaler, do you experience an analogy with Scripture in what you've written? How so?

What is your prayer about the spiritual practice of journaling? About the blank pages in your life?

chapter seven

SCRIPTURE

"Look into and heed the Scriptures"

*H*ow is your heart "washed with the rivulets of the Scriptures?" St. Hildegard speaks often and highly of praying with Scripture. "Look into and heed the Scriptures, which are rooted in the Holy Spirit . . . a mirror in which we see God by faith."[1] She opens our minds to the idea that "all these things pertain to you."[2] To her, the Scriptures are "a path which leads to the lofty mountain where flowers and precious herbs grow, with a fragrant breeze blowing over them, bringing forth their sweet aroma, and where roses and lilies show their bright faces."[3] How refreshing is her image.

St. Hildegard also relates God's promise: "To a person who willingly and with good heart receives the seed of My Word, I grant the gifts of the Holy Spirit in superabundance, as to a good field."[4] What might "the path which leads to the lofty mountain" involve? How do we "willingly and with good heart" receive the Holy Spirit's gifts? Gradually, I have found some stepping stones.

"Be perfect as God is perfect"

Are you perfect?

"Be perfect as God is perfect." (Matt 5:48) What does this mean? How is it achievable? When I read this verse in the context of the entire chapter, I could see that "being perfect" involved going the extra mile, loving my enemies, and praying for those who persecute me. In the context of the other readings for that Sunday (Lev 19; Ps 103; 1 Cor 3), it meant being holy, neither having hate in my heart nor bearing grudges, loving my neighbor as myself, being steadfast in love, appreciating that the Holy Spirit dwells in me, and engaging in loving service. The footnotes in my study Bible said *holy* means to be inspired and directed by God's nature and God's desire for us, and to express love concretely, as in good works. They also said *perfect* implies "whole, complete, mature," and following Jesus.

Using a biblical commentary, I went a little deeper into Matthew 5:48, and I found that the wisdom of love is to inform how I deal with opposition. Being perfect is about kindness, forbearance, generosity, and an open attitude toward others. Actions are important, but so are my heart and the sort of temple of the Holy Spirit I am. St. Hildegard says, "Let us, with our hearts washed with the rivulets of the Scriptures, cast out anything in our conscience that drives us to evil and let us search in the true words of the Scriptures for Who God may be and what God's works are."[5] For Who God may be. What a discovery that would be.

With my "heart washed with the rivulets of the Scriptures," I prayed with the verse that stood out for me: "Be perfect as God is perfect." I mulled over the insights I'd gained and invited God to show me what I was to see, that I might learn why I was so struck by this verse. Was it simply awakening the perfectionist achiever in me? As I grew silent and open in prayer, a scene from work came into focus—a scene in which I felt betrayed by a coworker who, in a difficult moment, threw me under the bus.

St. Hildegard says, "The Word of God also awakens the sleeping minds of humans, and makes them to see in the true vision of faith."[6] My prayer was developing; I was inspired to ask God's own reaction to the scene. I prayed for that glimpse of "God's nature and God's desire for us" the footnotes mentioned. I prayed for the wisdom of love I lacked.

Soon I was filled with sorrow for both parties. I saw the harm to both and the offense to God. For the first time, I felt genuine compassion for the other person and for me. I sensed that forgiveness was finally within reach, and the next thing to pray about. I desired, rather than resisted, the forbearance and maturity to go the extra mile. I wanted the Holy Spirit to dwell in a forgiving, not a resentful, heart. I began to "see in the true vision of faith" what God desired for me and my colleague. "Who God may be and what God's works are" clearly involved forgiveness. With grace, I could "be perfect as God is perfect" in this one little event, now that my "sleeping mind" had been stirred and my "heart washed."

"I will bless you"

Are you a blessing?

On another occasion, I read Genesis 12:2, in which God says, "I will bless you . . . so that you will be a blessing." The words remind me that God's gifts have a "for others" purpose; they are not for me alone. St. Hildegard says, "The likeness of the dove teaches you, and the Word of God is knowledge in you."[7] Her dove image suggests gentle nudging from the Holy Spirit. The knowledge that I am to be a blessing informs my prayer. Now, at the close of a prayer time, I sign myself and ask God to "bless me that I might be a blessing." If I am leading a group in prayer, I ask, "Bless us that we might be blessings." Repeating these words often as a Scripture-based spiritual practice helps me notice when situations tempt me to ways that will not bless. The words call me to a higher road of thoughtfulness, generous spirit, prayer, and deeper response.

"If you are patient"

What do you need to work on?

Praying with Scripture shines light on things that are important for self-knowledge and self-work. The Word is a seed. When I prayed with, "If you are patient when you suffer for doing what is good, this is a grace before God" (1 Pet 2:20), I had to admit I rarely suffer for doing good, that when irritations do arise, they are usually minor. I find a surprising (to me) patience with all that my work, ministries, and health issues require. I take a lot of things in stride. Yet when I think myself patient, I soon flunk tests of my patience. St. Hildegard counsels us to have patience and a tranquil mind in "both prosperity and tribulation."[8] I cannot take patience for granted, particularly in tribulation, so am I really patient? St. Hildegard advises, "Look to that light which you have tasted a little."[9] She counsels, "O human, who are not just a bundle of marrow, pay attention to Scriptural knowledge!"[10] The little seed sown by a verse about patience soon sprouted.

On the phone, my six-year-old godson explained his first grader's take on Lent and what he was going to do during the season. I said I was thinking about it, too, and asked if he had any ideas for me. Without a shred of hesitation he replied, "Well, Aunt Sue, I think you should try to be a little more patient." An arrow zinged into my heart.

I was mortified that my dear little godson experienced me as impatient. I was suddenly highly motivated to become a more patient person. I wrote "patience" in large letters on the whiteboard in my office and looked at it often. Throughout Lent, I took greater notice of this virtue and prayed for grace and the will to embrace it. It wasn't easy, but I felt helped. I realized that fatigue, overwork, and other self-care issues made me vulnerable to impatience. I saw why God and godson underlined the verse for me, and why St. Hildegard says, "God's grace touches and instructs."[11]

That Lent I learned to stop and pray when tempted to impatience. I learned to embrace balance and other practices that aided patience. I grew in appreciation of God's patience with me. I was impressed by the challenges and rewards that being patient brought. St. Hildegard says, "People work more strongly in soul and body than if they had no difficulty in doing it, since they struggle against themselves in many perils; and, waging these fierce wars together with the Lord God Who fights faithfully for them, they conquer themselves . . . and so know themselves to be in God's army."[12] Graced conquering of self and improved self-control grew my patience. I felt helped by God to inner growth.

The idea of Lent is that sacrifice brings us closer to God. I was brought closer to others, too. I grew in admiration of patient persons and in empathy for others who, like me, occasionally flunked patience tests. The latter were often "doing what is good" and suffering for it. I tried to focus on the good, just as I hoped they would do in my case. Praying with Scripture as a path to self-knowledge was etched into my mind.

"Imbue your perception"

How does Scripture awaken your imagination?

I also pray with Scripture in the Ignatian way, imagining that I am present in the scene. For example, in praying with the Annunciation (Luke 1: 26–38) of the angel Gabriel to Mary, I once imagined myself praying with Mary. I envisioned the details and what the experience might have been like for her. St. Hildegard says, "Imbue your perception with streams of water from the Scriptures and with the calling and way of life of the saints."[13] I imagined great light shining into the Annunciation scene, signaling the beginning of Light coming into the world. "[God] is the brightest light that cannot in any way be extinguished."[14] St. Hildegard refers to Mary as "Unclouded Brightness" and "Mother of Light."[15] She describes the Annunciation as the moment when Mary was "pierced by the light of God."[16]

Praying in this way, I realized that Mary did not know the Gospel story's end and all she was saying yes to. I felt compassion for her. Later, I reflected that this is also true for us. We are invited to share God's work and to say yes without fully knowing what we are getting into. As I reflected, I sensed God respecting and loving us for saying yes with courage and trust.

I return to the Annunciation often in prayer. St. Hildegard points to this story's importance: "The Scriptures were revealing God eagerly; they knew and revealed that God was to be incarnated; all the works of God were and are confirmed by the Holy Spirit."[17] This is still happening. When God seems to announce something to me, Mary's example helps me stare down my fears and trust. St. Hildegard says of Mary, "Such daring!" and "Priceless integrity!"[18] Mary moved beyond fear to trust and integrity. St. Hildegard says to Mary, "Your womb held joy."[19] Might accepting God's invitations be my greatest joy?

In praying with the Annunciation, I am renewed in awareness that I, too, am pregnant with the Word of God. Like Mary, I must carry, labor, and give birth to the Word. Just as Mary questions Gabriel, she poses questions to me—for example, "Do you think you can have the same relationship with God as I have?" That wonderful question humbles and enlightens me each time I reflect on it. Praying with the Annunciation takes me deeper into Mary's response (Luke 1: 47–55) and prompts my own magnificat. Imagining oneself present in a Scripture scene leads to much that is beyond imagining.

"A taste for the gifts of God"

How does Scripture inform your roles in life?

Scripture presents people who influence, lead, or steward. I turn to Scripture regularly to see how these models fulfilled their roles in faithfulness to God and to be inspired and strengthened in my own leadership and stewarding. St. Hildegard counsels us not to be "unmindful of God"[20] in our work. She has particularly strong respect and fondness for Paul and Moses as leaders. She refers to Paul as one who has "drunk deeply of God's wisdom"[21] and who can "keep himself together"[22] in adversity. She identifies both with Paul's visionary experience and his ability to remember that he is only human. I am encouraged to know that God can help me be a visionary leader even as I, like St. Paul or St. Hildegard, understand that I am human and dependent upon God to help me with the inevitable adversity a leader experiences.

Moses "brought the Divine Law into human hearts" and "broadened [justice] into more definite manifestations."[23] To St. Hildegard and to me, Moses models leadership that influences hearts and is just in concrete ways. Moses is God's "most cherished friend" and the recipient of God's "hidden miracles."[24] He is "inspired by the Holy Spirit"[25] and has "a taste for the gifts of God."[26] Moses inspired St. Hildegard to advise another leader, "Let your soul flow like the water God made to flow from the rock struck by the rod of Moses . . . that the day which shines in your spirit may grow."[27] Let your soul flow. What a message that is for a leader.

When the Israelites became "as numerous as the stars of heaven" (Deut 1:10), Moses needed leaders to help him. These persons were to be "wise, discerning, and reputable," as well as "fair" and "not partial," willing to "hear out the small and the great alike," and "not be intimidated by anyone" (Deut 1:15–17). Sometimes their job, like mine, was to scout out what was ahead and then help the others prepare (Deut 1:22). When those they led "grumbled in their tents," their leaders "cried out to God" (Exod 15:25), Who heard and helped. Often in my own leadership, when my team struggled with the hardships of our work, I too cried out to God for help.

Leaders must not be "puffed up" (1 Cor 4:6), "lord it over" (Matt 20:25) others, or seek their own advantage (1 Cor 10:24), but rather must have an "upright heart . . . [and] skillful hand" (Ps 78:72). They must "know well the condition of [their] flock" (Prov 27:23) and remember that all are one body (1 Cor 12:12–31). And, of course, leaders must abide by the golden rule, doing unto others as they would have others do to them (Luke 6:31). In stewarding, they must "be found trustworthy" (1 Cor 4:2) and be faithful in little as well as much (Luke 16:10).

All of the above constitutes a high standard. I, as leader and steward, fall short at times; when this happens, I, in my regret, turn to Psalm 51, a beautiful prayer of contrition and hope for God's mercy. Quoting God, St. Hildegard says, "If you fall, seek Me with a constant outcry, and I will lift you up and receive you. . . . Cry out and persevere in seeking Me; and I will help you."[28] What I noticed as I prayed with Scripture is that Moses, Paul, the prophets, Jesus, and Mary also prayed. A steward and leader must pray, for what is truly to be stewarded is "the manifold grace of God" (1 Pet 4:10). (Later in the book, I will relate examples of integrating prayer and work as leader and steward.)

"Humbly show Me the field of your mind"

Are you a psalmist?

The psalms help me to deeper honesty with God about my situations and feelings, for the psalmists are frank with God. St. Hildegard quotes God: "Humbly show Me the field of your mind and speak to Me with a flood of inner tears."[29] I recommend the psalms to directees struggling to name their feelings or open up to God about their lives. "Let them return to their own heart, and let them look back to their Creator and the Creator's work."[30] When I contend with psalmic language about "enemies," I remind myself that my spiritual enemies are not other nations or people but rather temptations, bad habits, poor decisions, distractions, neglect, or resistance to grace, all of which block my deeper relationship with God.

I write my own psalms, opening to gratitude and praise. For example, in my struggles to heal a broken bone, I was inspired to write:

Thank You, my Healer, for hearing my prayers
for help and healing,
for my progress toward health.
Such an ordeal, a hard time.
You give me hope,
and that counts for so much.
It is out of Your goodness
that I do so well.

You understand, lift me up,
heal and show mercy.

St. Hildegard wrote songs, including a few "songs without music."[31] In one of them, she describes God as "all-accomplishing Word" and, in her unique psalmic style, writes:

Your prescience hidden
in the heart of Your power,
Your power like a wheel around the world,
Whose circling never began
and never slides to an end.[32]

St. Hildegard used psalm verses to counsel others. She referred a woman experiencing turbulence in her life to Psalm 34:14, "Seek peace, and pursue it," and advised her, "Find quiet places for yourself, so that your soul will not wither."[33] I feel affirmed in suggesting that directees find quiet places and pray with the Psalms. The withering of one's soul is at stake.

"The grace of God shines"

How is the deeper meaning of Scripture discovered in prayer with others?

Twice a month in my parish, I facilitate and participate in *lectio divina* (sacred reading) prayer with Scriptures. (Many books describe variations of this method.) The two different groups allow me to experience diversity in how the Word is received and responded to. Our prayer involves reading each passage aloud, slowly and clearly, four times. We've found it helpful as readers to pretend that the listeners do not know how to read and depend on the reader for clarity. We listen rather than read along. After each round, we reflect in silence, write the fruits on a worksheet, and then briefly share without discussion.

The first round of lectio divina invites us to share a word or phrase that struck us. The second round focuses on the stirring of one's heart—the feelings or emotions that came. The third round invites details noticed or questions that surfaced. The fourth reading is followed by a lengthier silence and invites reflection on what the passage and God are saying, and also on what we desire to say to God in response.

"The grace of God shines like the sun and sends its gifts in various ways: in wisdom, in viridity, in moisture."[34] Often, a word, phrase, feeling, detail, question, or prayer offered by someone else in a round awakens me to what God is saying to me, and I am surprised, enlightened, and helped by what comes. Gratitude pours out regularly. The lectio divina experience is inspiring, strengthening, and mutually supportive. Our groups have been faithful to the practice for years. We have all noticed that we've grown to hear better at liturgies because of this practice.

"All the secrets of the Old and New Testaments are being shown to the faithful so they can be made manifest and can be strengthened."[35] St. Hildegard uses the word "secrets" to describe the deeper meaning of Scripture that unfolds when we pray with a text. Once we truly grasp the message, we can more readily embrace and manifest this deeper understanding in our daily lives. "The human being is nothing without the greenness of faith; and without understanding doctrine and the Scriptures, the human being does not bring forth any fruit."[36] Over time, the lectio groups have grown in faith and relationship; they are fruitful faith communities within the larger parish community.

Lectio divina can be done on one's own as well. I journal my responses for each round. I end by using a word or phrase from round one as a mantra for centering prayer.

For group or individual lectio divina, I sometimes use different Scripture translations for each round—for example, NAB, NRSV, Jerusalem Bible, and so on. Doing this frees us from the trap of thinking that we already know exactly what the passage says or means. The words and phrases translators differ over can have special potency.

A vivid example is the story of the man at the pool (John 5:2–15). In one translation, an angel stirs the water. In another, there is no angel. The angel's disappearance shifted our focus to the human beings, as often happens when angels depart in Scripture. We noted the failure of the community around the man to support him and, in contrast, the care and concern Jesus showed him. We realized God was drawing our attention to the plight of others in our community. As St. Hildegard says, "By Your grace, You Who can do it, shall lead me to know You as my God in works of justice."[37]

"Dwell in this place"

How important to you is routine for staying grounded?

I often traveled internationally for work. Praying the Liturgy of the Hours grounded me in whatever the time was at my new location and reminded me that all time is God's time. This way of praying with Scripture expressed my intent to "dwell in this place with all devotion and steadfastness, for [I] have chosen it as a place to serve."[38] I felt connected to all who prayed the Hours around the world. St. Hildegard says, "The eye of God looks upon the felicity of humankind in simplicity."[39] I prayed that God's blessings might permeate all the hours of my day.

St. Hildegard advises, "Although you find yourself among persons of various states of mind, learn how patient and how long-suffering Divine Goodness has been to us all."[40] The Hours kept me in touch with Divine Goodness amid the confusion and challenges of international work. The repetition, the frequent reencounter of certain Scriptures in the Hours, helped their message sink in.

In other times and situations, however, I seem to require variety and spontaneity. Very familiar passages do not speak to my immediate situation. When this is the case, I allow myself the freedom and God the opportunity to surprise me by sometimes praying with Scripture in a more random way.

"Like the woman who sought her lost drachma"

How does God surprise you via Scripture?

One time, when I felt discouraged and my hope was shaky, I paged through the books of the prophets. I searched these texts for something that was missing in my spiritual life. I was praying with Scripture—"Like the woman who sought her lost drachma"[41]—and, like her (Luke 15:8), I found what I sought.

I came upon the ending of Habakkuk, "Though the fig tree does not blossom, and no fruit is on the vines; though the produce of the olive fails, and the fields yield no food; though the flock is cut off from the fold, and there is no herd in the stalls, yet will I rejoice in the Lord; I will exult in the God of my salvation. God, the Lord, is my strength, and makes my feet like the feet of a deer, and makes me tread upon the heights" (Hab 3:17–19). These verses expressed my discouragement, and yet I received strength from God to transcend my situation in hope. I return to these verses now and then and offer them to others who feel discouraged. As St. Hildegard says, "Let the Fiery Illuminator enkindle your heart."[42]

"Through God's grace I understand"

How do you proclaim "inward things"?

St. Hildegard says of herself, "Through God's grace, I understand the profundities of the Scripture."[43] I pray with Scripture in preparation to proclaim the Word as a lector at liturgy. "These words use outward, visible things to teach us about inward things."[44] In this spirit, I begin by seeking the message of the passage. I study it and look at other translations. I reflect and pray. "Because a person chooses, she may choose wisdom. As long as she desires help . . . help will be given her, for if she calls upon God, God will help her."[45]

I work on proclaiming, which is not reading. Proclaiming requires directing one's energy into and through the message. It asks of me that I know what I am saying and deliver it with a style and pace that help hearers embrace the message. "The power of reason is in the bright goodness of God and brings out into the open and confirms the mysteries that have been gathered together in the Old and New Testaments."[46] I experience lectors who help me hear the Word. I feel called to "keep the hunger for God's justice [and] stay in the straight path" and to "be victorious in this shadowy world."[47]

"Look into and sift out"

What is your experience with studying Scripture?

Scripture prayer is helped by education. Scholarship in study Bibles, commentaries, concordances, articles, and books helps us understand Scripture and fruitfully apply it. "When we look into and sift out the Scriptures carefully, we worship God and esteem God's name."[48] Formal classes help us appreciate both the human and the Divine presence in texts, gain perspective on the Bible as a collection of books, understand the influence of culture and events on texts, notice literary devices, and become familiar with the strengths and weaknesses of translations. We learn about insertions from redactors that affect the original meaning of a text and gain experience with exegesis and the use of tools such as lexicons. St. Hildegard lauds "teachers of truth" who "reveal the mysteries . . . as if from a well," for through their work "the earth is sanctified outwardly and inwardly."[49]

The teachers, however, "will never be strong enough to empty this well."[50] Study is not the same as prayer. For the Word to be a living Word, we need the Holy Spirit, Who will "continually instruct the learned, making them joyful by the inspiration of Wisdom."[51] God speaks through scholars, and also in our prayer.

Prayer with Scripture can take many forms. We may simply feel blessed and calmed by the Word as the entry to another way of praying. However, to receive the message of a text, we must usually interact with it. Here I have illustrated (1) unpacking a phrase with a little informal study followed by silent openness; (2) appropriating a verse into one's spiritual practice; (3) reflecting on a verse toward greater self-knowledge and virtue; (4) imagining oneself present in a biblical scene, reflecting further on it, and opening to the questions it poses; (5) turning to Scripture for guidance and role models; (6) using the psalms toward deeper honesty with God; (7) writing one's own psalms or magnificat; (8) practicing lectio divina; (9) praying the Liturgy of the Hours; (10) paging through Scripture "like the woman who sought her lost drachma"; (11) preparing to proclaim the Word and to listen to others proclaim it; and (12) engaging in scholarship about Scripture and praying for the Holy Spirit to light up that learning.

"Now," as St. Hildegard says, "plow in your heart with the knowledge of sacred Scripture and receive the rain."[52]

Reflection Questions

Choose a Gospel scene to pray with. Imagine
yourself present in the scene. Imagine the details
and sensory information. Listen to the words
spoken. Describe what this was like and how you
reacted. Reflect on the experience and what it
meant for you.

"Find quiet places for yourself, so that your soul will
not wither." Choose a psalm to pray with. Allow it to
help you be honest with God and to express what is
going on with you. Or consider using the psalm as a
template for writing a new one. What was psalm
prayer like for you?

What is your experience of praying with Scripture
"like the woman who sought her lost drachma"?
How were you helped?

What is your prayer about "receiving the rain" of
Scripture?

chapter eight

————•••————

SPIRITUAL DIRECTION: ATTENDING GOD

*"[One] can know God by believing in God, by seeing God,
and by attending God."[1]*

S piritual direction is a way of attending God. Attend comes from the Latin *attendere*, "to stretch to apply the mind and energies." Spiritual direction helps us stretch to catch what God is up to in our lives. With our spiritual director, we listen for and pay particular attention to God's presence and action and consider how to respond. Here, spiritual direction is introduced as a practice for befriending the soul.

"Why do you not come?"

What is your experience with deep listening?

St. Hildegard says, "O slow people, why do you not come? Would not help be given you if you sought to come?"[2] She speaks of drawing toward Wisdom, but these words could easily apply to spiritual direction, a wonderful way to befriend one's soul. Spiritual direction flows from the *anam cara*, or "soul friend," tradition.

The Holy Spirit is our first and foremost spiritual director. St.

Hildegard relates the Holy Spirit as saying, "You can sow a word in human ears, but into the heart, which is My field, you cannot pour the dew of compunction, or the rain of tears, or the moisture of devotion, or the warmth of the Holy Spirit, through all of which the fruit of holiness must grow."[3] St. Hildegard reminds us that "the grace of God comes to people through the Holy Spirit."[4] In spiritual direction, both director and directee listen for the Holy Spirit. "When the gifts of the Holy Spirit pour forth upon them from above in pure and holy abundance, they teach them many things about heavenly and spiritual matters."[5]

We seek to consistently notice God's presence and action in our lives. "God is like a worker Who blows on a fire with a pair of bellows and then turns the fire every which way so that God can accomplish the work more fully."[6] Are we aware of God's constant, fiery activity? St. Hildegard says our spiritual journey is our work "because God is full Life, without beginning and without end, so a person's work is also life in God."[7] A spiritual director helps us with the work that is life in God.

Glimpses of God may cause us to desire more or to seek clarity about our experiences. God "revealed God's hidden Divinity to humans with great heralds and many signs."[8] Seeds sown by the Holy Spirit may give us the sense that we are not yet fully abloom in knowledge of God. As St. Hildegard says, "the knowledge of God . . . lies in human hearts without fully flowering in them."[9] A spiritual director helps us along the path of deeper knowledge of and relationship with God.

Our interest in spiritual direction may flow from the desire to live our lives in greater service, holiness, and happiness. "Both spiritual and secular people who desire to serve God and keep their souls in life ought to convert themselves to the dawn of a holy way of life and blessedness."[10] Such motivations for seeking spiritual direction often surface in Lent. Those already serving in church ministry or outreach may find a spiritual director helpful in their pursuit of holiness and happiness.

Occasionally, we experience crises in faith, turmoil, unhelpful images of God, uncertainty about our call, big changes that are difficult to accept, fear of going deeper in life with God, prayer life that is dry as toast, or decisions for which we lack clarity. "The Most Powerful Giver whom no one can resist has given you wings to fly with," says St. Hildegard, "Therefore fly swiftly over all those obstacles."[11] A spiritual director helps us work through obstacles and flex our spiritual wings.

St. Hildegard tells us that we "can know God by believing in God, by seeing God, and by attending God."[12] To attend, in her sense of the word, means to stretch a little in applying our mind and energy. How do we do the attending and seeing that support our believing? What if life events challenge our believing? "So too the earth is disturbed for a time like a chariot overturned."[13] When life feels shaken apart, "it may even be necessary that the human being keep herself together in sadness."[14] Where is God in our grief and loss? "God gathers those who are estranged and seeks those who are lost."[15] A spiritual director helps us feel a little less lost and a little more gathered.

My directees describe regular spiritual direction as providing "guard rails" or "a little extra motivation." Spiritual direction benefits me as well. It helps me stay on track with my spiritual practices and journey. The anticipation of the next session brings constancy in my spiritual life. Constancy "is the foundation of the other inner virtues in people, and by her discipline leads them to God."[16] A spiritual director cannot do our work for us, but can be a beacon and a motivator. The director is waiting to hear about our relationship with God and stands ready to help us with our journey. "Let people turn to the spiritual life . . . let them contemplate . . . under the direction of their spiritual advisor."[17]

"Wisdom is found in some people"

What do you look for in a spiritual director?

"[Wisdom] is found in some people of the world, in a mind that, instructed by the inspiration of the Holy Spirit, meditates on every heavenly thing. . . . What the soul holds in her mind is from Divine inspiration."[18] St. Hildegard notes characteristics we seek in a spiritual director—wisdom and inspiration from the Holy Spirit. She adds, "Be mild and gentle in your spirit and your heart."[19] We desire a director who also is gentle with our soul, does not intimidate, and has a good heart.

A spiritual director is committed to the ministry, such that she "faithfully and dutifully serves God."[20] A director is spiritually deep —that is, she has befriended her own soul and become a friend of God; is spiritually mature, wise, and prayerful; demonstrates a sincere, humble, genuine, and generous spirit; and has a deep trust in and love for God. "Some people . . . know God, and so they carry the treasure of good will and the sweet spices of virtue."[21] No amount of skill compensates for lack of spiritual depth. A director commits to growth in relationship with God and prays about her ministry. "Watch carefully lest your God-given viridity dry up."[22] A spiritual director is receptive and inclusive. St. Hildegard says, "Receive this woman . . . who has not yet completely shown her hidden wounds . . . and all others running to you."[23] A spiritual director seeks to "imitate the dove of mercy"[24] in her manner toward her directees.

How do we know we are called to this ministry? A common sign is the tendency of others to seek spiritual conversations with us. In my case, colleagues came by to converse about the struggle to find God in challenging situations, the impact of overwork on their spirits, how to be courageously honest despite fears, or how to discern new calls. When I casually mentioned the uptick in these conversations to my spiritual director, he said, "What do you make of that? Why not pray about it?" With time and discernment, I discovered God's invitation to become a spiritual director. I then trained to prepare for the ministry.

There are spiritual director training programs all over the world. Spiritual Directors International is one organization[25] that helps people find training programs or spiritual directors by geographic area. It also provides ethical guidelines for the ministry. Training programs and supervision form directors and help them develop critical interpersonal skills.

Spiritual directors are accountable to God, but also to supervisors or peer groups for their growth as directors. Spiritual direction experiences, if fruitfully reflected upon, help directors become more spiritually attuned and wise.

Spiritual depth and God-centered listening—what St. Hildegard terms "the inner spiritual law"[26]—are the most crucial characteristics of spiritual directors. We must have "ears sharp to hear inner meanings."[27] Even so, we know the fullness of what we hear is "known only to the Spirit of God."[28] Without abundant experience finding God in our own lives, we struggle to have the sharp ears to hear the inner meanings in others' experiences.

Spiritual directors pray to have "a heart of flesh" (Ezek 36:26) and a listening, understanding mind and heart, able to discern (1Kgs 3:9). We listen deeply and generously to the directee, and for God's mysterious presence and action in the directee's life. We pray to have "spiritual eyes . . . [by which we] see, and [to] know spiritual things through hearing."[29] We may hear insights, potent words, something emerging in the directee's relationship with God, or an inner truth beginning to shine forth. We listen to and observe God within and with the directee. "The fiery Holy Spirit will lend you Her aid in this."[30] To receive this aid, the director also listens to God within herself and prays, "May I be steeped in the gift of God's grace."[31]

How does the Holy Spirit guide directors? St. Hildegard counsels, "Watch over yourself, because the grace of God does not withdraw from you, but makes a sign to you."[32] A moment of quiet in the session can help us. "The admonition of heavenly inspiration appears in secret quiet. . . . What the soul holds in her mind is from Divine inspiration."[33] To listen to the directee, to God at work within the directee, and to God within one's self, we must "learn . . . to keep our minds pure."[34] We must be undistracted, prayerful, and fully present, saying, "Here I am, Lord, Your listening servant" (1Sam 3:10).

REFLECTION QUESTIONS

How have the wisdom, prayerfulness, and good will of your spiritual director mattered to you?

How have a spiritual director's depth and experience helped you entrust your deepest spiritual experiences to him/her?

What is your prayer about spiritual direction?

The Holy Spirit "breathes into her right ear"

What is your experience with a spiritual director helping you fulfill God's call?

In my early days of being drawn to spiritual writing, my spiritual director was a great help. I felt called, yet reluctant. The more I read about the women saints I loved, the more I realized I wasn't alone in that reluctance. St. Hildegard herself describes vividly the call from God to "Say and write . . . the wonders of God"[35] and yet she "refused to write for a long time through doubt."[36] She describes feeling compelled until finally she "set [her] hand to the writing."[37] I knew if I opened up to my director about God's call to write, I would have to respond to God. I would be on the hook. I would hear God's words to St. Hildegard addressed to me, "Cry out therefore, and write thus!"[38]

I resisted, yet felt terrible about resisting. I told my director I needed to speak in our next session about a call from God. I asked her not to let me escape from that conversation. My director understood and agreed. I think we both knew that "no one is able to resist God, since God alone is God."[39] She did not probe, but trusted God to keep the conversation going with me. "The gifts of the Holy Spirit . . . are in the person."[40]

Between sessions, I considered my successes with scientific writing, and then realized I didn't know how to do spiritual writing. *Is it nonfiction too?* I wondered. *Why do some people write and others not? Why me? Why do I resist? What will happen? Will my life be rearranged and changed?* Yet "sparks burn in the hearts of the faithful."[41] I realized the smoldering might never stop. I thought about St. Teresa of Ávila and all she'd revealed in her writing. I felt protest and panic about such revealing on my part. *Yet what if St. Teresa had not written and her insights were lost to me, to us all? But what am I doing, comparing myself to her and St. Hildegard?*

"The faithful impose constraints of the heaviest weight on their own . . . while inwardly they endure many sufferings in their hearts."[42] God urged that the Good News of my life be revealed. I imposed constraints. In my heart, I suffered reluctance and questioning. I felt lost, resistant, and inadequate. Yet I also began to feel certainty, the capacity to learn, held and guided by God, compelled, and a desire to serve. I needed to talk about how conflicted and yet convicted I felt. St. Hildegard expresses God's desire: "I wish to wipe away the thick clouds from among my daughters, because I am unwilling to be without them."[43]

In our next session, my spiritual director smiled across at me in lovely receptivity. I spoke briefly of other themes, and then out tumbled the sequence of spiritual events pointing to the call to write. It seemed that "the Holy Spirit steeped my power of reason."[44] Somehow, as I related my arguments against the idea, they seemed so trivial in the face of God's mountain of graces. "No soul has enough power to fight against God, Who resists their attempts."[45]

As I spoke, I became clear on what I was to do. The self-imposed "constraints of the heaviest weight" and "thick clouds" were gone. "Where Divine grace has worked, it banishes all dark obscurity and makes pure and lucid those things that are obscure."[46] I felt relieved and freer for having spoken about my conflict. St. Hildegard says, "Indeed, Divine Love and Humility exist in the purest divinity, from which the streams of blessedness flow . . . to free and set aright humankind."[47]

I abruptly surrendered my resistance. I declared to my director that I would do as God desired. Looking back, I surmise that my prayerful director wisely noted that my abrupt capitulation was not really a full-throated yes to God. "The tree that is full of flowers is beautiful to look upon," says St. Hildegard, "but it is far more useful when its fruit has ripened."[48] My director suggested I pray with the mix of themes I'd brought up: how did God want me to be with the writing, how was I drawn, what did love of self mean to me, and how did I feel about the looming Feast of the Sacred Heart. She wondered aloud if God might be inviting me to trust.

Bingo.

"[The Holy Spirit's] touch breathes into her right ear . . . [and then] into the hearts of believers that they may understand the Divine power of God."[49]

Left to my own devices, I would have worked on plans for writing and not explored the other themes. I would have missed things God wanted to say to me. Initially, I saw no relationship between the themes. But I felt an inner resonance with what my director said, and I fully trusted her. I often sensed that she and God worked in cahoots—"in the same hut," as the word's origin expresses. "God has infused human beings with good understanding."[50] How true of my director. I was committed to doing as she suggested. As an advocate of spiritual directors, St. Hildegard says, "Let [people] also be persistent in the purest prayers in the amount their spiritual director advises."[51]

When my director mentioned God's invitation to trust, I knew instantly that this was so. I expressed to God my desire to trust more fully. I prayerfully reflected on God's mountain of graces. I could see that God had been inviting, guiding, and preparing me for some time, and would undoubtedly continue to do so. "A river from the Holy Spirit will flow into you," says St. Hildegard, "and will water all these things in you, and . . . will cause a column of sanctity and good will to rise up."[52]

My director had said that God knew how I felt and what my life was like. Indeed, as I prayed about the invitation to write, I felt understood by God. A new insight, a bit of self-knowledge arrived. Some of my panic resulted from not wanting to let God down. Now I saw that God would stay with me and help me fulfill the call. I wasn't alone, wasn't without aid. "Keep in mind that God . . . holds the person who faithfully and dutifully serves God in God's sweet embrace, and God greatly loves her."[53] My trust deepened as I prayed, as did my confidence that just as I could trust God, God could trust me in return. I began to ask myself, *What if spiritual writing is important for the person God wants me to be, for my growth in relationship with God, and for my service to God and others?* It was becoming clear that spiritual writing wasn't to be my hobby but rather a serious matter, a ministry. *What if it is truly in the best interest of my soul, or someone else's soul, to commit myself to this path?* I pondered. *Might it be good for me to become a spiritual writer?* St. Hildegard says, "The burden of your labor, which God has given you to bear, is good for you."[54]

Next, God invited me to see my scientific writing background as relevant, not the opposite. A scientist plans, hypothesizes, does the simplest experiment first, and then communicates the results. Adhering to this model, I could figure out a reasonable place to start. "When a person's reason imitates God, she touches God."[55] I sensed God saying, "Yes, what is it you don't know?" My skills and experience would go a long way. *I must trust myself and my experience*, I realized, *for God would not call me to do what I am incapable of doing.* Suddenly I felt better, like I could breathe deeply again. "We live illumined in God and vivified by the breath of life, through which we know that God is God and our Creator."[56] I felt that I had returned to my true self.

I turned to the Feast of the Sacred Heart. I prayerfully reflected on Jesus's heart—how open, how consistently welcoming, how willing to endure heartache. I considered the sacredness of a heart that is aligned with God, a heart that is God's home. I remembered the traditional Sacred Heart image in which Jesus points to His heart. And then, I got it. "Clearly, joy was near, the joy of illumination."[57] *What sort of heart is a follower of Jesus to have?*

In that moment I offered my wholehearted alignment with God's call to write. I didn't want to be a mopey disciple, all wishy-washy and half-hearted. No. I wanted a proper spirit of adventure, enthusiasm, and all-out willingness. St. Hildegard says, "Let your spirit shine in God and your days burn bright in the Fiery Giver."[58] I wanted a heart welcoming to readers and a heart willing to be wounded for this cause. I wanted an open heart. I knew the Good News I could write about had sometimes been discovered in wounds. My heart must be vulnerable and courageous. I prayed to have the heart of Jesus.

The quality of our heart matters in the fruitfulness of our work. St. Hildegard affirms this. She doesn't write much about the heart of Jesus, a devotion popularized after her time. However, she does refer to Jesus as the "Pastor of our hearts."[59] She speaks of her own heart's response to God, saying, "My heart's knowledge recognizes a shining gem in the gentleness of Your sweetness."[60] We know her heart from her writing, how boldly and generously she pours out what is of God. The monk Guibert wrote, "This blessed lady . . . contemplates the one thing that is alone necessary, the glory of the Blessed Trinity, in the utmost simplicity of heart. Mild and gentle in heart, she drinks from that fullness within herself and pours it out of herself to relieve the thirst of those who thirst."[61] May we all be so.

St. Hildegard had the heart of Jesus. In turn, she noticed the hearts of others. For example, she said, "The cheerfulness of the human heart shows in the sound of the voice, which the human lifts up with the soul's breath."[62] May my writer's voice be lifted up with my soul's breath, for then it will ring true. "The Holy Spirit's gifts bring viridity into the human heart, to bear good fruit."[63]

Next I turned to love of self. This theme had come up in an earlier retreat, and yet I had not fully explored it. I mentioned it to my director merely in passing, as I still did not take it seriously. To my director, however, it was a theme for my continued prayer, and thus it became so for me.

The first thing that came was, "You are the strength of my heart and my Joy forever."[64] *The self I love is the self for whom this is true.* "God is in the strength of the soul."[65] *How can I not love the self for whom God is everything, the self that is the recipient of grace?* "The soul comes from God. The soul is fertile from God's grace."[66] *God dwells within me.* "The soul exists as something Divine in the person."[67] *To not love myself betrays that; to love myself is to be true to this reality. This is the truth of who I am.*

I have no self to share that is independent of God. Now God, Who is Love, desired to love me into becoming a spiritual writer. Because I am "human and like other people," and because I possess "so strong and so steep a desire for God"[68], I must love what God loves. St. Hildegard says, "[In] the figure of the human body . . . God's work lies hidden."[69] I saw that hidden within me was a spiritual writer, and God had been steadily drawing forth that writer. Would my relationship with God be deepened and enhanced through writing? St. Hildegard says, "God loves you so much that God wants your soul."[70] There are "different paths of the soul to attain . . . one desire in God."[71] This was now my path and my desire.

I returned to earth from these beautiful, lofty, inspiring thoughts. I journaled, "But what does it look like to concretely love myself as a spiritual writer?" *For one,* I thought, *I don't betray my call or the One Who calls. I give myself fully to the call. I give myself time, space, solitude, steadfastness, patience, openness, prayerfulness, trust, and training to fulfill my call. I learn what I must learn. I dedicate myself to this. With God, I love myself into the role. I befriend my writerly self. I lovingly do what benefits me as a writer.*

I realized, *I believe the God Who calls is the God Who gives us grace to fulfill the call.* "Divine grace enkindles them in the fire of the Holy Spirit."[72] *I must prepare for the ministry of spiritual writing.* St. Hildegard says, "God assigns to all of you the task of ministering to all the needs of this life, both the spiritual and the secular."[73] *I must embrace all the practical means of the spiritual writing ministry. I shall love my spiritual writer self to better love God and others.* I felt great peace, excitement, and fiery willingness.

I returned to my director amazed at the fruits of prayer with the themes she'd suggested. The Holy Spirit was at work in our sessions and in my prayer. "God is here. God is not a hidden fire nor a silent fire, but an effective fire."[74] I told her all that had happened, and that I'd not only grown in trust of God but also grown in trust of self. I told her my "yes" was fresh, and I must align with God to concretely love my spiritual writer self into being. My director suggested I continue to pray and seek confirmation from God in my discerning. This I did. The ultimate confirmation of course is in the fruitfulness and grace of fulfilling the call, and it is my joy that these were eventually realized.

Spiritual writing and spiritual direction require ongoing commitment to one's own spiritual journey:

It is fitting that the rays of the sun should shine upon that root which has been planted in the Holy Spirit, and that a gentle rain should moisten it, for a good field which brings forth good fruit flourishes in the sun and the rain and the dew. Therefore, blessed soul, maintain your temple with discretion, so that the fruitfulness with which you embrace God does not wither, because God greatly loves your soul, and God will gather you into Her bosom and will receive you into eternal felicity. Now, live forever, and with a vigilant soul sigh to God.[75]

"A manifestation of the invisible and eternal" and "Attending God"

Have you ever sensed there was more to a story?

Some scientists come to me for spiritual direction because of my scientific background. Together, we seek spiritual richness in their work. St. Hildegard is a great companion for us. She says that "God, for the glory of God's name, gathered together the world from the elements"[76], and that fire "pervades all of creation and supplies to it the joy of its light, signifying the power of God."[77] Whatever we observe is "a manifestation of the invisible and eternal."[78] St. Hildegard was fascinated by the natural world and wrote about it. The scientists I companion, like St. Hildegard, have been interested in the natural world since their youth. They experienced God's compelling call to become scientists. They desire to both fulfill their call and find God present with them in their work.

One scientist spoke about the story of the Syrophoenician woman in Mark 7:24–30. The woman was a Gentile who sought healing for her daughter. Jesus at first declined her request, saying, "I was sent only to the lost sheep of the house of Israel." The woman persisted, saying, "Even the dogs eat the crumbs." Then Jesus healed her daughter. I invited my directee to say more about the importance of the story to her. She said, "Somehow it spoke to me. I admired the woman's savvy and persistence. She really wanted to help her daughter." I said, "And that meant something to you?" She said, "Absolutely. I really want to help the people I serve as a scientist, too."

I sensed there was more in this story for my directee. I wondered what God might be saying to her through the story. I allowed a few moments of silence but did not sense the Spirit calling me to probe that.

Sometimes directees are reticent about God. They lack the words or the habit of explicitly speaking of God. "A person does not have the capacity to speak of God in the same way that she would speak of the humanness of a human being or the defining characteristic of a work made by human hands."[79] I felt called to simply listen.

The directee then spoke about a work experience. She described a large amount of experimental data that at first seemed like a sea of numbers. The analytic process, the graphing, and the interpretation of the data were laborious and unappealing, yet she kept going. The directee said, "Finally I started to really understand the data. I grasped something very key. I sensed God sharing it with me. I realized God reveals through science! Data show us something about the world that God is revealing, and I can participate!" St. Hildegard says, "The grace of God shines like the sun and sends its gifts in various ways."[80]

"How did you feel in that moment?" I asked.

"I felt closer to God," my directee said. "I actually teared up. I felt loved by God. I wasn't expecting that. It means a lot to me."

St. Hildegard says, "With an open heart, the faithful . . . consider the greatness of God's power."[81] I was touched by my directee's faithfulness.

At that point, our time had run out. Now I did feel the prodding of the Spirit. I suggested to my directee that she return in her prayer to the story of the Syrophoenician woman and to her experience with the data. I invited her to savor these and see if God had more for her. To slow down and savor God's graces is so important. "God mercifully waters a person with the hidden sweetness of God's grace to bear the fruit of good works."[82]

In prayer, I rejoiced in God's goodness to my directee. St. Hildegard says, "Great joy came upon them, since the person had help everywhere from God."[83] I prayed for even more grace for her. "May the bright light of God's grace never be cut off from you."[84] I had, after all, set God up. Then I let go and entrusted my directee wholly to God. "Our God . . . existing as Life, gives out unfailing life to God's own . . . and God has a mansion for them to live in. Who can do this other than God?"[85] Before the next session, I renewed my letting go, reminding myself that God and the directee might have gone on to new themes—that my job was to "hear the mysteries of God."[86]

"Persistence!" my directee began in this session. "Jesus responded to the persistence of the Syrophoenician woman, and to my persistence with data analysis. These things were connected. Maybe the woman's persistence inspired mine." She went on, "The woman gave Jesus a big thought to think—maybe He's here for Gentiles, too—and it changed His perspective. That's what the new data did for me. It changed my perspective, including about God."

"And how has that change in perspective played out for you?" I asked.

"I feel glad about my call and more willing to be persistent, to have discipline, for one thing," she said. "But I also started to consider where my mind is when I relate to Jesus. Thoughts are important. I'm trying to be more aware of my mind's habits, be more spiritually aware of my thinking, since it is part of how God works with me."

St. Hildegard says, "Good desire went up from what is customary. . . . It went up into the hidden way of knowing God, which is the soul's salvation."[87] My directee was, because of God's initiative, responding to God in a new way. She'd changed her prayer style.

"How has this influenced your prayer?" I asked.

"Oh, prayer is much deeper," she said. "I'm letting my scientific self be more present in prayer; I don't stifle it. I enjoy prayer more, and I feel fully present."

"And God?" I asked.

She smiled. "It turns out God desires my imagination, observations, and thoughts, and to reveal with me."

St. Hildegard says, "The human person cannot fully comprehend with her own knowledge what she is, and so the soul admonishes the battle-weary person to look back and reach out to her Creator with patience and obedience."[88] She should look, yes, and find out that what she is, is important to God. Wisdom "protects and guides the people who want to follow Her, and keeps with great love those who are true to Her."[89] In new wisdom, my directee discovered the importance to God of her scientific self.

As the spiritual director in this situation, I had not been sure that the two themes the directee initially brought up were related. I'd simply sensed there was more to each story and that both were worth savoring in prayer. St. Hildegard says, "Always examine the hidden things that pertain to the soul."[90] God graciously brought further enrichment for this person. "God is fire and living Spirit."[91] A spiritual director knows "she must zealously keep on guard, lest she ascribe these things to herself, as if they were of herself rather than of God."[92]

This example reveals that some directees lead with thoughts and thinking in their spirituality. New thoughts arrive as gifts from God. An emotional investment exists, but thoughts are spoken of first, not feelings. An analogy is the style of St. Paul, whose letters are full of reasoned thinking, but unspoken worry, concern, love, and zeal enter his message. If directees are open, the Holy Spirit enlivens their thinking and brings them into deeper relationship with God, which is the hope in the spiritual direction ministry. For every directee, "God established a road so that people might walk in it."[93] God establishes the road; the director invites the noticing of it.

We all have a crucial need, as this directee illustrates, to feel fully present to God in prayer. In her experience is a cautionary note for directors. It is painful for a person to feel that their profession or personality type (e.g., thinker vs. feeler) is not of spiritual value. It is also not consistent with the variety of professions among Jesus's first disciples. St. Hildegard says, "The omnipotent God moves the person with her own piety so that she sees the light of the highest blessedness in the flame and love of true holiness, so that she chooses this flame."[94] This directee chose the flame and befriended her soul.[95]

In St. Hildegard's time, monastics were held to be spiritual greats in comparison to ordinary laypeople. St. Hildegard challenged that bias, declaring, "The stars, clearly the good laypeople ... demonstrate that the grace of God is heavenly. Through it they are found in almsgiving and the most holy work."[96] Through her letters, St. Hildegard was a spiritual director for both lay and monastic persons. Her focus was always on their relationship with God. This is, as she says, "the pilgrimage you are on."[97]

REFLECTION QUESTIONS

When has a spiritual director's "God-centered listening" been a godsend to you?

How does your unique background affect your companioning of others or your insights into their spirituality?

Have you ever listened to someone's story and sensed there was more to it? What was happening within you as you listened? How was God at work in you during that experience? What did you do?

Are you more a feeler or more a thinker in your personality style? How does this affect your perception of another's style of interacting with you or God?

What is your prayer about being a spiritual director?

chapter nine

———••———

PRAYER

"There is nothing that is hidden"

ow is your prayer life?

"My house, that is, the human being, is a house of prayer."[1] How beautifully St. Hildegard invites us into prayer with words she received from God in her own prayer. To be a true and faithful friend of our souls, we must pray—we must connect with God, Who dwells within us. "The powers of the soul are very strong, for through them the soul knows and perceives God."[2]

There is no substitute for prayer, though there are many ways to pray. The point of prayer is our relationship with God. "When any faithful heart fixes its spirit upon God, it cannot be torn away from God . . . nor does [it] walk in an unstable whirlwind."[3] We can be in communication with God, sharing life with one another, helping one another. St. Hildegard says, "What good can I do without God? None. But then I look to God Who gave me life . . . [and] I am made a strong stone of God's edifice."[4]

God already knows everything. "There is nothing that is hidden from God or that God does not know."[5] So why talk about it? God desires to share in and help us with the very things God already knows about. In a close human friendship, our friend may observe and surmise how things are with us, but our friendship is sustained and enhanced when we open up to our friend about our life and vice versa. And, of course, it is most often in prayer that we realize our Friend is with us. "Indeed, the human person understands through the soul that she possesses God."[6]

Prayer is about utter honesty with God. Transparency is consistent with being in the image and likeness of God, for "God is truthful and without illusion."[7] We can be so as well. Prayer involves openness to receiving what God offers, in whatever way it comes. St. Hildegard relates God's promise that "I shall speak of My beloved children, who receive Me with open senses and willing mind and clear intellect, and touch Me with sighs and tears, and follow Me with joy to embrace Me."[8] Openness is key. God communicates constantly. We are wise to not limit our prayerfulness to one part of the day, and to sustain our receptivity, readiness to hear and notice, and alertness to God and to grace. Our generous God promises to hear us. We can address God in all hours with confidence in God's interest and loving response. "The grace of God is near you, and gives you blessings. . . . Do not cut yourself off from it."[9]

Those I see in spiritual direction already pray and view their spiritual lives as important. What is sometimes missing, however, is an emphasis on relationship with God. Frequently directees speak of what they want from God; much less frequently they speak of love for God or God's love for them. St. Hildegard relates God's words, "In her ignorance she does not know Me."[10] God is primarily the One Who gives them what they want or need. This is a very human and usual starting point. Often, our prayer is not integrated with the entirety of our lives. We select certain things to bring to God. Yet "no one is able to stand who wants to stand by her own effort."[11] To each of us St. Hildegard says, "Keep faith in God, entrust everything to God, and God will never desert you."[12]

Some directees do not initially name the grace they need or pray for themselves. Sometimes they have not prayed about the very crisis they reveal. Some have images of God that suggest distance or lack of intimacy. They experience inherited images as off-putting but haven't found a more life-giving one. They face a sizable leap to pray with and trust the God dwelling in their very soul, the God so intimately sharing their every experience, the God Who wants to help and, if allowed to, *will* help. With encouragement, willing effort, openness, and their own experiences of God, things change. St. Hildegard says, "The trust a person has in God also touches her with constancy, to trust continually in God and lift up her thoughts to God—for the minds of the faithful are strengthened by the virtue of constancy."[13] Trust comes, and with it constancy in intimate relationship.

What God does and says in response to our prayer is also God's revealing of God. St. Hildegard says, "Divine Love is beautiful . . . in the strength of unfailing Divinity, and wonderful in the gifts of [God's] mysteries."[14] We come to know God more deeply in our openness. What does an answer to prayer say about the Answerer? "This good is yours by the knowledge that lets you understand God by the inspiration of the Holy Spirit."[15] God's revealing is inexhaustible. There is always more. Through prayer we discover God's love for surprise and abundance. As the great mystic visionary St. Hildegard shows us, God reveals in ways that are well beyond our little requests and lives.

What sort of God converts Saul, persecutor of Christians, to St. Paul, founder of Christian communities and source of treasured Scriptures? The experiences of St. Hildegard, St. Paul, and others reveal the power of God working within us to make us more than we once were. They reveal God's love and desire to involve us in God's projects. God gives, reveals, changes, loves, and asks things of us if we are open and prayerful. "The Holy Spirit will pour forth the dew of Her grace among the people, together with prophecy, wisdom, and holiness, so that they will then seem to be changed into a different way—a better way—of life."[16] To pray sincerely is to open ourselves to change, deeper relationship, and service. To resist prayer is to resist becoming something more—to resist knowing the One Who invites us to grand adventure.

To pray deeply is to know and love the God Who dwells with us and in us, and thus to know and love our true self as the beloved dwelling place of God, as a house of prayer. In this dwelling place, God "imparts . . . power and strength . . . by the great clarity of Divine visitation"[17] and "makes us alive invisibly."[18] St. Hildegard says, "[We] live in the power of God just as a heart lives in a person."[19] God's loving power beats gently and constantly at the center of our being, our Life, our Hope, and our Love. To know God intimately in prayer is to know our true self intimately in relationship with God— the epitome of self-knowledge and befriending the soul.

"The right step on which to place their foot"

How important are traditional prayers to you?

Traditional prayers and praying communally often go hand in hand. We need the prayers we know by heart. St. Hildegard says, "Good will is the sweetest aroma to God."[20] We say these prayers in good will.

Years ago, I stood with my mother and eight siblings at my father's bedside as he breathed his last breath. I was inspired to intone, "Our Father," and we said the rest together. The beautiful prayer said what we needed to say to God and brought us together spiritually in the moment. St. Hildegard says, "Thoughts that proceed from faith with truth's simplicity [are directed] through the soul's sighing to the true King."[21] Your kingdom come in this moment; Your will be done. We forgive. Amen.

Looking back, the prayer honored the sacrifices my Catholic mother made to raise us in her faith, yet also honored my Methodist father's tradition. We all knew a prayer that was meaningful for both. God "gives people all the things they need."[22] We needed the gift and inspiration of Jesus's own prayer, and I feel gratitude for the inspiration to begin a prayer that was perfect in ways I couldn't think through just then. Who has their own words at such a time? We befriended our souls and invited God into our experience of Dad's death via the Our Father. Praying as one in that moment seemed to strengthen us. Wisdom "supplies what is necessary for the present moment and for life in general."[23]

From this experience I saw the gift of traditional prayers. The God Who inspired me to intone one surely finds them agreeable. They flow from our good will. God bends over to inspire our prayer when we most need inspiration. I grew in love and trust of such a generous and kind God, so wonderfully present in the hour of Dad's death. I recognized in myself the faith and openness the Inspirer requires. "A faithful person . . . shows her Creator the pious and holy devotion of her heart."[24]

The greatest prayer in my faith tradition is the Mass. I think of it as a meal the resurrected Jesus shares with today's disciples. As with His first disciples, Jesus shares His life with us—"Being Life, He gave Life to those believing in Him."[25] At this meal He not only gives Himself, but also addresses us, both communally and individually. St. Hildegard connects many God events in describing the Mass: "That same power of the Almighty, which overshadowed Mary and brought forth from her the flesh and blood of the Son of God, descends through the open wounds of Jesus Christ upon the offering of bread and wine so that this oblation is mystically transformed into the flesh and blood of Jesus Christ in the sight of God and of the holy angels, just as grain and wine grow through a hidden viridity that a human being cannot see."[26] She prays, "Thus may it be done in us, that we may see You in our souls through faith, and may receive You with praise and true love in the habitation of our bodies."[27] I am fed by the Word, by Jesus's self-giving in bread and wine, and by sharing life with Him and my community. "Through the seeds of His words the Son of God revealed to those who believe that, filled up with His flesh and blood, they can have life; and this, once hidden within the Divine secrets, He disclosed through Himself."[28]

Sometimes I arrive for Mass feeling hungry and thirsty for spiritual nourishment. I leave ready to be bread broken and wine poured out for others. "The Son of God will never be exhausted, but will always give the drink of life to those who thirst. For He is the Savior of life. And we, who formerly fell short, now are strengthened. . . . Through Him we eat the food of life and go on through knowledge of God to life."[29]

At other times I come to Mass aware of having gifts to offer, especially if I am serving as a Eucharistic minister, lector, or intercession leader. One of my joys is to lead the intercessions. The community so palpably prays its concerns for the Church, the world, those in trouble, and its own members who are ill or have died. My community has prayed for me during my health struggles. To know they were aware of my plight and praying for me gave me strength. St. Hildegard says, "God will always hear the cry of your prayers."[30]

In the intercessions, in the parish's numerous appeals to time, talent, and treasure, and in simply looking around at my diverse community, my heart is touched and enlarged. I hear the call of Jesus in the Gospel. I learn to be of service in concrete ways. St. Hildegard says, "Faithful people both small and great can find in Jesus the right step on which to place their foot."[31] She also says, "Through His humanity, the incarnate Son of God enlightened faithful and heavenly people. . . . And so He inflamed them with charity that they might faithfully assist all the needy."[32] Without the Mass and my community, I likely would not be as generous or as clear about the right step on which to place my foot in order to concretely love others.

Unexpected moments of grace occur at Mass. During a Lenten offertory, two women with beautiful voices sang, "Given to you that you may draw close to Me." (At least, so I heard it.) I received the message as: my life, all my experiences, even my great challenges and difficulties, are given that I may draw close to God. I knew in my depths this was truth. I felt tender consolation and deep gratitude for all that God had used to draw me closer. I gained strength for the journey in that moment.

That experience has had a lasting effect. I now look at new challenges as opportunities to draw closer to God. These women gave voice to the Word of God I needed to hear. "The beautiful human language that gives voice to the will and disposition of God is a great measure of human stature; and it makes music at the altar of God, for it knows God."[33]

The sung Word is blessed by God with special impact. I treasure participating. St. Hildegard, a composer of wondrous liturgical music, says, "It is proper for the body, in harmony with the soul, to use its voice to sing praises to God."[34] She articulates the power of song and the sense of wholeness and harmony we experience. "As the power of God is everywhere and encompasses all things, and no obstacle can stand against it, so too the human intellect has great power to resound in living voices, and arouse sluggish souls to vigilance by the song.... For the faithful creature rejoices to her Creator in a voice of exultation and gladness and returns God perpetual gratitude."[35]

At Mass, the Word and Eucharist sometimes come together powerfully for me. One Sunday we heard about the call of Isaiah, when a seraph touched his lips with a live coal (Isa 6:6–8). God asks, "Whom shall I send?" Isaiah responds, "Here am I; send me!" Later, as I approached the altar for communion, I realized the "live coal" on my lips was the very body and blood, the life of Jesus, preparing me to be sent, to be prophetic. I said, "Here am I; send me!" The moment called me to reveal the presence and action of God in my life, especially through writing, and, like Isaiah, to abandon my reluctance. St. Hildegard says, "[The resurrected Jesus] touched His disciples with that fire from which He was conceived in His mother's womb: in tongues of fire He poured upon them the mightiest force. . . . The Holy Spirit changed them into a different form of life that they had not previously known. . . . They were inwardly strengthened."[36]

Traditional prayers and praying communally go together and help us in many circumstances and states. Reflecting on the Mass with St. Hildegard deepens the experience. She fluidly brings in the overshadowing of Mary by the Holy Spirit as relevant to the transformation of grain, wine, and us. The Fire by which Mary conceived is the same Fire with which Jesus touches us in this meal. St. Hildegard says that here is the right step on which to place our foot. She says singing arouses our souls, brings harmony within us, and conveys God's will. Through this greatest prayer, we know more intimately the One whose disciples we are and receive the grace to live as such.

REFLECTION QUESTIONS

What is your reaction to St. Hildegard's image of you as "a house of prayer"?

In your view, what is the point of prayer?

What is your prayer about your prayer life?

"Bitterness . . . gnashes its teeth"

What life experience has tempted you to bitterness or another un-promising attitude?

Attitudes we develop toward our lives, our work, others, or situations present spiritual risks to us if we persist with them. We cannot be a good friend to our soul with a bad attitude. Here I focus on the spiritual risk of bitterness, but one could easily substitute negativity, blaming, judging, cynicism, greed, distrust, jealousy or any number of unpromising inclinations. Any of these would certainly "leave blessedness behind."[37]

If prayer is part of being a faithful friend of one's soul, then to be bitter is surely to "unfriend" one's soul. St. Hildegard touches on bitterness with such wisdom that I suspect she confronted it and prayed about it in her own spiritual life. She has deepened my reflection on it, particularly with her insight about the connection between our individual struggles with bitterness and the broader impact on justice. A release from bitterness came for me via an insight, a little written prayer, and praying with a spiritual classic.

The injuries I sustained in the wood when I was very young gave me physical and emotional problems for the long term. I could no longer run, and even walking presented some challenges. I often endured physical pain. In my teen years I brooded over these things. St. Hildegard says, "Bitterness . . . gnashes its teeth . . . flees from wisdom, [and] leaves blessedness behind."[38] I believed I'd lost out on who I could have been. Something of that was true.

My struggles convinced me my whole life would be like my present experience. All around me were healthy teenagers. I felt alone in my misery. I constructed my own cross. I lost my hopefulness, cheerfulness, and enjoyment of much that was still possible for me. I felt shriveled and joyless inside, for, ironically, bitterness "does not desire any joy out of life."[39] Everything bothered me. I felt I was slipping away from God. St. Hildegard tells us, "Bitterness rejects God ... it does not seek God's mercy; it does not love God's judgments ... [and] does not plant anything that can be reaped in faith."[40] It plants nothing but more of the same.

Yet, in the midst of this spiritual crisis, one thing stood out in my mind: *I am extremely fortunate to be alive and to walk.* I believed I had God to thank for helping me. In a moment of insight, I realized that I did not want to waste the life I'd almost lost. St. Hildegard says, "Bitterness also kills."[41] I began to see that for myself. I, like St. Hildegard, thought, "Who will help me but God?"[42]

So, having been drawn to pray, I pulled out my earliest journal—a pocket-size spiral notebook I always carried around—and in it I wrote a prayer. I asked God to keep me from becoming a bitter and resentful person, to not let the life I'd so miraculously held on to be lost to negative attitudes. I did not believe that God would have been so very present to me as I clung to life, only to later allow me to be lost to hard feelings about that life. I trusted God to help me with how I felt. St. Hildegard says, "God does not stop fulfilling whatever petitions are just."[43]

Even in the 1960s it was odd and old-fashioned for a teenager to read Thomas à Kempis's *The Imitation of Christ*,[44] but I was drawn to it and I did. I felt invited to take up my real cross: the sequelae of my injuries that troubled, complicated, caused pain, and demanded attention. St. Hildegard writes, "I feel my wounds. . . . So with great care I will seek the narrow ways."[45] The narrow way the book suggested was to seek spiritual richness in my situation. I dared to think that there could be a path to holiness in all this. I asked myself, *Can I draw closer to God instead of moving away? Can I find meaning and purpose where emptiness and painful questions abound?*

Gradually grace seeped in. Bitterness and resentment receded. As my heart reopened, I experienced God comforting me in my pain and struggle, and I did not resist. Courage and hope deepened within me and became, along with determination, consistent features of my character. I found I was free to have a different attitude toward my path through life. I discovered how much God desired to go with me, consoling, helping, and inspiring. St. Hildegard says, "Now that you are freed . . . from that oppression, go from strength to strength and take care not to admit into your consciences . . . [that] which does not strengthen but bitterly weighs down your heart."[46]

Decades later, I remain necessarily vigilant and prayerful that I not succumb to bitterness and resentment. St. Hildegard encourages "vigilance and zeal, not with bitterness, but with great compassion."[47] I enjoy a deep relationship with God and a spiritual richness I might not have had without what happened to me, or without the grace to pray in the midst of my struggles, or without my openness to grace. I now can readily see that God cares, has compassion, and desires my happiness. St. Hildegard's statement that God gives us God's hand and "changes bitterness into sweetness"[48] rings true.

I thought God's help against bitterness was mainly about my attitude and happiness. St. Hildegard opened my eyes to another reality. She says that many people "cast away the good desires they should have for [God] and the knowledge of the true God . . . [and] they embrace bitterness and contradict the good, and so despoil themselves and steal from themselves the good treasures."[49] I realized that bitterness could have alienated me from God and caused me to be an unpleasant person, one very different from what God intended. It could also have prevented me from working with God to do good. When I first prayed about bitterness, I ignored the "good treasures" I still had. In the throes of bitterness, I did not look beyond myself or imagine I could help someone else. "A bitter and unpleasant person flees from wisdom, leaves blessedness behind, and flees from charity."[50] I underestimated the spiritual stakes in the bitterness I prayed about.

St. Hildegard tells us, "Hard-heartedness should not be allowed to harden itself against God or others. For this is the worst evil of all evils. It spares no one and shows no mercy."[51] Hard-heartedness is evil, plain and simple. "Neither does it think that charity is necessary nor does it do any good works."[52] Bitterness is a torment so implacable when rooted within us that it hardens our hearts. I know, decades later, that grace lifted me out of bitterness. Grace allowed me to do good in the world and to enjoy spiritual richness in the life I nearly lost. God's compassion for me helps me be compassionate in turn and to have joy.

"True mercy answers hard-heartedness."[53] That mercy is from God. "Who . . . will take away from us . . . the hardness whereby we do not want to do good deeds? . . . With God's grace hardness is removed so that afterward we would have joy in the good."[54] That's just it, isn't it? When we are bitter or invested in another non-spiritual attitude, we do not even want to do good deeds. We are joyless. I find that scary. St. Hildegard helps us to see the great spiritual risk of our negative attitudes.

God is just, in individual lives like mine and yours, and in more global ways. God finds unique ways to raise us up, give us great grace, and make us "friends of God and prophets" (Wis 7:17). We need not remain in bitter victimhood. In the graced desire to not be bitter is also the desire for God's justice. Bitterness, by definition, flows from a sense of an injustice toward oneself. St. Hildegard says, "Injustice calls forth justice."[55] In other words, God has already heard, in the injustice of devastating injuries to an innocent child, a call for God's justice. "How dangerous injustice is to one's soul and one's felicity."[56] We can easily overlook the profound, long-term spiritual impact of devastating events.

God's justice to me helped me be more just, to share in the imperative to raise up others. St. Hildegard advises, "Reach out and grasp mercy, which comes not from you, but only from God; and so do not withhold it from those to whom it should be extended."[57] *Singular justice* is the term I use for God's unique way of raising us up person by person. "I will always hope. . . . My mouth shall declare Your justice. . . . I will treat of the mighty works of the Lord; O God, I will tell of Your singular justice" (Ps 71:14–16).

In this little story one sees the connection St. Hildegard makes between "the strengths of the soul" and justice. She says, "For the beginning of just desires fly into the soul . . . and the taste of good will plays in the soul. . . . This is all according to the wisdom of the highest mysteries . . . since wisdom begins to work good things in the soul of a just person and it also finishes these works in the soul."[58] Thanks to St. Hildegard, I have a bigger picture of God's wisdom in answering my prayer to not be bitter. I see a larger purpose in God's response. "Let good people, then, not grow hardened or embittered toward God's justice; let them be mild and prepared to receive every good."[59]

"Get rid of everything that does not contribute"

How does art bring spiritual gifts to you?

Occasionally I do art as part of my prayer. Though not a trained, skillful, or even talented artist, art opens me to grace and insight. For example, I once drew the three crosses described in Luke 23:39–43: the crosses of Jesus, the criminal who derided Him, and the criminal who asked Jesus to remember him. Coincidentally, I made the art at a time when I was writing about forgiving someone who was complex and contradictory, especially in regard to their sense of culpability. St.

Hildegard says, "Humans are more changeable in their actions than any other type of creature, and this fault protests against honesty."[60]

The artwork drew me into Jesus's experience with the two men. I then saw the person I forgave as hanging on not one, but both of the crosses to either side of Jesus. This version expressed the person's on-again, off-again embrace of culpability. My mind had wanted to neatly settle on one version, one cross. But truth, as St. Hildegard says, "has none of falsehood's shadow."[61] The one-cross version was false. In reality, there were endless contradictions in the person's words and behaviors. In making this art, I was freed to see that the truth lay in two crosses, not one. St. Hildegard says, "Look to the One Who established you in freedom."[62]

I did. I felt helped in my perception and my writing, and accompanied by Jesus, Who is the Truth. I'd felt both internal and external pressure to embrace a one-cross story. I'd mistakenly believed that God and my readers demanded a Pollyanna-type version with only a "good thief." This version would have made reconciliation easier. But my art prayer reminded me that God saw the same contradictions I did. "All things are in view of the Seeing Eye, which is God."[63]

A soul is befriended by truth. St. Hildegard counsels, "Get rid of everything that does not contribute to the health of your soul or lift your spirit up to God."[64] The single-cross version was gone. Jesus quite literally hung with both men. In truth, I do as well.

Forgiveness means not seeking revenge, including on the page. Authors of true stories encourage writing a troublesome character both well and with compassion, even while telling the truth of one's experience. As I prayed with my art, I imagined the person I forgave on either cross, suffering terribly. I grasped something of the pain in the person's life and I thought, *Who would want to live in this way? How can there be peace? How will God's mercy be known? How can there be love of self?* St. Hildegard says, "You shall also love yourself. How? If you love God, you love your salvation. And, loving yourself in all this, you shall also love your neighbor."[65]

"You love your salvation." I wanted not revenge, but what was in the best interest of this person's soul. I felt genuine sorrow. In the genius of God, art prayer bore fruit in compassion. "The mercy of God bends down to humans and has compassion on their miseries, and so is available to those who seek it."[66] I felt God's own compassion for the other being shared with me.

God was not finished. I was reminded of my own failings, my own tendency to hang on first one cross and then the other at times. St. Hildegard says, "O how lamentable is the fact that God makes such fragile vessels which cannot refrain from sin, save through the grace of God."[67] So often I am in need of forgiveness in my own contradictions. "We have not fulfilled what we promised in baptism, for we have transgressed . . . thrown away our innocence."[68]

A little humility arrived. St. Hildegard tells us that in humility, "You gather unto yourself beautiful flowers from the thorns . . . after all, we are all full of thorns."[69] God delivered me, "not by power but by mercy."[70] I renewed my forgiveness, saying, as St. Hildegard did, "Forgive us . . . according to Your loving-kindness; as we also . . . forgive those who wrong us for the injuries they have done us."[71] Compassion means appreciating one's own failings and need for mercy. "Mercy demands prayer, which God loves. May the Holy Spirit make that prayer fiery."[72]

God tossed still another log on that fiery prayer. As I returned to writing the story of forgiveness, I found I could be sensible, real, and truthful about the good and the bad simultaneously present in the story. I was free. I did not demonize the person. I wrote truth with compassion. Staying with my art prayer at length ironically removed the person's centrality in my thoughts and in my writing. Instead, Jesus, the Source of my forgiveness and compassion, became the true central figure of the story. I was saved by all three crosses. St. Hildegard says, "Soon the soul sets before her the cross and all the sufferings of Jesus Christ . . . to lift her up in hope."[73] Through art prayer, during which my "soul set before me the cross," I arrived at the balance, truth, deep insight, and shift in focus I needed.

The experience gave me a wondrous sense of God's interest and involvement in my writing, God's continued work in redeeming the story, God's upholding of truth and affirmation of my truth, and God's efforts to help me grow in compassion and freedom. God will even use a bit of sketchy art to save us. St. Hildegard's words are so true: "Do not trust in your powers alone, but see to it that you flee to the grace of God."[74]

REFLECTION QUESTIONS

What "good treasures" and good works might have been lost if you'd succumbed to a spiritually risky attitude?

How has God's "singular justice" toward you played out in more global justice?

Has art led you to truth and freedom? How so?

What is your prayer about attitudes and art?

"Vessels . . . adorned with the stars"

How does your body "prepare your soul for God"?

Engaging the body in prayer—through prayerful postures, gestures, or other physical motion—helps us connect with God. We move in silence or with music. We express ourselves to God and receive from God through the body. St. Hildegard says, "How wondrous that these . . . vessels are sometimes adorned with the stars of God's miracles."[75]

During my scientific career, a company merger was a stormy time that kept us on edge. "The work of people . . . is stormy and . . . has many limitations and tribulations."[76] We all had questions: *Will some of us be offered early retirement? Will we have a brutal workforce reduction? Will we need to relocate?* None of our speculations were reassuring.

St. Hildegard says, "Acknowledge that you have no power except in God and through God."[77] Feeling threatened and powerless, I followed the saint's advice to "call upon God and seek God's goodness."[78] One weekend during this anxious time, I walked a labyrinth for my prayer. At the entrance my prayer was simple: "I need help dealing with this merger crisis. I trust in You." Simply moving forward on the path of the labyrinth felt good. "A person extends trustful hope through the soul to God."[79] I realized part of my merger angst resulted from not having made a plan for my own future. I was letting a ruthless corporation decide it. I recalled the saying, "You can love the corporation, but it will never love you back."

As I slowly walked along, the tension in my body lessened. I felt quieter inside. "People may have quiet amidst the turbulent adversities. . . . God will be a peacemaker."[80] I felt more open as I recalled that the twists and turns of my life had always involved God. The repetitive steps along the set path freed me to focus on God. St.

Hildegard says, "Let the faithful person walk to God in her faith and seek God's mercy, and it will be given to her."[81] I desired intimate time with God at the center of the labyrinth.

I let go of distracting thoughts and worries along the way to prepare for that time. "O illustrious and wise ones, prepare your souls for God."[82] When I arrived at the center, I felt grounded and receptive. God "makes people into creatures of peace."[83] My body indeed felt relaxed and peaceful. I thanked God for grace in the twists and turns of my life. I reiterated my trust in God's love and mercy. I spoke to God of my contentment and happiness as a scientist and my desire to continue serving God as such. St. Hildegard says, "Be content with the labor which you have done for God, and are still doing. But as far as you can, direct your mind and thoughts toward God."[84]

My time with God at the center of the labyrinth was simply peaceful. The gift of peace and the return to my own heart were wonderful fruits of prayer. St. Hildegard says, "Let them return to their own heart, and let them look back to their Creator."[85] As I prepared to leave the center and walk out the way I'd come, I prayed that the fruits I'd received there would be sustained in me, especially when I returned to the tense corporate environment.

I turned to go out. Just then, a voice reverberated deep within me, saying, "How many lively years do you think you have left?"

I stopped in my tracks. "Because [the soul] is fiery, it recognizes God."[86] I believed God had posed the question. With the literal approach of a scientist, I began to calculate the answer. I knew roughly how long I might live, give or take. *But how many years will be "lively"? How can I know?* The God I knew and loved didn't ask trick questions; rather, God made me think—in a loving way, of course. "God embraces with great love all things."[87] My unpreparedness, my failure to discern my future, my ignorance of when I could afford to retire, my procrastination in planning for my remaining lively and not-so-lively years, were causing me to feel threatened by what the corpora-tion might do.

God "penetrated the abyss like a manager Who does not allow any of her things to be lost."[88] God, my real manager, would be with me no matter how the future unfolded. Yet it could unfold with my options clear. On the slow walk out of the labyrinth, I prayerfully considered the information and discernments needed. God "gives people all the things they need."[89] I felt freed from my resistance to an honest, forthright consideration of the end of my scientific career. The Holy Spirit "strengthens people . . . so that they put the love of God before all other things."[90] I desired to serve God in whatever way God called me. St. Hildegard says, "The will arises and imparts its taste to the soul, and its lamp is desire."[91] I marveled at the love in God's question, the anticipation in it, how helped I felt, and how in touch with my deeper desire I was. I walked out of the labyrinth a different person.

Walks in nature also help prayer. St. Hildegard says, "The Creator is known through the creation."[92] I visit local gardens when all is in bloom. As St. Hildegard reflects on plants, she notes that God "placed all the sprouts of the virtues"[93] in us, and provided "food for the soul's refreshment."[94] Who would not desire these? I often walk to Lake Michigan and up and down the shore. The vigor and color of the lake constantly change. I feel its power some days and its peaceful-ness on others, and am mindful of God. The beauty of the lake fills me with gratitude. I marvel at the creation of such a large body of water. St. Hildegard says, "God . . . cannot be seen; rather, God is known through creation. . . . Neither is God seen by any mortal creature—rather, God is understood by faith."[95]

Every bench along the lake path is a prayer spot. I offer God my all, pray for others, ask for grace, guidance, and strength. "That Lofty Strength never fails that founded all the sources of strength."[96]

Vastness of lake and sky reveal how small I am in the scheme of things and what a marvel it is that God pays attention to me. I respond with love and humility. "[One] should not neglect to love God above all things and to humble [oneself] in all things."[97]

Sometimes I visit the lake at night to see the moon over the sparkling water. St. Hildegard says, "Behold the sun, moon, stars, and all the embellishments of the earth's greenness, and consider what great prosperity God gives to humankind in those things."[98] How amazing that we can see heavenly bodies when all is darkness around us. "Let these lights also be for her, inner signs for how to sigh, pray, and weep for God, and to call upon the Holy Spirit for aid."[99] I would know I was truly spiritually deadened if I did not feel awe and Presence at this sight. I also come here after the Easter Vigil to see the first glimmers of the sun rising to bathe the whole earth in new light.

I am a medical physiologist by background and, like St. Hildegard, am fascinated by the human body. Our physical nature reveals God. Our body is a place of gradients: one pH in the stomach, another in the small intestine; a positive charge this side of a membrane, a negative charge on the other; a high pressure in this vessel, a low one in another. Nothing is neutral. Maybe we are to note that God is not neutral. Maybe we are to grasp the wonder of our physiology and rejoice with God, imagining God's delight in us. St. Hildegard says, "So too creation was as Wisdom's vesture, for She caresses Her handiwork as one feels one's clothing."[100] If you'd sewn a fine garment, would you not touch it in a certain way? Why would God not admire and touch the fine physical and spiritual beings we are?

Is our nature a messenger of God? We can become weighed down, obsessing over aging, flaws, and vulnerability. Or we can see our bodies as God's revealing, "like a painter showing people invisible things by the images in his painting."[101] These "vessels . . . adorned with the stars" are vital to our prayer.

"A fountain does not flow for people who . . . do not come"

Where are the fountains in your prayer life?

"A fountain does not flow for people who know of it but do not come to it," says St. Hildegard, "They have to approach it if they want to draw its water."[102] Years ago, I went on my first silent weekend retreat during Lent. I arrived with mind revved, obsessing about work. The first night I slept poorly, frequently waking, mind going strong. All the next morning, it was the same. St. Hildegard says, "She cannot live free . . . for in her . . . exile, she cannot glimpse the full joy of her heavenly homeland, unless she strives for it from afar in the shadow of faith."[103] There was no joy for me at that point, only distance. Faith alone kept me engaged in the effort to pray. I was frustrated and sobered by my state. The silence exposed my head full of noise. I felt chagrin over how I must appear to God. St. Hildegard says, "Tell us Your Name again, lest we forget."[104] It was nearly thus for me. I prayed, "Remind me of You. Bring me back to You."

The retreat director gave me tips for centering prayer. She proposed a Lenten fast from my own thoughts and opinions in order to be present to God. She reminded me that God seeks me, too, and will help me. "God saves everyone who devoutly and chastely seeks God out."[105] St. Hildegard quotes God's promise: "Cry out and persevere in seeking Me; and I will help you."[106]

At first, prayer was hard work. The moment my mind generated a thought irrelevant to prayer, I disengaged from and let go of it. I had to be quite vigilant. With shocking persistence, my mind returned to its favorite topics. St. Hildegard says, "With a vigilant soul, sigh to God."[107] With vigilance, I chose not to pursue these topics. I imaged my mind as having several well-established, easily triggered, reverberating circuits that could only be disrupted by prayer. Gradually I felt peaceful, relaxed, present to and helped by God. St. Hildegard says, "Prayer has great power with God, and as a result of it God throws down the wheel of captivity of souls."[108] God, the Great Circuit Interrupter, released me from captivity.

Late Saturday afternoon, I sat in the tiny chapel in my newly centered state, happy to be quiet inside. I was humbled by my experience and grateful for the grace and faith I was given to persevere. St. Hildegard says, "Faith herself shows the devotion with which each soul has sought God."[109] She emphasizes adhering to our desire for God no matter what difficulties we face: "The soul leads the constancy and security within a person . . . [and] causes her to cling to heavenly desires in both adversity and prosperity."[110] I thanked God, the Source of my desire and faith, the God Who drew and called me and penetrated my powerful distractions. "God draws human beings back to God."[111]

Why was God so helpful to me, someone who'd gotten into such an unprayerful state? St. Hildegard quotes God: "Humbly show Me the field of your mind and speak to Me with a flood of inner tears."[112] At times, that is all we can do. Even St. Hildegard has been there: "In my anguish, God is giving aid to me, a poor little form of a woman."[113]

As I sat in prayer, I saw God's grace in my decision to do the retreat, and in my persistence in prayer. St. Hildegard quotes God: "You are ever in My sight."[114] She is right when she says, "Stretch Your hand out to God, and God will aid you."[115] God had been even more persistent than I was in getting me on track. I felt humility, gratitude, and love for God. Humility is "a strong and victorious protector. . . . No one falls who loves [humility] with a pure heart."[116] I desired to experience it often. St. Hildegard says that Love is "a valuable and desirable defense . . . very slender and subtle and . . . seek[s] out in those who revere [it], the smallest openings, and deeply penetrate[s] them."[117] I gave Love the smallest opening in my mind and heart, and Love penetrated it.

"Contemplate the charity with which God freed you . . . the number of good things God constantly gives you."[118] I felt like a person released from a terrible fever into wondrous peace. I remained in silence, gratitude, humility, love, and desire for God. "God comes to rest upon one who is humble and quiet in heart."[119] At last I felt God's presence. All that had gone before flowed from my desire for God and God's desire for me. St. Hildegard says, "With full desire a person gazes upon God within her soul."[120] I praised God for this desire, a special strength of the soul.

Next, I heard, clear as a bell, "I am yours" (Ps 119:94), and then, "You are mine" (Isa 43:1). I hadn't been thinking those words, but there they were, sounding as though piped in. But the tiny chapel had no sound system. No one else was there. My inner spiritual experience seemed external. St. Hildegard says, "The soul is filled with beautiful air that makes it sound like a symphony."[121] Well, perhaps in her case. In mine, the message that came from God was a simple one, and I was deeply touched. It came again: "I am yours . . . You are Mine." How exquisitely beautiful it was—ethereal, sparkling with joy, and far beyond the mundane. I was convinced of its Divine origin. "What the soul holds in her mind is from Divine inspiration."[122] I felt deeply loved, desired, and accepted. Despite the time I'd wasted on my own troublesome thoughts and the poor quality of my prayer, there was God, in overwhelming generosity, letting me know I was loved. *I belong to God*, I realized, *not to all that distracts*.

During the silent evening meal, I prayerfully savored my experience. My thoughts returned to the desire for God that had drawn me to retreat and sustained me through my struggles in prayer. I realized my desire had its origin in God's drawing, for, as Jesus says, "No one can come to me unless drawn by the One Who sent me" (Jn 6:44). St. Hildegard writes of the origin of our desire: "I [Heavenly Desire] come to each and every creature with grace because I am the life and greenness in all good works. I am the jewel of all the virtues, I am the delight and understanding of the love of God, and I am the foundation of all desire. . . . I am the Psalter and harp of God's joy. But I am also a representative from heaven in all causes."[123]

God's message that God is mine and that I am God's, and the idea of desire, connected for me. My desire for God and God's desire for me became, "*My desire is yours. Your desire is Mine.*" *God desires me, and I desire God. Desire is mutual.* God made the point clear, and deep joy arrived.

Before we left on Sunday, the retreat director encouraged reflection on carrying our graces forward into daily life. Silence had exposed my state, helped me befriend my soul, and prepared me to experience God's love and desire for me and mine for God. I committed to more silence in my life. A big "what's missing" in my prayer was listening. I talked too much. St. Hildegard says, "Do not regard God as your servant, but look to God faithfully."[124] I hadn't been making myself available to hear the God Who desired me. "God wants you. See to it, therefore, that you do not withdraw from God."[125] The proper response to God, Who "wants you and knows you," is "seeing and hearing."[126] I committed to more of these in prayer.

My life then was intense with the demands of scientific research and I had intense habits to go with it, designing experiments as I showered in the morning and pondering results into the evening. But God desired me, and I desired God. In silence, I continued centering prayer, using a mantra to return my focus when distractions came. "With God's help, keep your mind from wandering about."[127]

This prayer style was an act of obedience. St. Hildegard says, "Obedience is indeed a fire."[128] My struggles were humbling. "A faithful person glorifies her Creator with every effort of her mind and body, with a spirit of humility."[129] Constancy and discipline are essential for scientists, and they came to my aid in prayer as well. The virtue of constancy "is the foundation of the other inner virtues in people, and by her discipline leads them to God."[130]

I noticed that inner quiet arrived late in my prayer time. I disliked the battle within myself to get quiet. I began to simply imagine myself walking through a garden, stopping at various shrines to say traditional prayers. The practice gently signaled my mind to be prayerful. St. Hildegard says, "Remain in the garden where you presently are until your mind has fewer flaws."[131] The garden is my inner self, available only to God and me, closed off from surrounding noise. "Enclose your garden with a high wall."[132]

Once prayerful and quiet within, I enter a little chapel in the far corner of my imagined garden. "Let a person understand God and let her take God into the innermost chamber of her heart."[133] The chapel is my deepest self, where God dwells. St. Hildegard says, "You ought to be the little habitation redolent of myrrh and incense, in which God also dwells."[134] In silence and listening, I open to God. "God is eternal. And fire is eternal. And God is here."[135] With this inner chapel prayer, I see St. Hildegard's wisdom in describing the human being as a house of prayer.

Deep in God's little habitation, the promises of God are fulfilled. St. Hildegard quotes God as saying, "O human, if you love Me, I embrace you, and I will warm you with the fire of the Holy Spirit. For when you contemplate Me with a good intention and know Me by your faith, I will be with you."[136] All my waking hours were greatly affected by the fruits of prayer. St. Hildegard says, "God's grace will soon look upon her. If that grace then sees her reaching out towards the light and lifting herself up out of the shadows, it will be present for her in all things and inspire in her what is just and holy."[137] Exactly. I changed. I became a calmer, more centered person, such that others commented on the change. "What flows from the fountain of eternal life cannot be obstructed or hidden."[138]

Years later, I cannot remember what I obsessed about on that weekend retreat, but I remember vividly the encounter with God—how wondrous it was, and the impact it had. God was so faithful to me that I became more faithful to God. I learned the truth of St. Hildegard's insight: "If by seeing and hearing, you call upon God, God will not abandon you."[139] One need not talk to call upon God; seeing and hearing are also prayer. Silent prayer is listening, not batting away thoughts. There is a difference. I sometimes try to hear liquid dripping in my heart, so intent on listening I become. I know myself as an intimate dwelling place of God. I realize the mutuality of desire. The struggles were a tiny price to pay.

Now I teach the garden prayer to my directees, guiding them through it the first time. The extroverts especially find it a help. St. Hildegard says, "Be vigilant in mind, and God will love you and will never desert you."[140] The call to a new prayer style is also the call to deeper relationship with God.

REFLECTION QUESTIONS

What does your body reveal about God? How is it "the garment for wisdom"?

Is there sufficient silence in your life? How is silence helpful to you?

What is your prayer about connecting with God through your body and the silence of your being?

"Contrition is a blessing"

How do you feel about contrition?

St. Hildegard wrote plentifully on contrition. "Contrition should be thought of not as an affliction but rather as a blessing."[141] Contrition is vital to our spiritual journey and our prayer because "humankind is ever sinning,"[142] and "when a person fails, every creature is darkened with her."[143] Our failings hamper our relationships with God, others, and self. "The soul commits suicide when it does not seek to cling to God."[144] Contrition is about the very life of our soul. "After desiring to reach to God, she lives again for God."[145] God is there to help. St. Hildegard says, "God has mercifully remembered God's great work and God's precious pearl, the human being. . . . How? By devising the life of penitence, which will never fail in efficacy."[146]

I am not writing a book of confessions, though I have sufficient material. I am flawed, unfaithful to God at times, and prone to be other than my true self at my best. Often our sinfulness flows from our woundedness, and deep healing (discussed later) is God's principal means of helping us. But sometimes our sinfulness results from our personality and willful ways. That sinfulness is a misuse of our gifts and is more in our control.

An upside of being an extrovert is the willingness to speak up when someone must. Extroverts are often willing to go first with difficult topics. We can move a group toward greater honesty and transparency about the elephant in the room. We can start conversations and keep them going toward fruitful outcomes. We can be spokespersons, including for those on the margins. We are energized by expression and interaction. We emphasize communication. We are not easily intimidated by large groups. However, there are many downsides to extroversion, as any introvert will tell you, and these are not harmless.

I am prone to speak bluntly and with insufficient prior reflection on my message, words, or tone, or the impact these will have. I offend others and God through my careless words. In one example, I grew frustrated with the low priority given our team project by one department of our research organization. When, once again, the team member from that department had no progress to report during a team meeting, I spoke angrily in a burst of rash words. Then I saw the stricken look on my teammate's face, stopped, and instantly felt terrible. I apologized, but the damage was done, not just to him, but to the whole team. "Who can measure the destruction caused when a person abandoned God?"[147] What I said was not of God. St. Hildegard says, "The person . . . is led by sin to forget God."[148]

Part of me wanted to justify my angry words—after all, I was responsible for the team's progress—but another part of me wanted to hide, especially from God. St. Hildegard says, "I fear God, knowing that I, too, was created pure and honest."[149] She portrays the soul as saying, "So, I, too, am afraid and hide myself from the face of God when I sense that my works . . . are contrary to God."[150]

After that meeting, I dragged myself to my prayer space. "If I cannot stand in the sun, at least I will drag myself out of the mud and wash my garments clean."[151] There seemed a huge wall between me and God. I felt shabby. St. Hildegard terms this feeling *compunction*, a grace. She says, "Compunction of heart . . . [is] that memory in the mind that bemoans and weeps for its exile with intense contrition."[152] Compunction is simultaneously feeling self-created distance and longing. "When a person is sometimes touched inwardly by the Holy Spirit's grace to consider how weighed down she is in the soul by the burden of her sins, she sighs unto God."[153]

My experience could not be shrugged off. I loved God. I loved my team. God had always helped me with my work as team leader. Now this. St. Hildegard says, "The one who commits sin is a slave of sin."[154] I certainly didn't feel free. I felt like a betrayer. The more I'd grown to love, the more intense had become the compunction. "In Your love, You infuse a person with the dew of the heart's remorse.... You are present, my Deliverer and Savior,"[155] says St. Hildegard. Imagine: feeling compunction is a sign of God's liberating presence. That should give us hope.

"Who could lift up [the lost human being], who was deceived and forgot her Creator, except the One Who, overshadowed by no fog, took compassion upon her ignorance?"[156] I confronted the improper use of my gifts. My sinfulness involved this incident, yes, but also a pattern of extroversion sins. *How little restraint I exercise*, I realized. *I hurt others. Some voices aren't heard. I often speak prematurely and confuse people. Indeed, God must be grieved by my vast ignorance.* My sorrow deepened.

St. Hildegard offers hope: "To the miserable and weeping hearts of the faithful grace comes in great abundance and fruitfulness."[157] She also points to forgiveness—"[God] forgives each debt that a person confesses from the heart"[158]—and expresses God's plea, "Touched by My grace, which reaches you in the paths of your inner vision, at once cry out, pray, confess and weep so that I will help you."[159]

I confessed from my heart all the abuses of my extraversion gift and told God how contrite I was. Repentance "is stirred up in a person through the grace of God as from a bright fire."[160] I expressed my sorrow and regret for hurting others and offending God. "The human being apprehends God by faith in a small container, the interior of her contrite heart,"[161] says St. Hildegard. And what happens next? "The mercy of God bends down to humans and has compassion on their miseries, and so is available to those who seek it."[162] I did not feel deserving, but I sought mercy. I told God that I could not fix the harm I'd done and needed help to change. Heeding St. Hildegard's admonishment to "turn to God, beg, pray, and promise,"[163] I promised to make amends and to be an extrovert in the way God intended.

"The all-surpassing goodness of Divinity, which is without beginning and end, brings aid and comfort to the faithful."[164] Perhaps God had long been concerned about my behavior and yet exercised restraint. St. Hildegard says, "And so those human deeds, which the true Trinity does not let go unexamined, are not punished or crushed as severely as that power could if it willed."[165] I was grateful that God did not "let go unexamined" my deeds, and that God chose this time for my transformation. I did not want to go unmindfully on. St. Hildegard says, "Let a person search carefully for the garment that she tore so that she may again wear it with joy."[166]

God will "raise up the ones who repent"[167] and "receives a repentant person."[168] In fact, St. Hildegard says, "God is indeed greatly praised by their repentance."[169] Imagine that: in repentance, we praise. I felt God's forgiveness and loving embrace. I felt reassured that God would help me improve and repair the damages. St. Hildegard quotes God: "I . . . exist like medicine for everyone . . . I heal what you wound."[170]

Though I still felt sorrow, hope seeped into my heart. I recalled that even the great saints struggled with sin. "For even Peter . . . was himself not safe. The same was true of many other saints, who fell in their sins. Yet these were all, afterward, made more useful and more perfect than they would have been if they had not fallen."[171] I prayed fervently that God, Who can do all things, would bring good out of this and help me be the woman and leader I should be.

"Those who had fallen would rise again through repentance and be renewed in a holy way of life, adorned with a variety of virtues as with the viridity of flowers."[172] I made changes. I prayed before speaking. I held a coffee cup in meetings and imagined it filling with others' words before I dared speak. In team meetings I invited everyone to write their thoughts before speaking, and did so myself. The participation of introverts, who dominate in science, grew. I gained from their wisdom and perspective.

St. Hildegard says, "In the jealousy of the Lord are marvels and wondrous Divine judgments, such as no person weighed down by sins can know."[173] I felt new spiritual freedom. I was released from the burdensome perception that introverts never stick their necks out, always leaving that to the extroverts. I also saw that my changes created room for others to develop along these lines, and felt chagrin that I'd previously blocked their growth with my style. "A beautiful flower arises from the destruction of sin."[174]

St. Hildegard says, "Penitence is the soul's illuminatrix."[175] That was my experience. I was enlightened in prayer to see my failures and the harm I'd done. It was uncomfortable, but also fruitful and necessary. I prayed to always be given the painful graces of compunction and contrition. I felt gratitude and love for God, Who showed me my larger sin via the smaller incident. St. Hildegard says, "[The penitent] love God more than if they had not needed rescue through repentance."[176] The pain of these graces is important for our permanent change. "The faithful person who is touched by the integrity of grace can resist her own sinful desires; she can put virtue in front of her."[177]

St. Hildegard provides another insight about the prayer of contrition: "You shall not waste yourself in matters alien to God, but collect yourself in the sweetness of God's love."[178] You shall not waste yourself. Wrongdoing is a waste of our very selves. She is saying that we are too valuable to continue as we were. We could be "stronger than before."[179] In a bit of rare humor, St. Hildegard prays, "Creator of all, You know me and therefore, if You wish, You can convert me away from my contrariness toward You."[180] This will hurt a little, but it is a good kind of pain. "May God give you that sweetest mother Mercy as your assistant."[181]

"Attending God"

Is contrition relevant to spiritual direction?

Contrition and sin rarely come up in my spiritual direction practice except during Lent. When I first began spiritual direction in a parish setting, person after person said, "I hate Lent." They disliked the focus on sin and repentance. They felt dry and empty. They were eager for Lent to be over and often skipped Good Friday liturgies, though they did love the Easter Vigil.

I was impressed by their honesty and willingness to seek spiritual help. I felt grateful for my own positive experience with contrition. But how could I be a helpful Lenten guide?

"God wishes your soul,"[182] says St. Hildegard. I proposed that Lent could draw us closer to God. Like Jesus, we could be led by the Holy Spirit, Who shines light where it is needed. We explored together how we understood spiritual freedom and how we notice our unfreedom. We spoke about obstacles to sincere prayer, fasting, and almsgiving. St. Hildegard says, "May the Holy Spirit enkindle us with Her grace, and strengthen us in Her service."[183]

When signs of unfreedom surfaced, I reminded my directees of God's love, mercy, and invitation to stay with prayer even when it is painful. St. Hildegard says, "As it pleased Almighty God to make humankind, so too it pleased God to redeem the one who trusts in God."[184] In times of painful realizations, directees need compassion, reassurance, and the admission that we, too, have been there, as have the great saints. But, as St. Hildegard says, "We do not perish who have hope in You."[185] We all have times when we "forgot we were sacred souls."[186]

The embrace of Good Friday then came naturally. Through repentance, we are "restored to a radiance greater than when first created."[187] Until reading St. Hildegard, I had never considered that our radiance, which we receive from God, could increase through repentance. "The Divine Pity . . . manifests God's many mercies and God's abundant compassion . . . [and] looks upon the sorrows of the people who try to follow God. And that radiance is all alive to console and save."[188] The radiance we share may console another. St. Hildegard relates Jesus's words, "O human being, rise up and bring light to your spirit through Me, so that you may vigilantly search Me out. Then you will have life."[189] And what is Easter if not the radiant season of new life?

"Whoever seeks God . . . will find God"

How do you assimilate the gifts and fruits of your day?

At day's end, I prayerfully mull over with God how the day has unfolded. In Ignatian spirituality, this is termed an *examen*. Many books and articles describe this prayer. The awareness that I am not reflecting on anything God doesn't already know helps me. St. Hildegard says, "God is watching you through the windows because God is faithful and merciful."[190] In fact, the examen helps me see how God has been faithful, merciful, and loving, and how I have responded to God. It reminds me that "Whoever seeks God with proper invocations will find God in all places."[191]

I begin by remembering that God and I have a relationship of mutual love. I review my day. "I remember where my soul is from; I sift the barley . . . from the wheat."[192] I notice how God's love touched me, the gifts of grace, the goodness I encountered, and all that swells my heart with gratitude. St. Hildegard says, "God is good and all things that come forth from God are good."[193] I often feel humbled by all God has done in my day. "In the descent of true humility one attributes whatever good one has done to the One Who is

Susan Garthwaite

the Highest Good and through Whom one possesses the good."[194] I invite the Holy Spirit to help me see more deeply, especially where I have lacked insight or need transformation. As St. Hildegard says, "Acknowledge that you have no power except in God and through God."[195]

Sometimes I realize my choices did not honor my relationship with God, and I ask God's forgiveness. I trust in God's love and mercy. I recognize God at work here and now to bring spiritual freedom. St. Hildegard says, "Contemplate the charity with which God freed you."[196] As I look ahead to the next day, I pray to be stronger and alert to the grace available to me. "For the grace of God, in its strength and piety, bends down to the faithful and lifts them on high to heavenly places."[197] Often I journal the fruits of the examen and bring these to spiritual direction. The prayer supports befriending my soul and growing in relationship with God through intimate sharing.

"Following the example of the saints" and "Attending God"

Who is your confirmation saint? Why did you choose this saint?

St. Hildegard deeply appreciated the saints. She wrote hymns to honor them in personal and communal prayer. "You have . . . saints who in their lives shone like the sun in its might. . . . Sing and be joyful in the merits of these saints, and . . . strive to be part of their company."[198] I reflect on the saints' writings—St. Hildegard's and St. Teresa's in particular—and seek to fruitfully follow their inspiration and example. Taking their example, we can "advance rightly in soul and body."[199] We can trust them, for "All the saints are comprehended in God's brightness; they have loved God and remained with

---

Susan Garthwaite

the Highest Good and through Whom one possesses the good."[194] I invite the Holy Spirit to help me see more deeply, especially where I have lacked insight or need transformation. As St. Hildegard says, "Acknowledge that you have no power except in God and through God."[195]

Sometimes I realize my choices did not honor my relationship with God, and I ask God's forgiveness. I trust in God's love and mercy. I recognize God at work here and now to bring spiritual freedom. St. Hildegard says, "Contemplate the charity with which God freed you."[196] As I look ahead to the next day, I pray to be stronger and alert to the grace available to me. "For the grace of God, in its strength and piety, bends down to the faithful and lifts them on high to heavenly places."[197] Often I journal the fruits of the examen and bring these to spiritual direction. The prayer supports befriending my soul and growing in relationship with God through intimate sharing.

"Following the example of the saints" and "Attending God"

Who is your confirmation saint? Why did you choose this saint?

St. Hildegard deeply appreciated the saints. She wrote hymns to honor them in personal and communal prayer. "You have . . . saints who in their lives shone like the sun in its might. . . . Sing and be joyful in the merits of these saints, and . . . strive to be part of their company."[198] I reflect on the saints' writings—St. Hildegard's and St. Teresa's in particular—and seek to fruitfully follow their inspiration and example. Taking their example, we can "advance rightly in soul and body."[199] We can trust them, for "All the saints are comprehended in God's brightness; they have loved God and remained with

God in faith and deeds through the good perseverance of their ministry."[200]

The saints provide sound advice. As I recovered from serious illness, I encountered the words of St. Jane de Chantal: "Take my word for it, God is more pleased with our accepting the relief our body and soul require, than by all these apprehensions of not doing enough and wanting to do more. . . . God expects you to take care and not demand of yourself what God, in gentleness, does not ask for."[201] St. Hildegard says, "Following the example of the saints, and observing their character you will learn the nature of the righteous God."[202] The saints reveal God. St. Jane revealed God's nature and attitude toward my situation. Her words were exactly what I needed. She went on to say that God asks a "calm, peaceful uselessness, a resting near God . . . faithful, simple surrender."[203] All that I was capable of, and yet resisted.

Wisdom, St. Hildegard says, "is found in some people . . . instructed by the inspiration of the Holy Spirit."[204] The gifts of the Spirit are given for all. St. Hildegard sings of St. Boniface, "Friend of the Living God, your goodwill gleams in our path like crystal, lighting ways you traveled in zeal for right."[205] She praises God for the saints: "You are the sun with innumerable spheres, that is, Your saints and Your elect, whose number no one can reckon."[206] In my faith tradition, we are fortunate to know some saints and benefit from their light on our paths. In spiritual direction training, I was required to select a saint as my spiritual director. I chose St. Teresa of Ávila. She truly became a light on my path, as St. Hildegard is now.

I learned to pray intimately with the saints. I picture myself praying beside Mary as she opens her heart to God. We are simply in silence together. I feel wonderfully close to her and to God. Once, when I was drawn to pray this way, my desire to be a wise spiritual director for a directee who struggles with depression weighed on my mind. I felt frustrated, troubled, challenged, and ineffective in the face of the "stuckness" manifested in our every session. We had the same conversation every month. I wondered if we should quit, and yet I hated to give up on a man who so desired God's help.

As I prayed, I unexpectedly found myself with Mary at the foot of the cross, sharing her utter helplessness before Jesus's suffering. All Mary could do was be compassionately present. Then I understood: that was my simple, holy role with my directee. I must accept my helplessness and simply be compassionately present. My directee showed me what it looks like when Jesus suffers from depression.

St. Hildegard speaks of Mary as "Mother of Light," "Gladdening Sign," "Unclouded Brightness," and "Priceless Integrity."[207] She says, "That power which descended into the womb of the Virgin . . . remains up to the present day."[208] Why not? I felt enlightened and relieved. Mary was a gladdening sign for me in this situation. St. Hildegard says, "People benefit each other with the saving grace of prayer."[209] I agree. St. Hildegard says Mary is the "Self-portrait of the Maker, Masterpiece of God's hand."[210] Mary helped me see the hand of God in my ministry, that I might share in her priceless integrity.

I now attune to my directee's suffering and do not focus on spiritual movement per se. I simply make our sessions prayerful, positive, and even enjoyable. I seek to ease his burden and help him connect with God during that hour. St. Hildegard encourages, "Hold on to mercy firmly, the companion of humility."[211] She says, "Love fulfills God's entire will."[212] I help this directee see grace in his endurance. I affirm his faith and generous ministry to others. Seeing his witness, I know God is with him and I say so. "Faith herself shows the devotion with which each soul has sought God."[213] I am helpless to change his situation, but Mary's witness and example changed my heart, and I am now able to be compassionately present. "May the citizens of the skies rejoice in those who imitate their lives."[214]

REFLECTION QUESTIONS

What has it been like for you to encounter God in "the interior of your contrite heart"?

How have the saints inspired, advised, or been examples for you?

What is your prayer about "attending God" in situations involving contrition? What is your prayer about directing others with depression?

"Cry out and persevere" and "Attending God"

Is prayer difficult?

Directees with depression quickly abandon forms of prayer that seem arduous. In truth, many directees without depression are unreliable with forms of prayer they find difficult or not suited to them. When God calls us to new prayer forms, we are given grace to embrace them, but without God's call, we may flounder in practices that are hard for us. Must prayer be hard in order to be fruitful? That is a surprisingly ingrained notion. Are directees who undertake reading the entire Bible front to back for prayer following God's lead? Or actually avoiding God? Or resisting giving themselves to God in prayer? Or thinking of prayer as achievement instead of intimacy with God? The examples of prayer in this section show that our method must support our regular, undistracted availability to God and our openness to God and grace. St. Hildegard quotes God's promise: "Cry out and persevere in seeking Me, and I will help you."[215]

The point of prayer is relationship with God. "One should not neglect to love God above all things and to humble oneself in all things."[216] We give God our openness, honesty, heart, longing, seeking, and need in the best way we can. We listen, receive, and respond in gratitude as we embrace all God offers to us in prayer and subsequent to prayer. St. Hildegard says that the person "who perpetually looks in the mirror of her heart at God from Whom she has her body and soul, is wise."[217] God desires relationship and helps us to the deep openness essential to that. St. Hildegard says, "Drawing the person in, the grasp of God's love lifted her up. . . . Through the Holy Spirit's gifts the ears of her heart opened, and God gave her the sweetest taste through the rationality of the soul."[218]

But what if our openness is blocked? Sometimes we need different images and names for God. These may have an impact on our prayer and our trust of God.

Some of my most profound spiritual experiences have involved a feminine sense of God. "The gifts of the Holy Spirit are manifold."[219] God may provide the images and names for God that help our relationship develop, or we may find our own. St. Hildegard says, "Reason discovers God through names, for reason itself, by its very nature, is full of names."[220]

St. Hildegard called God "Sophia," "Pastor of our Hearts," "Voice Primordial," "Maker," "Life of All," "Spirit of Fire," "Sacred Breath," "Current of Power," and "Teacher,"[221] in addition to more traditional names. We all need the name and image for God that allows a person to "extend trustful hope through the soul to God."[222] In my experience, prayer opens up with a new name and image for God.

What if we don't know what blocks our connection to God? Spiritual directors seek to help directees navigate such situations. For many, praying with psalms opens the mind and heart. The frankness of the psalmist encourages one's own frankness with God. Art, music, or a walk in nature may open us to our deeper selves. To simply sit in the dark with God may also help. Faithfulness requires our willingness to discover what is in the way. I ask myself, what is it I don't want to talk about with God or with my spiritual director? St. Hildegard says, "You do not say, rejoicing: God in God's great mercy will receive me. But God will. Believe, have faith, and hope, because God loves you and wishes you, and God will receive you."[223] Remind directees of this often.

At times it is in spiritual direction that we discover what blocks prayer. Directees tend to save troubling matters for late in the session. Often I sense we haven't gotten to the heart of things. I say, "Is there anything else on your heart and mind today or that you would like me to help you pray about?" With this explicit permission and support, out tumbles their biggest concern. Then, "the all-surpassing goodness of Divinity, which is without beginning and end, brings aid and comfort to the faithful."[224] Even if the concern is heart-wrenching, I know that God has begun lifting up this person. "The lost person lives again in the honor of life, redeemed in God by healing grace."[225]

In this chapter we encountered many ways to be "a house of prayer."[226] Openness to God and God's grace is the crucial attitude for transformation and relationship. Later, we will go deeper into how God draws us to forms of prayer that are beyond our expectations and more difficult to articulate. However, we never cease needing the methods and simple openness we've just reviewed. For now, "Let a person rise up quickly with the breath of the soul by which she can stretch to God. Let her ascend quickly with the desire of the soul by which she can embrace God, and let her hold strenuously onto the will of the soul by which she can love God . . . [for] God will fill your soul with heavenly joy and light."[227]

Reflection Questions

What forms of prayer have you quickly abandoned? Why?

What images and names for God help you "extend your trustful hope to God"?

Describe what it is like for you to be "a house of prayer" and "a faithful friend of your soul."

What is your prayer about befriending your soul through perseverance in prayer?

chapter ten

———•••———

DISCERNMENT

"The Spirit will reign in you" and "Attending God"

ow does God guide you?

Discernment is critical for befriending our souls. In discerning, we know ourselves and know God. It is a way to "pray without ceasing" (1 Thes 5:17) and to sustain consciousness of God. St. Hildegard emphasizes the gift from God that discernment is: "Look to the Fiery Giver Who endows humankind with discernment."[1] She points out that discernment is about paying attention to our feelings. "When you act with wisdom and discretion, you feel God in your reason."[2] The lively activity of the Spirit within keeps us aware that we have a soul, a Presence within. "The Spirit will reign in you, and then you will understand God in your soul."[3] Discernment is about integrity and God's defense of our spirit. St. Hildegard says, "In the Divine power exists the integrity of holiness, which fortifies on every side the inner spirit of the person who joins herself to God."[4] How do we discern? How do we experience God's defense of our inner spirit?

"Just like all other creatures, humankind cannot live without help and service from above."[5] And so, God provides. "Fear not, because God, by Whose grace you are endowed with wisdom and knowledge, will never abandon you."[6] By definition, to discern is to perceive or recognize or distinguish, often with a degree of difficulty. Discernment and discretion mean we judge well and, in freedom, choose what should be done in a situation. Spiritually, the purpose of discernment is to choose to love. "God said in the admonition of the Holy Spirit, 'Let there be lights within discretion by the Holy Spirit's gift, that a person might love God and her neighbor as herself.'"[7]

Ignatian spirituality books describe how to discern in daily situations and in making significant decisions; I highly recommend these. St. Hildegard preceded St. Ignatius by centuries, however, and most of us, like St. Hildegard, do some discerning without having explicitly learned the Ignatian path. What St. Ignatius formalized, he experienced naturally first as he befriended his soul. I believe the two saints would have understood each other well and have written in different ways about identical spiritual experiences. Both speak of the Holy Spirit's activity within us. St. Hildegard says, "When the gifts of the Holy Spirit pour forth upon a person from above in pure and holy abundance, they teach her many things about heavenly and spiritual matters."[8]

A common spiritual experience is our reaction to gossip. St. Hildegard described gossip as "the vain attacking the harsh, and the harsh, the vain."[9] She says "whispers" can topple even "a strong warrior."[10] Gossip is an age-old, harmful problem. The focus is not on building up. Some people enjoy gossip and seek others to participate in it. St. Hildegard says, "Yet in the great foolishness of your character, you enjoy gossip and seek it out. This does you no good at all."[11]

Some people gossip in spiritual direction. In reaction to this, I've felt dismay, lack of peace, a sense of not-rightness, uneasiness, sadness, and confusion. These feelings are the hallmarks of what St. Hildegard and St. Ignatius term "desolation." As St. Hildegard says,

Wisdom "supplies what is necessary for the present moment and for life in general."[12] Desolation is necessary. "Watch over yourself, because the grace of God does not withdraw from you, but makes a sign to you, and if you are willing, stretches out a hand to you."[13] In desolation, one feels as though God and grace have withdrawn. But, if we remember God is the defender of our inner spirit and desolation is a sign, we know desolation is God's hand stretched out to help. Desolation is there to remind us that gossip is not of God, and St. Hildegard exhorts us to "preserve yourself from that which is not of God."[14]

St. Hildegard grounds discernment in what it is to be made in God's image: "God, in Whose image and likeness the human being was created, gave the human the knowledge of good and evil."[15] Even in a simple case such as gossip, "The day grows dark for one who does not labor in the straight path of the journey."[16] St. Hildegard encourages, "Turn from darkness onto the straight path and shed some light on the feelings of your heart."[17] She says, "Rise quickly, therefore, and walk the straight and narrow before the sun sets on you and your days wane."[18] To her, desolation is actually a dawn of sorts, eventually leading to bright sun. She says, "I see in my soul that the concern you have about the distresses of your soul is like the dawn that rises in the morning. Therefore, may the Holy Spirit make you a burning sun."[19]

My desolation due to hearing gossip persisted long after one session. I explored my feelings in prayer. I saw my responsibility to firmly disallow gossip in spiritual direction sessions. *I must confront that behavior,* I realized. *My duty as a spiritual director is to act in the best interest of the directee's soul, not to mention my own. Isn't that why the person seeks direction? Surely I am not called to enable what isn't of God.* A person's ears are made beautiful "when she turns away from listening to wicked whispers."[20] With wicked whispers rejected, "She flies with all speed towards the good."[21] I had a choice in this situation.

"You will be either the day or the night. Choose, therefore, where you wish to take your stand."[22]

Once I decided to take a stance against gossip and prayerfully chose direct but kind words to use in the situation, desolation abated. I felt more tranquil, though still challenged with my discomfort at confronting another. I understood that discomfort not as desolation but as a normal feeling one has in taking a risk with someone. St. Hildegard says the faithful "do not turn themselves away from [right desires], but with every devotion cling to them without pause."[23] I felt strengthened to follow through and confront gossip, and not initiate, participate in, or enable it. I name as "consolation" the consoling, strengthening grace that helps me move forward as I ought.

Desolation comes to help us be wise and discreet. Discretion "is the wise sifter of all things, holding what should be held and cutting off what should be cut off, as the wheat is separated from the tares."[24] St. Hildegard's words underline gossip's obstruction of the good that is possible when we seek God in spiritual direction. She says, "Let the person who wants to dwell in the house of God think and act accordingly."[25] The "dawn" of desolation in this case led to the "burning sun" of freedom to focus on good and more loving and just ways.

"I only stir up great sadness in myself"

What happens when you bring your struggles to God?

Spiritual writing provides opportunities to experience desolation and consolation while discerning one's direction. I once struggled with a short paper I felt called to write. I felt dry and uninspired, as though I'd lost my connection with God. I began to doubt my call to write it. St. Hildegard describes her experience of such desolation:

"I doubt as to whether or not the Holy Spirit has given this to me. . . . I only stir up great sadness in myself, so that I do no works, either on the heights of sanctity or on the plains of good will; but I bear within me the disquietude of doubt, desperation, sadness, and oppression in all things. . . . Ach! How unhappy is this struggle . . . depriving me of all happiness."[26] She describes an experience we often share: "When I do a good work, I fear that it is not perfect before God; for I do not see it clearly, but as in a glass darkly. Sometimes I know it in the spirit, but sometimes I do not know it because of being weighed down."[27]

In the midst of desolation, it is hard to remember that things will improve. But "the grace of God looks upon you with wide open eyes."[28] We have hope for change. "Consolation will empty desolation of its power."[29] St. Hildegard says God will not hide and "a great light of consolation will soon come into your soul and into the joy of your body, in God's own good time. For God lives in your tabernacle, and God's grace is not overshadowed there."[30] How normal for a writer to struggle. Indeed, the light does come "in God's own good time." When God calls us to do something, God is generous with grace to fulfill the call. St. Hildegard says this as well: "God helps you in everything you have undertaken with God's guidance."[31] I began to doubt my own doubt. What I needed was God's guidance. Desolation is a call to prayer.

I finally opened up to God about my struggle and feelings and felt the goodness and peace of simply being with God. St. Hildegard says, "The grace of God awaits you, and God will gather you to Her bosom like a book."[32] I expressed to God my desire to fulfill what I felt called to do. I asked God to help me persevere, transcend doubt, and more fruitfully envision the paper. St. Hildegard quotes God's promise: "For what flows from Me is a sweet and delightful taste to the soul; [the soul] goes forward in perseverance and does not look back in indecision. Therefore, blessed is the one who, confiding in Me, puts her hope and the beginning and end of her works not in herself, but in Me. She who does these things will not fall."[33] I asked God's guidance in my writing and continued to talk it over in prayer. "People know in their heads that God will help them."[34]

Finally, I stopped talking. I remained in prayerful silence. I trusted in God's help but assumed it would arrive in a future writing session. For now, I simply dwelled in gratitude for God's listening ways. As I gathered myself to get on with my day, something shifted. St. Hildegard says, "Through the Holy Spirit's gifts the ears of her heart opened, and God gave her the sweetest taste through rationality of the soul."[35] A fresh picture of the paper suddenly entered my mind. I felt guided and clear about the change needed. What was now required challenged me, but I sensed the rightness of the approach. Doubt evaporated.

St. Hildegard quotes God: "It pleases Me that people who know and love Me should understand what to do by the gifts of the Holy Spirit."[36] I felt relieved, like I could again breathe deeply. New energy filled my being. Again quoting God, St. Hildegard writes, "For when you seek Me in your inmost soul, as you were taught through faith in baptism, do I not do everything you desire? . . . And when you sought Me, did I reject you?"[37]

That describes my sense of God speaking to me—what did I expect? Of course God would help. I felt gratitude and happiness, humbled that God would be so kind, affirming, and helpful. "In God's sublimity I know the sweetest good, which is humility, and feel the sweetness of the unfailing balsam and rejoice in the delightfulness of God as if I were amid the fragrance of all perfumes."[38] I was delighted by God's generous response to my prayer.

"The creature was kissed by the Creator when God gave it all the things it needed."[39] I was kissed by my Creator and renewed as a collaborator with God in creating a written work. I felt valued by God. St. Hildegard says, "God values human beings."[40] The feelings flowing from my encounter with God were consistent with consolation: peace, trust, gratitude, and relief. I was inspired, excited, and confident, even though I felt challenged. I was liberated from doubt. I sensed God's goodness in guiding me. My spirits lifted and I was filled with positive energy as I embraced my new direction. I delighted in God. The contrast to desolation was indeed "a sweet and delightful taste."

With the illumination I received for the new thrust of the paper, I completed and published it. St. Hildegard says, "The mercy of God's grace, like the sun, will illumine the person; the breath of the Holy Spirit, like the rain, will water her, and so discernment, like the tempering of the air, will lead her to the perfection of good fruits."[41]

REFLECTION QUESTIONS

How do you experience the lively activity of the Holy Spirit within you?

When has desolation led you to right action?

What is your prayer about becoming wise and discreet?

"Weigh carefully little by little"

Have you ever gotten enmeshed in something because you didn't think it through?

St. Hildegard and St. Ignatius both note that we can be deceived into thinking a choice is good when it isn't. A choice, says St. Hildegard, "can appear heavenly and then deceive."[42] However, "those who truly pay attention to and inquire about what is shown to them are not deceived so easily, but persisting with the strength of truth, they shun those things that they weigh carefully little by little."[43] By definition, evil is not always what is plainly immoral, malevolent, or wicked; it can also be what is harmful or undesirable. "Evil . . . is nothing but a false choice, an opinion contrary to God's will."[44] We might head down a path that is harmful or undesirable for us because we've made a false choice.

During spiritual direction formation, I had a couple of profound experiences while walking the labyrinth and while tending it for others. In the glow of these experiences and without "weighing carefully," I chose to become materially and ministerially invested in a labyrinth. Good came for many participants and for me. For example, I learned to make sacrifices for the sake of others' time with God. God did not abandon me in my poor decision. However, I could barely handle the large canvas labyrinth. I was set back physically each time I worked with it, such that my other ministries were affected. The setbacks exacerbated my disability. The labyrinth required large spaces that were hard to find consistently, therefore people could not walk it as a regular practice. With proper discernment, all these issues could have been foreseen.

God knew what was right for me, even if I paid poor attention to that. "God knows what the human being can accomplish."[45] And it was less than I thought. "If you undertake greater toil than you can endure, you will fall . . . deceived."[46] My path began to look like that. St. Hildegard says, "O servant and close friend of God, consider the example of a day which begins clear and beautiful and remains so until the evening, never clouded over by storms, as opposed to a day which dawns brightly but soon becomes a dangerous stormy time, so that the foul ending destroys the promise of the beautiful beginning."[47] The glow of the labyrinth ministry had clouded over. St. Hildegard and St. Ignatius encourage a look back over our path. Perhaps we were deceived about its rightness.

As I reflected on my labyrinth situation, I felt uneasy. The fact that I'd not discerned a call came home to me. St. Hildegard says, "For as a person looks to the beginning of her deeds, so too should she consider carefully their end and merits."[48] *How did I get here?* "Take care to see in your solicitude what is of God and what of man."[49] I'd wanted to share the wonders of labyrinth walking with others. My path sprang from my lovely experiences, my ego, a false sense of my material autonomy, and oblivion to my true physical capacity. I now felt unfree in what I'd undertaken.

Feelings of unease, doubt, falseness, and unfreedom are signs of desolation. "The human being's essence is perfect, because something of that original light remains in her, although she is filled with misery and woe."[50] In that remaining light, I prayed about my situation. I realized my desolation was actually a sign of God's grace, presence, and defense of my spirit. St. Hildegard says, "Fear not, because God, by Whose grace you are endowed with wisdom and knowledge, will never abandon you."[51]

I prayed to understand more clearly what had happened. The truth was, I had not involved God in my decision. I'd felt, *I want to do this*, but not a true sense of God's call. St. Hildegard says, "Trust not in deceptive vanities but in God."[52] With the grace of self-honesty, I admitted I'd ignored little cautions along the way. The whole project had become disconnected from God, and therefore empty. St. Hildegard says one feels "that You withdraw from me, because I have traveled away from You."[53] It was I, not God, who had traveled away. In labyrinth work, I did not have joy. Instead, I felt burdened. "When the sun has been darkened by a cloud, creatures . . . are left joyless."[54] But I knew that desolation was a sign that God had not abandoned me and wanted to help. St. Hildegard says, "I pray to God that you not consider God's help as something foreign to you."[55]

I discerned what to do. In peace, I sold the labyrinth to a church. The experience convinced me that some "good ideas" only masquerade as such. One is spared much trouble by discerning. St. Hildegard says, "God is truthful and without illusion."[56] We are vulnerable in the "glow" of lovely experiences. The glow is not a sign of one's direction per se. Never in my life had God, the defender of my spirit, called me to do what I hadn't the capacity to do. Instead, God has steadfastly defended my body and spirit. Everything God calls me to brings joy, happiness, and growth, even when there are challenges.

I thanked God for my new freedom. With God's help, "a person's thoughts are shifted."[57] I regretted my mistake and its cost, but as St. Hildegard says, "No one can have peace without anxiety in this present life, but only in life everlasting."[58] To discern is to hold oneself in the balance that supports good hearing. "Each person should . . . lift herself up . . . not unduly exalted by the good or prostrated by the bad. She should gaze on God in purity of heart, and therefore rise upward and not cast herself down to earth."[59] I am human. "If human beings were created such that they could do neither evil nor good, they would be like trees."[60]

Humility is not about berating ourselves; it can mean accepting the truth that we make mistakes, but learn from them. My mistake reinforced the importance of discernment. "Rationality was given to the human, so that with it she might discern when she ought to listen to God's command."[61] I was humbled by the fact I'd betrayed my body through lack of discernment. That realization enhanced my zeal for day-to-day discerning.

How could I improve? I prayerfully considered God's call versus the ideas that spring from my enthusiasms, attractions, or ego. When God calls, I sense God loving and drawing me toward what is of God. I feel close to God, intimately touched, and guided. I have a spirit of humility and undeservedness, even a little reluctance. My perspective enlarges as I see more as God does in contrast to the narrower scope I typically have. I sense a larger purpose. I feel alive and valued by God. What I want seems unimportant compared to saying yes to God. My energy and enthusiasm are neither momentary nor weak. I find satisfaction in service. I am sustained by grace and joy as I fulfill the call. St. Hildegard says, "Be true to your calling because this is what the grace of God wishes."[62]

"Minute thoughts and deeds may be jewels of virtue"

Are there little things in your life that you ignore at your peril?

St. Hildegard says discretion "encloses everything that is apt and suitable, that our most minute thoughts and deeds may be jewels of virtue."[63] Minute thoughts and deeds have great impact for a type-2 diabetic. When first diagnosed, I pictured a life of deprivation and complications. At first my blood sugar went wild due to some food choices. With medication, exercise, weight loss, careful eating, and prayer I have stabilized.

"As people are going along the way of truth, disposed to walk in the Divine commands, they are met by many temptations."[64] I desired to be strong against temptations. I also desired to share this new journey with God and deepen our relationship. St. Hildegard says, "The human spirit is the certain cause of the knowledge granted a person by God, and permeates everything else God gives the person, being true and faithful life and not false or deceptive."[65] I reflect on the "human spirit" that should permeate my being as I manage my disease in true and faithful life.

Our deeper response to a situation benefits our relationship with God. St. Hildegard says, "In the work of God wisdom and discretion are like two walls. . . . And God imbues the whole of the human mind with these, an equitable and just gift, that the mind may know God."[66] *Imbue* comes from the Latin for "moisten" or "keep wet." "For God in the power of God's goodness profoundly imbued the human being with reason and knowledge and intellect, that she might dearly love God and devotedly worship God."[67] We are soaked, saturated, or permeated with wisdom, discretion, knowledge, and intellect that we might love and worship God. How can I use the gifts with which I am imbued to love and worship God in deeper response to diabetes?

I have chosen little moments of testing my blood sugar as moments of prayer. I pray for those stabbed by racist remarks, sexist comments, and unkindnesses. I pray for those tested by greater trials. I pray for those whose blood has been shed by violence or war. I pray for others with diabetes or blood disorders. These are "minute thoughts and deeds," and yet they are a deeper response undertaken to share the journey with God.

Jesus said, "My food is to do the will of Him Who sent me" (John 4:34). The diabetic journey requires faithfulness to God in how I eat. I renewed my understanding of the human body and how it handles food, uses its insulin, and responds to exercise. As I renewed my knowledge of my inner world, I sensed I was sharing in what God knows about me. I felt wonder and gratitude. I saw complexity in what goes awry in diabetes and what exacerbates it, the harm minute deeds do. I began to hear my body and hear God in new ways. St. Hildegard says that Jesus "put the Holy Spirit's gifts into the human being's ears, so that she could obtain a sense of hearing different from what she had had before."[68]

Next, I became crystal clear on a diabetic's meal—that is, "what is apt and suitable." I noticed that desolation comes with poor choices. Now, I eat only those meals I feel pure-hearted in praying over. It is that simple. St. Hildegard says, "The soul indeed loves discretion in all things—and as often as a person's body eats or drinks without discretion, or does any other such thing indiscreetly, the powers of the soul are torn apart. For all things must be done with discretion."[69] Discernment in the minute deed of choosing food is one way the diabetic can love self, God, and others.

I am at peace if get the exercise I need. St. Hildegard says, "The soul in a person is strengthened by the Holy Spirit's fire for good works, and weakened by the cold of laziness and neglect."[70] I have never heard a spiritual directee point to lack of exercise as a cause of desolation. Yet exercise is essential, "apt and suitable," and a rightful part of a "true and faithful life." Surely it is a "jewel of virtue" to undertake it and a desolating force to not do so.

At this point on my journey as a diabetic my emphasis on the right spirit, a deeper response, closeness to God, and managing the disease with discretion works. I don't feel deprived or burdened. I have befriended my soul. I feel acceptant, faithful, and helped by God. St. Hildegard reminds us, "Do not trust in your powers alone, but see to it that you flee to the grace of God."[71] Discerning or discretion in this example involves "minute thoughts and deeds" and embracing the grace that God offers. "The grace of God is near you, and gives you blessings, for it wishes to keep you."[72] I find truth in St. Hildegard's words, "If you seek God's grace, it will not flee from you."[73]

Reflection Questions

> Recall a time when you got involved in something you did not "weigh carefully little by little." What happened? What were the signs God "never abandoned you"?
>
> How has God been the defender of your body as well as your soul?
>
> What is your prayer about "thoughts and deeds" that could become "jewels of virtue" for you?

"We live illumined in God and vivified"

How do you know when to say yes and when to say no?

No one discerns for us. Parish life brings numerous requests for participation in events, funding, or ministries. Some may be right for us and some not. To say yes to every request is to say no to balance and moderation. "Discernment strengthens holy works with moderation."[74] Some activities, such as counting rummage sale proceeds for two hours, might simply be undertaken as a helpful parishioner without formal discerning. The intellect, St. Hildegard says, "sifts things . . . inquiring whether they are useful or useless . . . [or] pertinent. . . . It chooses among the various works wisely."[75]

Other requests require deeper commitment and potently affect others' experiences of Church and God. For making decisions about how to respond to these, I hold discernment in high esteem. St.

Hildegard refers to it as "the Ladder between [the active life and the contemplative life], on which human minds ascend to heaven."[76] To her, discernment is part of being made in God's image and likeness. She says, "The human understood all things, because she has rationality, since God created her in God's image and likeness. . . . Rationality was given to her, so that with it she might discern."[77]

The Rite of Christian Initiation for Adults (RCIA) is a ministry that runs from autumn to early summer each year with several meetings per month. When asked to join this ministry as prayer leader, discernment guide, and catechist, I carefully and formally discerned whether to say yes. I prayed to know if God was calling me to support RCIA. St. Hildegard says, "Divinity's excellence . . . illuminates all things."[78] Though attracted to the ministry, I expressed to God my willingness to say yes or no. I believed my greatest happiness, not to mention the benefit to others, was in God's call. "If a person works in accordance with the soul's desire, all her works become good."[79]

Both St. Hildegard and St. Ignatius propose that we follow a process or rule in discerning important decisions. St. Hildegard says, "The spirit raises itself in two ways: sighing, groaning, and desiring God; and choosing among options in various matters as if by some rule, for the soul has discernment in reason."[80] She believes order is of God: "Strength of the everlasting, in Your heart You invented order."[81] In my experience, careful discernment brings fullness and wholeheartedness of commitment and freedom from wondering about my choice. My life is ordered positively. St. Hildegard quotes God: "For what flows from Me is a sweet and delightful taste to the soul; it goes forward in perseverance and does not look back in indecision."[82]

I have not discovered a formal rule for discernment in St. Hildegard's writings despite her above reference to such. I discerned the RCIA request in the Ignatian style. After my prayer of willingness, I sought to be open to the Holy Spirit. St. Hildegard and St. Ignatius agree that one begins by holding the options in balance and desiring what God desires. St. Hildegard says, "Every creature looks back to God with her own talents and does not do anything without God's instruction."[83] How often I have violated her admonition. But this time, I spent a few days imagining both the yes and no possibilities. I tried to sense how the Holy Spirit was drawing me.

First, for a few days, I imagined saying no, with Monday nights free and someone else serving RCIA fruitfully. I imagined that it wasn't my call. I dwelled on other wonderful things I could do with my time and energy. During those days, I felt dryness, low energy, a little sadness, and disappointment, even though my life was otherwise fine. I felt out of alignment with God. St. Hildegard expresses the sentiment, "What good can I do without God? None."[84] I felt disconnected from partnering with God in good.

Next, I spent a few days imagining my yes to serving RCIA. I pictured Monday nights spent at the parish, driving through snow to get there at times. I imagined preparing materials. I imagined studying my faith, preparing to answer complicated and challenging questions. I assumed a deficit in time for other things. I considered how hard it would be when some participants rejected my faith tradition. During those days, I felt a paradoxical lack of consternation about the sacrifices involved. Instead, I felt energy, excitement, a sense of rightness of the request, and generosity in my heart. I felt aligned with God. A former spiritual director's words came back to me: "One shouldn't be casual about requests to minister." The contrast with the previous few days got my attention. I was surprised by the result. St. Hildegard says, "We live illumined in God and vivified by the breath of life."[85] I felt illumined and vivified.

I named as desolation my experience of imagining no and as consolation my experience of imagining yes. I believed I was called to serve RCIA. I knew I could be deceived, as I'd sometimes made mistakes in the past, so I prayed for confirmation from God, another Ignatian step. St. Hildegard says, "Because a person chooses, she may choose wisdom. As long as she desires help with her will, help will be given her, for if she calls upon God, God will help her."[86] We can and should trust that God will confirm a choice aligned with God. St. Hildegard says, "God hides no counsel from me."[87] Still, in my experience, confirmation is a surprise. It never comes in the way I imagine God will bring it. St. Hildegard says, "Keep your eyes open and walk in the straight way."[88]

Two days later I spoke with someone who'd been through RCIA and who also was keen on my writing. I happened to mention the RCIA request. She vehemently opposed my saying yes, which she perceived as a threat to my writing work, and put forth all the reasons I should say no. They were valid and I took them seriously, but with a paradoxical result: inside, I recoiled from the advice. In my experience, I do not react to the Holy Spirit by recoiling. St. Hildegard says, "The Holy Spirit comes softly to a faithful soul . . . just as . . . a certain moist air moves."[89] That is also an Ignatian understanding.

I grew more certain I should say yes. The reasons this woman put forth didn't erode, even a little, the mysterious conviction that had unexpectedly solidified within me. St. Hildegard says, "Take care not to abandon the fiery gifts of the Holy Spirit because of the timorous advice of others or because of the discouraging opinions of this world."[90] Later, in prayer, I understood this experience as confirmation of my call. God's grace had already strengthened me. "The Creator is present to the creature when God gives her greenness and strength."[91]

When I said yes to the requestor, waves of joy and confidence in God's help came. St. Hildegard says, "My heart's knowledge recognizes a shining gem in the gentleness of Your sweetness."[92] She describes the endpoint of careful discernment: "O daughters of God, God does not scorn knowledge rooted in holy rationality, because God made the human being in God's own image. . . . And so rejoice, and entrust what you propose to do to God."[93] What God calls us to do God gives grace to do. "With the grace of the Holy Spirit assisting, humans accomplish what they chose according to the will of the soul."[94] We are fired up by the Spirit's own fire. "Because of the good desires which God loves in you, God enkindles you with the fire of the Holy Spirit to do good works."[95]

Further confirmation that I had discerned correctly came in the fruitfulness, joy, fulfillment, endurance, and growth I experienced for years in RCIA ministry. St. Hildegard says, "When God sees that the person has begun to do the good and that her house thus gleams, God knows and sees the beginning of goodness within her and looks upon her with God's loving embrace."[96] I thanked God for calling me to a ministry that was a good fit for me. Truly, my greatest happiness was in going the way God asked me to go. "Reason . . . holds the means of gladness."[97]

Alignment with God through discernment, says St. Hildegard, is one way that we, like Mary, "magnify" the God within us:

> For the soul in which God is . . . contains the sighs, prayers, and holy works that lead to God. . . . All the beauty and embellishment of Divine inspiration, as it were, the flowering and embellishment of the virtue of God, as well as Divine inspiration itself, are glorified through the soul. For when the soul in which God is, performs good works, God's glory is magnified with heavenly praises since the soul comes from God. The soul is fertile from God's grace and sprouts blessed strengths and virtues. . . . The soul exists as something Divine in us.[98]

Eight years into my RCIA work, however, something shifted. The class that year presented many challenges. My spiritual direction and spiritual writing ministries had grown, and I was busier. Little was new for me in the material we covered in RCIA. Yet these were minor factors. In reality, I wasn't myself. Something was going on. St. Hildegard says, "There is darkness in some part of you. Why do I say this? Because your heart is bound up in that sadness which is encircled by doubt, like a millstone, questioning."[99] I did not question my original discernment; I trusted the Holy Spirit. "The Holy Spirit is a fire, but it is not an extinguishable fire that sometimes blazes up and sometimes is put out. It permeates eternity."[100]

During a short retreat, I opened up to God about my desolation. I admitted I was not myself. I did not have my usual joy and fulfillment. The RCIA work seemed harder than it should, and I was not as positive as I typically was. I wasn't depressed. I didn't feel this way in other parts of my life. St. Hildegard says, "You will frequently experience great tribulation—not like a prodigal son, but like the friend of God."[101]

As I prayed, I finally considered leaving the RCIA ministry—and as I did, a rush of relief and peace came over me. St. Hildegard says, "She will feel the change in her mind, and . . . raise her eyes to see and her ears to hear and her mouth to speak and her hands to touch and her feet to walk."[102] The consolation was compelling. I worried about leaving what I'd felt called to do; but could I ignore this? "Whoever has knowledge in the Holy Spirit and wings of faith, let this one not ignore God's admonition, but taste it, embrace it, and receive it in her soul."[103]

Discernment is complex when a mix of feelings, concerns, and commitments is involved. This is why we need the Holy Spirit's help. St. Hildegard says, "God does not cease to work with the human"[104] and "Divinity's excellence . . . illuminates all things."[105] God coaxes us into discerning anew. I humbly conceded that God decides what we should revisit. "God discerns whatever ought to be discerned and divides whatever ought to be divided."[106] I continued to pray. I offered God my willingness to continue or to leave the RCIA ministry. I discerned the decision, just as I'd done at the beginning of the ministry.

Clarity and consolation came. St. Hildegard says, "For the Holy Spirit, with heavenly power, emits diverse rays, which are gifts to humans; and these rays, more brilliant than the sun, diffuse and penetrate the recesses of humility in the clear vision of faithful souls. And thus the Holy Spirit enlightens their minds and senses that they may gain a deep understanding in everything of what they should rightly do in God."[107] I knew what I should rightly do. I stepped away from the RCIA ministry. The God Who calls us into something can also call us out of it.

Desolation prompted my search for clarity. St. Hildegard says, "Divine Love is saying to you, I long to remain with you, and I want you to . . . love Me diligently."[108] Joy, good energy, renewal, and ever deeper trust in and gratitude for God's wisdom arrived. "When You created me, You gave me to act following You, as You also made me to be Yours."[109]

"Her soul will be joyfully filled"

Has it ever seemed that God took a particular interest in your effort to serve?

"The grace of God comes to people through the Holy Spirit."[110] The Holy Spirit provides consolation to strengthen and inspire us in ministry. St. Hildegard says, "God sometimes speaks to a person when God opens up her heart. How? In the Holy Spirit's sweetness, because in that person, the place of the Spirit's dwelling shines."[111] I once facilitated a group discussion of St. Thérèse's *Story of a Soul*. In this parish activity, I received strengthening, inspiring consolation that enlarged my heart and aligned me with God's agenda.

To my amazement, thirty people signed up. Before our first meeting, I happened to read, "Wisdom is close to those who seek Her, and the one who is in earnest finds Her" (Sir 51:26). I was abruptly ambushed with deep feelings of love, joy, and closeness to God. St. Hildegard says, "The Spirit will reign in you, and then you will understand God in your soul."[112] The "sweetness of the Holy Spirit" seemed to reign in me.

I reflected on the Sirach verse. I realized the readers of St. Thérèse's book were seeking Wisdom, Who was close to them. Another wave of consolation and tears of joy came. St. Hildegard describes such experience uniquely: "The fire . . . is Divine power, which vivifies and sustains all things. This fire is sweet and mild, and the human soul is inspired by it. It is a fire that does not consume (although it is mighty), but sets hearts ablaze with love."[113] I was invited to love the readers. I prayed that God's desires for them be fulfilled. "The Holy Spirit's gifts bring viridity into the human heart, to bear good fruit."[114] I prayed that the fruits be all that God desired to bring forth.

Consolation kept my focus on God's desires for the readers. I felt strength and zeal to dedicate myself untiringly to their earnest seeking. St. Hildegard says, "When a person works according to the soul's desires, she becomes a flourishing garden on which God feasts God's eyes."[115] I felt joy in serving. "The desire to do good works gives joy to the mind."[116] I truly was single-hearted, a wonderful benefit to consolation I'd not grasped before. For "the person who turns toward the good and with God's help embraces it in works of faith . . . her soul will be joyfully filled with inner holiness, for she is serving her Creator in well-disposed and ordinate single-heartedness."[117]

We experience spiritual joy because "virtues are beginning to show themselves."[118] Here, the virtue was to focus on God's desires as the way to love others. I was affirmed, guided, and accompanied as I worked to bring St. Thérèse's wisdom to others. In the mystery of God's consolation, I glimpsed God's love for the readers, God's extraordinary regard for St. Thérèse, and God's desire to speak to the readers through her. "There is another lovely kind of joy, which is kindled . . . by the Holy Spirit, and the rejoicing soul receives it faithfully."[119] Our fruitful response to God's consolation and grace begins with our openness to receive and to savor in gratitude.

REFLECTION QUESTIONS

> When have you sensed "darkness in some part of you," a time when you weren't yourself but weren't sure why? How did clarity arrive?
>
> When has God, by opening up your heart, spoken to you?
>
> What is your prayer about discerning choices and deepening commitment?

"Do not withdraw from God" and "Attending God"

Do your own thought patterns ever take away your spiritual freedom?

During a retreat I was wound up and defensive about something someone had said to me. I was preoccupied with all I wished I'd said in reply. St. Hildegard says, "Sometimes various thoughts cause in that person so great an uproar that her soul's hearing . . . can neither understand nor recollect."[120] Exactly. These thoughts obstructed my soul's hearing. They distracted me from the Scripture prayer my director had suggested. My state was desolating; I lacked tranquility and freedom. "Although the peculiarity of the human will seeks strange gods and drives holiness away, those who choose God do not act this way."[121] I did not like the feelings that arose from not being prayerful and showing love for God. I resisted telling my director about my strange god thought-storm. Fortunately, God draws us back to God, and I did tell her.

My director simply said, "Is this how God is calling you right now?" And of course it wasn't. Instead, as St. Hildegard says, "God wants you. See to it, therefore, that you do not withdraw from God."[122] My director saw my lack of perception, withdrawal from God's call, and desolation. A wise guide is vital when we are spiritually not seeing and not hearing during desolation. St. Hildegard says, "Daughter of God, act like those on board a ship who heed the ship's pilot so that the pilot can bring them safely to harbor."[123]

Clearly, I had self-work to do and a false self to say good-bye to— but those could wait. My challenge would be to reject my temptation to obsess over the troubling conversation instead of engaging the retreat. I named the problem as a "temptation," because that objectified it and separated it from what I was really about.

In St. Hildegard's time, objectification was accomplished by pointing to the devil. She says, "I give this answer to the Devil's tempting: 'I will not yield. . . . For I must not let myself be struck by the Devil's arrows.'"[124] Both she and St. Ignatius refer to "enemies." St. Hildegard says, "The God of all creatures will give you the grace necessary for you to resist your enemies. God will do this for all eternity so that your enemies may no longer dominate you. . . . God will fill your soul with heavenly joy and light."[125] My enemies were the forces tempting me away from retreat graces, just the opposite of what the defender of my spirit does.

In my newly perceptive state, "I will not yield" was a good mantra. My temptation recurred in unguarded moments, as if I were indeed struck by little arrows. I recalled St. Teresa of Ávila saying that such things stir when we are engaged with what is of great importance to God. Ironically, my very troubles illustrated the importance to God of my retreat. That gave strength to my heart.

My own ego is sometimes the enemy. It is threatened and hyperactive when it encounters God, Who is far bigger and more important than it. My ego knew no humility at this stage of my journey. Fortunately, "the soul . . . teaches a person to abstain from unruly thoughts and . . . [not to] despair of God's grace . . . [and] to throw herself at Jesus's feet in true humility."[126]

When I was young, I assumed my thoughts and feelings were not a choice. Some of my directees struggle in this way. But to be victimized by our own thought patterns is not spiritual freedom. With growth in wisdom and self-knowledge, I've learned I have choices. St. Hildegard says, "God has illuminated me with two eyes . . . where I can choose which path to enter. . . . I think about Whom I shall call upon to lead me . . . into the path of light. . . . The cords of my captivity will be burst."[127]

I can choose to reject tempting, disquieting thoughts, and in this I have God's support: "The omnipotent God moves a person with her own piety so that she sees . . . the flame and love of true holiness, so that she chooses this flame, and . . . rejects the blindness and darkness of the temptations of the devil; she does not volunteer to subject herself to the devil."[128] I can consciously choose my Leader, the path of light, and the flame of true holiness.

I chose to shelve the issue, to recognize God as my guide and not yield to the temptation to obsess. I attained peace, calm, a sense of the rightness of this path, and a feeling of closeness to God. An abundance of richness flowed in my retreat. "The sweetness of the Holy

Spirit is boundless and swift to encompass all creatures in grace. . . . The Holy Spirit Itself is a burning and shining serenity, which cannot be nullified, and which enkindles ardent virtue so as to put all darkness to flight."[129] I no longer felt the spiritual unperceptiveness and darkness of desolation. I was drawn deeply into prayer and the experience of God's loving-kindness.

St. Hildegard says, "The Spirit lifts up the spirit. How? The Holy Spirit, by Its power, draws the human mind . . . that it may share in the vision of the Spirit, Whose eyes are not obscured . . . and Who sees the inner things. What does this mean? The Holy Spirit lifts the human spirit upward to the mountain of heavenly desires, that it may clearly see the works to be done in the Spirit, the great works of God."[130] Sharing in "the vision of the Spirit" and in "the great works of God" were at stake in choosing "which path to enter."

The experience revealed the dramatic contrast between my ego's noisy, annoying, obsessive, distracting defenses and the Holy Spirit's gentle, loving, peaceful defense of my inner spirit. I saw how critical a wise guide is in the midst of desolating unfreedom, and I realized the spiritual stakes. St. Hildegard uses humor to emphasize that our return to God is in our makeup: "All good rises from God and returns to God. The faithful should contemplate the profoundness that when God created the human being, God made us like a wheel in the spirit of life so that we roll back to God."[131]

"Attending God"

How does discernment unfold in spiritual direction?

In my spiritual direction ministry, directees often generously say, "I just want to do God's will," or "I'm not sure what God wants me to do," or "I wish God would give me a sign so I'd know if this is God's will." St. Hildegard says, "The soul is hungry for dutiful action."[132] Such desires, with consciousness and prayer, sponsor spiritual deepening. "Rise up quickly with the breath of the soul by which [you] can embrace God . . . [and] can love God."[133] I hear the directees' statements as their souls' hunger and desire to embrace and love God, but also as their unfamiliarity with discerning the Holy Spirit's actions. We start with the source of their desire and what that says about their relationship with God.

Who has created our desire, and why? "Temporal things cannot understand eternal things unless God in God's mercy wants to reveal such things to them."[134] God wants to reveal to us what we want to know. God does not play guessing games. St. Hildegard says it is virtuous "to see the example of Christ and how to follow in His steps, and . . . to anticipate with fortitude and reverence the will of God."[135] God's desire to reveal manifests in our desire to anticipate God's will and to follow Jesus. We desire God's support, and "all creatures are supported by God."[136] God does not intend us to be unaware of what God wants, and thus "the work of the Spirit is shown to the faithful and holy soul."[137]

Directors draw out this awareness by exploring directees' experiences of consolation and desolation. "God has so constituted you that, when you act with wisdom and discretion, you feel God in your reason."[138] We invite noticing how God communicates through drawing, guiding, loving, and defending their spirit. St. Hildegard says, "Take note that you dry up in evil things and grow verdant in good."[139] In this exploration, evil is simply what is not of God. St. Hildegard counsels, "Be mindful daughter, to make your paths straight in the discernment of your good intellect. . . . Choose the straight paths for yourself, and keep the eyes of your mind clear so that you are not deceived."[140]

Most directees recall a time when they knew with great inner conviction what they should do or choose. They also can describe a time when their inner spirit confirmed that they were on the wrong track. Their inner atmosphere at these times is key to their naming experiences of consolation and desolation. We then explore how the Holy Spirit brings clarity. The point is that discerning is in our very makeup, as St. Hildegard said. We can use it consciously and consistently toward deeper trust and love for the One guiding us.

Sometimes a directee confronts a decision and mentions difficulty in knowing the choice to make. I often comment, "The Holy Spirit does know the answer." St. Hildegard adds, "No one, save God alone, can know all things."[141] Through discernment, we learn what the Holy Spirit desires to share with us about our path. St. Hildegard says, "Discernment is part of the reason with which God inspired the human being when God breathed life and soul into the human's body."[142] What if we ignore this gift? "When a person's reason imitates God, she touches God."[143] What if we choose not to touch God? Not to be the person God intended? Not to love God? "You cannot plead as an excuse that you lack any good thing that would inspire you to love God in truth and justice."[144]

At times a directee fears accepting God's invitation to put out into deep water (Luke 5:4). As the director, I may feel a little pang of desolation at that revelation, a sign to me of the risk that God's invitation may be turned down out of fear. My inner pang invites me to help God defend the directee's spirit. I reassure and suggest Scripture readings to help the directee stare down fear and to trust. I also invite the directee to reflect on prior experiences of the Spirit's guidance and how they unfolded in grace and good. Past experiences of consoling conviction help the directee trust God's track record. If a significant decision is involved, we review a reliable method of discernment (such as the one described earlier).

Spiritual direction is the premier setting in which discernment unfolds. As directors, we help our directees satisfy "the soul's hunger for dutiful action."

"Flooding the heart with the fragrance of good"

How is your life enriched by discernment?

As we've discussed throughout this chapter, discernment supports being a faithful friend of our soul. It fulfills something of what it is to be in God's image and likeness. We discern what God desires to reveal to us that we might love, magnify God, serve, and be Christlike. Discernment involves listening to God more than to competing voices, such as that of our ego. Day-to-day discerning is part of praying always; loving God, self, and others; and noticing and embracing the grace already offered. It is refusing to yield to the little arrows of temptation and distraction that cause neglect of what is important to God and us.

God, the Source of our deepest desires, calls us to discern commitments of our God-given time, energy, talents, and treasure. The Holy Spirit helps us navigate complex decisions and align with God. Carefully discerned and confirmed choices bring happiness, wholehearted and single-hearted commitment, balance, moderation, and order to our lives. We may have to make sacrifices, but God always provides the grace we need to fulfill our calls.

To discern, we rely on desolation and consolation. Desolation disturbs our peace, saps our energy, and causes us to feel disconnected from God and our true selves. Desolation clouds our spiritual perception, and a wise guide is vital. Desolation is a gift and sign, however, that God defends our spirit and seeks to help us. It is an urgent call to honest prayer, and also a dawn of sorts, leading to the bright sun of consolation, for, as St. Hildegard says, "God is the day that never grows dark and never changes through the times and seasons."[145] Rolling back to God is in our makeup.

Consolation is joyous strength, a sense of God's love, an experience like the water within us changing to wine. It brings humility, a sense of undeservedness, and gratitude, for we cannot produce it in ourselves. Consolation transforms us in ways that are of God, bringing increased faith, hope, and love; it brings inspiration and a share in God's desires. We rejoice with St. Hildegard in praise: "Fiery Spirit, fount of courage, life within life of all that has being! . . . O Sacred Breath, O Blazing Love . . . flooding the heart with the fragrance of good. . . . Mirror of God Who leads wanderers home and hunts out the lost. . . . Armor of the heart and hope of the integral body."[146]

REFLECTION QUESTIONS

How is discernment part of being made in God's image and likeness?

When have you become wholehearted and free through discernment?

How has a wise guide brought you "safely to harbor" in a time of desolation?

What is your experience with "recoiling" from what you are hearing? With a message coming "softly . . . just as . . . moist air moves"?

What is your prayer about befriending your soul via discernment?

PART III

───────✦✦✦───────

BECOMİNG THE FAİTHFUL
FRİEND OF GOD

"Be such that you become the friend of God."[1]

chapter eleven

---•••---

INTEGRATION

"Become a living stone"

W hat is a living stone like?

Being a faithful friend to our souls inevitably brings us into more conscious relationship with God. St. Hildegard says, "Be the special friend of God so that you may become a living stone."[1] She refers to 1 Peter 2:5, "Like living stones, let yourselves be built into a spiritual house." Ephesians 2:19-20 says, "So then you are no longer strangers and aliens, but you are citizens with the saints and also members of the household of God, built upon the foundation of the apostles and prophets, with Christ Jesus Himself as the cornerstone."

Living stones abide in the spiritual house with saints, apostles, prophets, and Jesus. Living stones are not static or inanimate. We experience a secure and intimate relationship—a friendship—with the cornerstone. We are called to be special friends, living stones, solid and true, embodying and living our relationship to the cornerstone. A living stone is a living stone at all times and in all things. We must integrate all aspects of our living and being. "Be true to your calling, because this is what the grace of God wishes."[2]

"*God gives you the best of treasures*"

What do you leave out of prayer?

Integration means we bring everything to prayer and we bring our spiritual life to bear on all that engages us. All aspects of life count spiritually. For example, disappointment can be spiritually rich, though it tempts us to abandon constancy and faith. "If a person deserts the viridity of these virtues and turns toward the aridity of neglect . . . her soul's powers fail and dry up."[3]

I once led a research project that failed. I was devastated. I'd been so hopeful and had invested years of effort. To develop the same strong commitment to a new project challenged me. I was to lead others in the work, yet I struggled to get fired up. I desired grace. I went on retreat to regroup from my disappointment. St. Hildegard says, "Do not trust in your powers alone, but see to it that you flee to the grace of God."[4]

At the start of retreat, I said to God, "Nothing came out of this. All those years, all that work. What a waste." Over many hours I shifted from flat numbness to genuine sorrow, and I poured out my disappointment to God. I finally felt a little peace.

During prayer the second day, the image of a bicycle came to me. The front wheel, the failed project, was missing. The back wheel, the scientists who'd moved the project along, was still there. God showed me that the project wasn't a total failure. The people were more than they had once been. A little hope seeped into my heart.

The project had demanded of me a thorough and intricate grasp of cardiovascular science, as well as growth in leading and guiding others. I had become a better researcher and leader. St. Hildegard says, "God gives you the best of treasures, a vivid intelligence."[5] In the extravagance of God, the research had called forth the vivid intelligence of the scientists, and we had become treasures.

I revisited my call to be a scientist working on new medicines. "You must think every hour about how to make so great a gift . . . useful to others."[6] Many projects would fail, but all is not lost. St. Hildegard asks us to multiply our gifts in "praise and thanksgiving," for "God will make you burn yet more for love of God, so that, strengthened by the Holy Spirit, you may wisely discern the good and do greater deeds, and ardently glorify God, Who gave you these things."[7] Her words describe the wonderful change within me, the renewal I felt. Any gifts I'd discovered and developed belonged to God and God's people. To my surprise, I felt inspired again.

What better way to "make so great a gift useful to others," not to mention "multiply it," than to launch a new project? I desired to be the inspired leader that the project, the team, the patients, and God deserved. I trusted that "God, in the sweetness of God's love, will give me grace to overflowing and will make me burn yet more for love of God."[8] I was fired up anew. My dwelling in disappointment had transformed to a time of preparation for the new. I recalled God's words, "I am about to do a new thing; now it springs forth, do you not perceive it?" (Isa 43:19). I sensed that God was way ahead of me, already at work with my team and new project, and I needed to catch up.

Who would invite people to a "Holy Disappointment Retreat"? Yet it had been so for me. A living stone, a special friend of God, "must grow up in every way into Him Who is the head, into Christ" (Eph 4:15). I felt more integrated—felt I'd matured in handling disappointment. I was "renewed in the spirit of my mind" (Eph 4:23). St. Hildegard says, "It is natural for you to frequently have weariness of mind, but you need to learn to be generous through the grace of God."[9] That's just it, isn't it? Whether disappointment or some other challenge stops us in our tracks, we are called to a deeper, more generous response. With God's grace, the experience is preparation for new work to which God invites us. I was befriended by God in my disappointment and not doomed to stay stuck. God cultivated my new readiness to serve, to "burn yet more for love of God."

"Your striving for God and your labor . . . are the same thing"

Are you praying about your work?

I reflected and prayed about my team, the new project, God, and my spiritual life. I saw that my continued spiritual growth was at stake. St. Hildegard says, "You do not understand that your striving for God and your labor for God's people are the same thing. For your eager panting after heavenly things and your care of the people in God's name can be perfectly integrated."[10] I was a project leader with a strong, persistent focus on research objectives. Now I opened up to a more explicit focus on who we were to become. "God's work is the human being and this work is from God."[11]

My vineyard was secular, but my work as a research leader was nevertheless spiritual. "Because God is full Life without beginning and without end, so a person's work is also life in God."[12] If God had called me to this, God would help me do it. St. Hildegard says, "Secular people are the embrace of God's arms."[13] I would help God nurture the spirit of my team within the secular boundaries of a pharmaceutical company. "God assigns to all of you the task of ministering to all the needs of this life, both the spiritual and the secular."[14] Together, we would research the promise of a new molecule to bring new benefit to patients.

Prayer and openness regarding my daily work brought the inspiration and commitment I'd so recently not thought possible. I filled with gratitude. I felt more whole and integrated as a researcher and team leader. I trusted God to be with me, my team, and the patients we served. I felt ready to lead, renewed in fervor. The spiritual and the secular were now integrated in my perspective. I felt I could be true to my calling. My prayer life would encompass my entire work life. This was the vineyard to which I'd been sent. Where had I been?

"Reason praises God"

Do you and God reason and plan together?

A feeling of fervor hasn't the lifespan of a plan. St. Hildegard says, "God indeed ordains, while the human person thinks."[15] She never looks askance at reason as spiritual activity. She says, "Reason praises God in all good things. Reason is like a trumpet with a living voice."[16] She regards reason as God's gift, part of being made in God's image, and not to be neglected or disparaged. "The human being is alive with the wings of the power of reason . . . [and] speaks with her power of reason."[17] We needed to reason our way to a robust project plan. "Reason stands forth as the loud sound of the soul, which makes known every work of God or humans."[18] I prayed God would guide us.

Our team was blessed with diversity in membership, and our project was intended for patients around the globe. Diversity strongly influenced our plans. Indeed, our reason was "the loud sound of our souls." We were determined to research the merits of the molecule for patients who looked like our team. We discovered a scientific basis for especial utility in women, Asians, and African Americans. St. Hildegard says, "God does not scorn knowledge rooted in holy rationality. . . . Rejoice, and entrust what you propose to do to God."[19] I was convinced God was guiding us. I had a mental image of God's oily fingerprints all over our unique project plan.

Early studies revealed the molecule's potential to help patients with more significant cardiovascular disease, such as kidney disease and heart failure. These patients needed new options. St. Hildegard says, "A person should make for herself a garment with the heart-strings of mercy and come to the aid of each who seeks it, as far as possible."[20] We had been entrusted with a molecule of extraordinary potential. Everything we had and could become and all our intellectual gifts were being called forth by the challenges of studying sicker patients. St. Hildegard says, "Look zealously after the things God has entrusted to you so that you may bring your talent back to God doubled in value."[21]

Our reasoning, planning, thinking, and examination of data helped us develop a creative and integrated project plan. I myself felt more integrated as all these aspects of work entered my heartfelt prayer. St. Hildegard says that the human being was "made in the likeness of God to know, to think, and to act," and that we "compose our works in our hearts before doing them."[22] God utilized my intellectual gifts in new ways, challenging me to grow and be my true self at my best.

REFLECTION QUESTIONS

When you reflect on integration, what comes to mind?

How have you transcended disappointment to arrive at new readiness to serve?

How can "both the spiritual and the secular" become integrated in your life?

What is your prayer about God's utilization of your gifts?

"Words hurled . . . are like a dangerous wind"

How has God helped your relationships?

With plans in place, relationships with all who must approve their execution became the new frontier in my prayer. Our expansive plans were expensive. Company management saw our rationale but balked at the price and came across as adversarial. The team felt hurt, unsupported, and set back by their comments. St. Hildegard says, "Words hurled . . . are like a dangerous wind, suddenly assailing a person's heart. . . . These onslaughts often afflict even a person . . . whom God cherishes highly."[23] But she also says, "God fulfills God's signs in the fierce and the vigorous as much as in the mild."[24] I prayed that God's desires not be resisted. "There is no one who can resist [God's] will and justice."[25] I prayed about my role as a leader. Finally, God's answer came: *Improve the team's relationship with management for the sake of the patients.*

I journaled, "When you come to serve the Lord, prepare yourself for trials. Set your heart right and be steadfast, and do not be impetuous" (Sir 2:1-2). We were tempted to impetuous overreaction to management. What if the team "set its heart right and was steadfast"?

I asked the team how we could improve our relationship with management. First we had to process and transcend our hurt and anger. But the patients also called us to set our hearts right. We battled to the high road and grappled with God's idea.

The team proposed that we always be thoroughly prepared, respectful, open, and transparent; that we always present data in easily understood form; and that we position decisions clearly for management. We would stand for the patients in all interactions, reminding everyone of why the company existed. We asked an executive to mentor us and advocate for the project. St. Hildegard says, "Let your mind be pure in God, keep the hunger for God's justice, stay in the straight path, and God will receive you."[26] Gradually, we acquired a palpable humility and "set Justice upon the throne."[27]

I prayed mightily about funds. I told the team, "If you are at all religious, light a few candles or something." The day arrived to try again for funds. We went into the meeting with a sharpened budget, new data, refined plans, a clear picture of the potential benefit to patients with few options, a well-positioned decision, and a humble, respectful demeanor. Our executive advocate spoke up for the project. St. Hildegard says, "The Holy Spirit enkindled their hearts as the sun, beginning to appear from around a cloud, shows its burning heat by its shining light."[28] We were granted the money to include more seriously ill patients. "God does not stop fulfilling whatever petitions are just."[29] I saw that "with God's grace hardness was removed."[30]

We were sustained by our focus on the patients even as we tended our relationship with management. Integrating these relationships into my prayer life was so fruitful that I kept to that path. St. Hildegard says, "In the secret place of the heart one is good in the presence of God and humans when one dwells openly with them."[31]

The next relationship challenge soon arrived. Our Japanese colleagues were doing the first study in Asian patients. We knew our Japanese teammates pretty well. Both parties cherished the relationship. We interacted frequently. Even so, we had a big miscommunication and the Japan team went down a path that cost us time. We figured out our mutual mistakes, but getting back on track relationally wasn't easy. St. Hildegard says, "Have confidence in God and [do] not think God's mercy worthless or for naught."[32]

Despite our bumpy path, the results of the Japanese study were amazing. We all rejoiced. Yet our Japan teammates remained devastated by their mistake, apparently feeling embarrassment or loss of face. During our videoconferences, they literally hid their faces from the camera. I was saddened by the setback and realized how fond of them I was. St. Hildegard says, "Now, sweet daughter . . . see to it that you do not lay aside the office entrusted to you."[33] I was the leader. *What am I going to do?* I prayed to know.

As I prayed about our relationship, the wedding feast of Cana (John 2:1–11) came to mind. In my journal I wrote, "I sense the jars filled with water are persons. Jesus turns the water in us to something richer. . . . I suddenly felt filled with a certain richness, a rich energy. . . . Hard to describe. I felt that my concerns were God's and the saints' concerns, that we would be helped. We'd be shown the way." St. Hildegard says, "Rise up now because the grace of God is hastening toward you."[34]

Indeed, the grace of God did hasten toward me. In Japanese language class that evening I learned the phrase "*Ganbatte kudasai*"— roughly, "be encouraged." Perfect. The next morning, I sent large flower bouquets to our Japanese teammates. The card said, "*Ganbatte kudasai.* Congratulations on your beautiful study." Soon, emails arrived with pictures of our smiling teammates posing with their flowers. Their faces were back. St. Hildegard says, "The Holy Spirit enlightens human minds and senses that they may gain a deep understanding in everything of what they should rightly do in God."[35] Amen. I thanked God for the inspiration and for my colleagues' response. I glimpsed God's love for them.

Relationships with teammates, management, colleagues in other countries, regulatory authorities, consultants, department members, the patients we served, friends, family, neighbors, church members, spiritual directors, and others all became part of prayer and integration in my spiritual life. In each relationship, even during conflict, "the grace of God hastens toward me." I also discovered that praying together integrates us as living stones in the same spiritual house.

Susan Garthwaite

"We acknowledge God"

Have you ever prayed with your colleagues?

Our trips to Japan usually included a temple visit, often with our colleagues. We wafted purifying incense over ourselves, tossed coins in the offering box, bowed, folded our hands, and silently prayed. We imbibed beauty, spirit, and peace. The visits became more about prayer than tourism. I treasured these moments with my colleagues. Our little custom seemed natural and helpful.

A Japanese colleague told me that her people tend to be spiritual. They cherish their temples and shrines and often have small shrines in their homes. She was delighted to discover that Americans could be spiritual, too. I prayed that God would be manifest in our work together. "We acknowledge God, Who is just in all things and so must not be concealed but made manifest."[36]

During trips to Europe, I went to Mass with teammates. That opened the door to spiritual conversations about our work, an unexpected and welcome freedom. Eventually, we discussed our desire for a patron saint for our project. I proposed St. Hildegard due to her healing ways, scientific bent, and wisdom. She says, "You should have mercy and benevolence and virtue. . . . And also, you should stretch out your hand to the weak and those prostrated with troubles."[37] From then on, we appealed to her often to pray for the patients and for us. She says, "Direct your mind and thoughts toward God. As for me, I will constantly pour out my prayers to God for you."[38] I believe she did so. St. Hildegard became an integral part of my work and life.

Conducting clinical trials that include seriously ill patients means that a team endures their tendency to get worse and die. Experts outside the company periodically unblind data, checking to be sure that the test drug is not making patients worse. The company and the project team, however, are not permitted to know which patient is on what medicine.

To determine definitively if the test drug is helping or is ineffective takes years and thousands of patients. During such long waits, the team worries about the patients and doubts about the test drug's merits creep into their thoughts. Spirits go down. St. Hildegard encourages prayer: "Seek God, therefore, in the anxiety and anguish of your spirit."[39] I prayed daily for the patients.

One day as I prayed, all of the above abruptly came together in my mind: *Why not pray for the patients as a team?* What a delicate plan for a secular workplace—but we followed all the rules and were able to arrange a prayer service for the patients. St. Hildegard says, "The taste of good will plays in the soul."[40]

On the day of the service, we filled a third of a big old church near our labs. As the prayerful, beautiful music of St. Hildegard played, we lit tapers and wafted incense as we had in Japan. "Now it is fitting for you . . . to look to the smoke that ascends. . . . This is prayer, which ascends from our hearts. We ought to spread it liberally among ourselves."[41] We read inspiring texts. We prayed for the patients and for all those working to help them. We prayed for our industry, so tainted by greed. We prayed for strength and perseverance.

Team members offered aloud prayers from their own traditions and languages. A spirit of holy togetherness, good will, and humility permeated us. St. Hildegard says, "The Holy Spirit will pour forth the dew of Her grace among the people . . . so that they will then seem to be changed."[42] I looked at my team and thought, *Living stones, friends of God.*

At the end, no one wanted to leave—we were all still savoring the experience. Some of my colleagues were tearful. The patients were more present to us; they could never be simply data. I was profoundly moved, strengthened, inspired, and renewed. "For what flows from

God is a sweet and delightful taste to the soul."[43] I felt a deeper bond with my teammates, a bond that would help us through all our remaining work. St. Hildegard says, "Let your spirit be strengthened by God."[44]

Months passed. We were inspired to pray together again. Our Japanese colleagues were in town and joined us, as did members of other research teams. We filled more than half the big church. A clinical teammate read aloud letters received from patients. Some revealed that they were praying for us. Team members recited prayers from their own traditions in nine different languages. Directly behind me, a physician prayed for the dead in Hebrew. St. Hildegard says, "This life is a time of exile and . . . you sigh in expectation of another life."[45]

Those letters and prayers brought patients from around the world into the space. The patients' words of gratitude and encouragement filled our hearts, an unexpected and treasured outcome. "Divine grace will extend to every good deed, which is made up of two parts, God's love and the doer's."[46] I pondered the mystery of God in the great rewards of my work. "The Mysteries of God say to you: 'Whoever, for My sake, gives aid to someone who suffers in My Name will herself be aided—this is the reward of praise.'"[47] Our prayer and work for others circled back to bless and aid us. I went home that evening with prayer and work more integrated in my being than I'd dreamed possible.

Eventually, we celebrated the success of the new medicine in prolonging and improving patients' lives. St. Hildegard says, "Wisdom begins to work good things in the soul of a just person and it also finishes these works in the soul."[48] Many team members commented that it had often seemed we were helped "by something bigger than us." The stereotype of scientists is that they are not the most likely people to give such witness, but they did. "God saw them in their holy works and they will see God as well through them."[49]

I thanked God that our journey had not been a soulless, abstract drug development process—that it had instead been life with God. We were aware of Mystery drawing near to help us. St. Hildegard says, "Beware lest you attribute to yourself alone those good qualities which are yours in both your spirit and your works. Rather, attribute them to God, from Whom all virtues proceed like sparks from a fire.... Give God the honor which you owe God for the gifts which you acknowledge in yourself."[50] I sensed that was what my team was saying. I was deeply moved by their truth.

As I reflect on these experiences of holy integration, I realize that the epitome of spiritual integration is to help others integrate their work and their spiritual life. "The shoot of the spiritual life will . . . be made manifest by God's grace."[51] I believe a team that prays develops an inner eye for God's work with them—a God Who reveals "like a painter showing people invisible things by the images in his painting."[52] We were not "strangers and aliens" but "living stones . . . built into a spiritual house." We followed St. Hildegard's advice to "be the special friend of God so that you may become a living stone."[53] No doubt our patron had prayed for this to happen.

"Attending God"

How does spiritual direction aid integration?

The above examples of integration are from my work as a researcher and team leader. Many directees need encouragement to bring work to prayer, especially if their work is in a secular arena. Often, they do not think of their work as their call or ministry. In what we do we form ourselves; grow and mature; learn to cope fruitfully with struggles, conflicts, and relationship challenges; and find meaning and purpose—and yet secularity challenges the very idea of God's involvement in work. Directees express feeling dispirited by stress, difficult bosses, overwork, the endless focus on the bottom line, and so on.

We spend a high percentage of our life working. What a loss for it not to count in our friendship with God. When work is integrated into spiritual life, the story of work becomes the story of God with us, a story of movement and grace, a story of "special friends of God becoming living stones." At minimum, St. Hildegard says, we should "avoid the sin of being unmindful of God."[54]

Work is not the only aspect of life to integrate into our spirituality. Integration also means paying prayerful attention to facets of self that seem neglected, troubled, underutilized, underappreciated, unexplored, unhealed, or blocked. Our jobs may shine a light on these, as we shall see later. All of life, inner and outer, is our work, our "striving for God." As spiritual directors, we may sense the need for integration in our directees' lives and God's desire to "display My wonders"[55] in them.

My directees bring to spiritual direction their angst about performance reviews and other feedback at work. In advance, they fear what they will hear; post-hoc, they are upset by what they've heard. They have inner debates about the truth of it. "Disquieting battles arise"[56] after they hear another's opinion of what needs attention and integration in their lives.

How transformed the feedback process would be if directees' working lives and prayer lives were interwoven—if they felt they were working with and aligned with God in their work, and that the Holy Spirit was guiding them gently to integration. We can encourage these paths. St. Hildegard says, "Imbue your perception with streams of water."[57] A life-giving, non-disquieting path to integration is available.

One of my directees described low motivation in fulfilling one aspect of her work. Her delays brought unfavorable feedback. She felt disappointed in herself and stuck. I asked, "Is that telling you what you need from God right now? Where is God in this?" She was surprised by my questions. She said she had always kept her faith life and work life separate, "like two different worlds." She agreed to pray about her work struggles. St. Hildegard says, "If you will run to God, God will aid you."[58]

Over time, the directee accomplished what she'd once felt unmotivated to do.

"Prayer helped," she told me. "I felt like God helped me. . . . I think God cares about my work."

"And is there more?" I asked. "How does God regard you?"

She responded that God loved her in her work.

Her "two different worlds" comment revealed her need for integration. Spiritual directors listen for such disconnects in directees' experience. We seek to foster integration so directees become whole and enjoy greater fruitfulness. The "two different worlds" comment also signaled an "image of God" issue. My directee did not see God as caring about her work or about her as a worker. This was a flag of great relational significance. Integration is ultimately about the relationship with God, and so spiritual directors listen for arbitrary limits placed on God. We assist the Holy Spirit's integrating ways. We encourage prayer about all aspects of life and self. We pray with St. Hildegard, "May God give you God's blessing and God's help in all your works."[59, 60]

REFLECTION QUESTIONS

How have your "striving for God and your labor for God's people" become the same thing?

What aspects of self have become more integrated for you through spiritual direction?

What is your prayer about integration?

chapter twelve

———•••———

SURRENDER TO GOD
IN PRAYER

"What is born is called."

W hat do you and God want from each other?

Some people "think it possible to be what they wish without recognizing what they are and what they are capable of. But they remain unaware of Who made them and Who their God may be, wishing only to have God as their servant and do their will."[1] For a long time, in much of my life and work, I prayed primarily for what I needed from God. There is nothing inherently wrong with that. God wants to help. That aspect of the relationship is lifelong. But it doesn't necessarily lead to intimate friendship with God or the radical change needed for that. Eventually, certain prayer experiences shifted my ways and called me to deeper intimacy with God. St. Hildegard says, "What is born is called, as it were, aroused by the Spirit."[2]

One evening in deep winter, I sat in prayerful silence in my living room. I had been doing this often. I felt drawn to solitude and silence more and more. I was happy and peaceful in it. I was seeking God. St. Hildegard writes, quoting God, "When you seek Me in your inmost soul, as you were taught through faith in baptism, do I not do everything you desire ... and when you sought Me, did I reject you?"[3]

What has happened to my extrovert self and my season tickets to many things? I wondered. *I am just sitting here with God. Often.* My mother would have said, "You're unusually quiet these days." I might have dared to respond, "What can I do? God is magnetic." Indeed, "no one is able to resist God, since God alone is God."[4] I awaited God. St. Hildegard says, "The strength of our souls awaits Your coming in the tent of meeting."[5] So compelling was the call to solitude that I struggled to accommodate all else that needed tending. My priorities had shifted.

During one of these prayer times, I realized that God was calling me to God for the sake of relationship more so than to do something. Lent had arrived, so I decided to spend it focused on our relationship. *How exactly does God love me? What is God like? How do I love God back? What am I like to God?* As I prayed, I recalled my best friend's love for me. *In friendship with God there must be even more generous abundance.* St. Hildegard describes saints as "Friends of the living God."[6] That affirmed my Lenten strategy. I journaled, "If I develop my friendship with God it won't be hard to relate or to believe in God's love. I also feel very warmed by God's love in this realization."

At first I struggled to keep a relationship focus and to not slip back to old images and habits. I wrote, "It is important to keep focused on my relationship with God. After all, it makes all else possible anyway." St. Hildegard says the Holy Spirit strengthens the faithful "so they put the love of God before all other things."[7] I got a little traction with the friendship analogy. I wrote, "Jesus is like other friends. You can't force anything or have things the way you want when you want. The commitment has to be deep, meaningful, and is not to be failed. I am doing little concrete things with greater meaning now, like pausing in my day to be attentive and see what God is up to here and now. Prayer is much more about what is going on between God and me."

I kept going and soon wrote, "A relationship lesson about God: God cannot bear to be angry, wants to be involved, is interested in everything, and likes to surprise and delight me. If you know some endearing things about your friends, you know the same things about God."

In the weeks that followed, I more regularly sought awareness of God and God's ways. Our relationship felt more mutual. I was fully invested and determined not to turn away. I felt joyful and happy. St. Hildegard notes that "when a person who wants to be subject to Divine Love cherishes what is in God, looks upon God in the purity of faith, and does not set anything ahead of God, she prepares for herself a seat among the joys above."[8] Mid-Lent I journaled, "God has my heart. I am on the path once and for all. I have a passion for God."

On retreat late in Lent, the director invited reflection on what gift Jesus wanted for us. As I prayed, I realized Jesus wanted me to have the same relationship with His Abba as He had. That was the gift I wanted, too. I saw that my desire was the best gift I could offer. Yet I was now aware of issues within me that made me a suspect friend for God. St. Hildegard says, "I breathe in the love of God. . . . How do I deserve to share in the highest of joys?"[9] I wanted to live a holy and pure-hearted life in friendship with God, but I wasn't nearly as faithful as God. I must become my true self at my best to be consistently faithful in friendship. People like me, says St. Hildegard, are "asked by God if they had not seen God in the shadows of their heart."[10] There were shadows. "Every creature, and the human is one, has a shadow of itself, which signifies that it must be made new for unfailing life."[11]

I couldn't leap directly from spiritual insight to improvement. I spoke honestly with my Friend, God, about my failings. Every time I brought these up, God was right there with me in my struggles. I felt comforted. But finally I wrote to God, "Look, I don't want to be comforted! I want to be different! I want to be free! I want to be a better friend to You! I want to do what is hard for me. You know I will have a pretty meager life and showing as Your friend if I do not do what is hard for me." St. Hildegard says, "If someone looks in a mirror and finds that her face is very dirty, she will want to wash it clean."[12]

Coincidentally, at work we were examining "the way we always do things" with an eye to changing for the better. We discovered that the greater our frustration with what is, the greater our willingness to endure the havoc and pain big changes require. That's where I was spiritually as well.

"God alone . . . is able to free"

Do you respond to or react to God?

At this point I read somewhere that responding and reacting are two different things. I wrote, "I have many, many limitations and weaknesses, many more reactions than responses. If I were in better touch with my resistances I could recognize when I am not accepting and using my gifts. I want to respond, to give up my richness of fears. I want to let go of my fears and respond to God. Such a desire, I think, is evidence God is drawing me." I sensed, as St. Hildegard says, that "God alone and no one else is able to free me."[13]

God's initial response to my plea was to invite me out of my boat into the deep (Matt 14:28–33). It was night. The water was deep and dark. Jesus, the Light in the scene, beckoned me to get out of my boat and approach Him. My response was not promising. I journaled, "Like Peter, taking my eyes off Jesus and sinking as I concentrate on my fears—fear of letting go, fear of being 'illogical,' fear of giving over my very self, fear of changing. The stakes of vulnerability are high. Jesus grabs me and steadies me when I am sinking in the sea of my fears." Jesus was true to His promise. St. Hildegard quotes His words, "If you fall, seek Me with a constant outcry, and I will lift you up and receive you."[14]

The prospect of greater intimacy with God stirred up my fears. I was now in touch with my resistances. Like Job, I wanted to interact with God without fear. Job said, "Would that God's terrors did not frighten me; that I might speak without being afraid of God. . . . This is not the case with me" (Job 9:34–35). Nor was it the case with me. I wrote, "I'm trying to think of this as one of my turning points, not a place where I am stuck. Jesus did not reject His humanness, nor should I reject mine." Now, as I reflect on my journal entry, I see my respect for my human trepidation, but also my sense that humanness was key to being Jesus-like. St. Hildegard says, "God mercifully drew the human toward Godself. . . . For God . . . continued to love humankind very much, whom God knew beforehand as the clothing for God's own Word."[15]

I wrote, "I present the obstacles to intimacy. I'm the one holding back, and I can tell that I am." I knew I must stare down and name my fears. At my best I didn't let fear be my motive. I embraced bold graces and loved to move forward versus staying stuck. I saw courage as a sign of God's presence. St. Hildegard says that fortitude is "the great virtue arising from God's Divinity. . . . It is by great fortitude that people believe . . . what they cannot see with their bodily sight."[16] I was not yet fully open to this gift from the Holy Spirit.

An image, challenge, and invitation came whenever I entered prayer. I wrote, "I know there is a Divine invitation to let go of all and fall in/through an abyss, a seemingly bottomless chasm that is actually safe and of God. It is as though I am on a ledge in prayer and invited to fall off that ledge into the pitch-black mystery of God and allow myself to be taken nowhere or somewhere by God. A profound act of trust is required to let go and fall into Mystery, into not knowing what will happen, into zero control." But so far I hadn't been able to do it. "Who will help me but God?"[17]

Scripture has this clarity: "If the Son makes you free, you will be free indeed (Jn 8:36)." Intellectually I knew that was true, so I prayed, as St. Hildegard did, "Preserve me, body and soul, from every doubt that arises."[18] Only God could free me to do as God asked. "Who can do this other than God?"[19]

Good Friday came. I tried to stay with Jesus in His terror, dread, and utter vulnerability. I grasped that He fully understood the terror and vulnerability I'd experienced as a little girl confronting my own death. With sudden insight, I saw I had been unable to distinguish profound vulnerability in prayer from dying. Psychically, they felt the same to me. I wrote, "I cannot stay with it as Jesus does. But now I know I must. This dying is living. This vulnerability, this always dying, is the Way." St. Hildegard says, "Led to His passion, [Jesus] . . . knew in His body the darkness of death"[20] but then "rose again to serene immortality. . . . So joy unmeasurable by the human mind arose."[21] I understood the Way as the route to joy.

A new stage in my prayer life had come. *I resist and am afraid, but I must go ahead. I must not love my fears more than God.* St. Hildegard speaks of this spiritual "night"—or, as I put it, pitch-black Mystery. She says, "Night speaks knowledge . . . [and] provides the opportunity to make useful choices."[22] She points to light coming in the darkness: "God knows that you are in the dark night of your experience, but that you also see from afar in your mind a brightness."[23] The brightness is a relationship of deeper trust.

One morning shortly after Easter, prayer put me on the ledge over the dark, bottomless chasm once again. In that moment, I made one of the most "useful choices" of my life: I let go in loving trust, let myself descend and descend and descend into pitch-black Mystery, the inexhaustible depths of God, and ever-deeper trust. The descent continued until the prayer spontaneously ended. All was well.

I had this same prayer experience of descent into Mystery several times. I got so I readily took the plunge. It wasn't painful or disorienting. I was in the vastness of God, Who "has neither a beginning nor an end."[24] This was God's way and beyond my imagining. St. Hildegard says, "None can act and none has such power as God."[25] I experienced vast, pitch-black Mystery; I couldn't understand it or perceive a circumference to it. "No human can understand fully the profound mystery of the Divinity."[26]

Now I name the descent a mystical experience, but then I knew nothing of mysticism. The experience grew my trust of God enormously. I surrendered all in letting go. I floated in Mystery with nothing but my naked self. What if I had not let go? I was naked before and in God, the very thing Adam and Eve feared and "hid themselves from" (Gen 3:7–8) and which made it hard for them to "seek God . . . [or] rise to true knowledge of God."[27] In my descent, all was God.

St. Hildegard says, "God does not stop doing God's work until God has brought it to perfection,"[28] and "God will remove the shackles."[29] Such were my hopes. My growth in trust was essential for addressing the flaws that kept me a suspect friend of God. The God Who grew my trust to be more genuine and lasting could resolve other traits that were obstacles to intimacy. I must continue to surrender completely, with no holding back.

I journaled, "I am convinced that it is my heart and mind that need changing, and I have implored God to help me." My prayer became, "Dear God, change me and I shall be changed," an echo of St. Hildegard's prayer, "Prove me, Lord, through faith and hope. . . . Try me . . . that I may . . . become Your loving friend. . . . Cause me to be always aflame with the fire of the Holy Spirit."[30]

REFLECTION QUESTIONS

How has your relationship with God moved toward greater intimacy?

What obstacles to intimacy with God have you discovered?

What is your prayer about surrendering to God, holding nothing back?

"I will prepare many hearts"

How effective is your firm resolve in helping you to change?

How can we change deeply, genuinely, and more permanently when firm resolve repeatedly fails? Imagine God watching this struggle. A God Who loves to change mourning into dancing (Ps 30:12) and to clothe us with gladness (Ps 30:12). A God Who is the strength of the people (Ps 28:8), gracious and merciful (Ps 116:5). A God Who is our courage (Isa 12:12). A God Who is Light and in Whom there is no darkness (John 1:5). A God Who is love (1 John 4:8). A God Who "burns . . . brightly with every kind of goodness and justice"[31] and says, "I will prepare many hearts according to My Own Heart."[32] Imagine God's compassion for our struggle to be more loving and compassionate. How the will and desire to help are in the very heart of God, if only we are willing, ready, and courageous enough.

Many experiences in my young life fostered my developing into a tough woman, and my career in a male-dominated profession reinforced my toughness. For a long time I did not desire to be otherwise. Toughness was as essential to me as my lab coat. But I became a godmother, supervisor, team leader, colleague, and friend. Toughness was not suitable for these relationships. I struggled to not be so tough. St. Hildegard says, "Blessed spirits should cast their opposites away,"[33] that is, reject what is contrary to true happiness.

Given time, I could find words to express to others my encouragement, empathy, kindness, and understanding. I desired to more fully feel and spontaneously express these. Yet I felt so consistently tough and held back. St. Hildegard says, "God, in true justice, had foreseen all these things."[34] God would help in ways I could not have anticipated, but first I tried firm resolve.

Day after day, I resolved to be gentle, but wound up blunt, uncompromising, defensive, and easily provoked into inappropriately tough stances. I asserted control as if my life depended on it. I was utterly frustrated by my inability to be different. St. Hildegard says, "By her own strength, she has not been able to extricate herself."[35] I was acutely aware that my behaviors were not of God and were unhelpful to others, to me, to what needed to be accomplished, to the team's energy, and to my relationships with God, self, and others. I was pained by my repeated failures and the disorder in my being and doing. St. Hildegard says, "A fierce storm has come upon you."[36] That's how the disorder felt. I wrote, "Inner change is preferable to the exhausting and often ineffective firm resolve."

In prayer I apologized to God almost daily for what I was like outside of prayer. I felt shabbier by the day. "It is just that You withdraw from me because I have traveled away from You."[37] Was this pattern coming to a head in prayer? I was afraid to not be tough, but I was even more afraid to never change, to never become truly free. I grasped that "God alone and no one else is able to free me."[38]

I prayed for my freedom to my Creator. "I am the work of God,

173

and so I turn to God."[39] I wrote to God, "I cannot change myself! Here is my humility and my honesty, God. Surely You know best what I need. I will go wherever You want me to go or suffer whatever I need to suffer if only You will change me. May I not be stuck forever with this thorn in my side!" With Job I prayed, "This is my final plea; let the Almighty answer me!" (Job 31:37). St. Hildegard says, "No creature is so dull of nature as not to know what changes . . . cause it to attain its full growth."[40] I wrote, "If I am to get from bluntness to gentleness, 'tough' may have to go. When I empty of this, God fills the space. God promises to fill what's empty."

St. Hildegard says, "She dashes her wretchedness upon the Rock that is the foundation of beatitude."[41] Maybe that was what God desired of me. The next day in prayer, I sensed something big was coming that was not my doing. I felt my resistance stirring, but I wrote, "That's an old habit and not a reflection of my real willingness! I am committed to my own good. By now I know trust in You is brought about by actual trusting. I trust that whatever is most loving will happen in response to my prayer." I promised God I would hold still and stay in prayer no matter what. "I abandon my falling and sinning nature to You so that You can wash that part of me with Your mercy."[42]

I wanted God to work on me. St. Hildegard says, "God is like a worker who blows on a fire with a pair of bellows and then turns the fire every which way so that God can accomplish God's work more fully."[43] God has a process and is thorough. "None can act and none has such power as God."[44] Perhaps what God does is unique to the person; I suspect so.

What happened next was heart-wrenching, excruciating. An entire layer of self was pulled off one tenacious strip at a time, like thick, sticky, head-to-toe strips wrenched loose and torn away. I remained still and passive. The experience seemed physical, emotional, and spiritual all at the same time. I felt great mercy and great loss simultaneously. All the while I was held in the great compassion of God. I knew what was stripped away was my long-held toughness.

When the stripping away was over, toughness felt thoroughly gone and unavailable to me. I sensed I couldn't assert it. God had removed it. I wept and wept in tender consolation, pain, loss, and hope. I was left trembling, naked, fragile, and new. St. Hildegard says, "God has made her a new person, with a life in her different from what she had had before."[45] I did not know what to do with myself. At first the result did not seem a gain. I felt utterly defenseless, like a new fawn. St. Hildegard says, "Acknowledge that you have no power except in God and through God."[46]

Who am I now? "Humankind has been led in soul and body to the fullness of pure integrity, though they are very often moved away from an upright and steadfast posture."[47] Integrity is being true to one's core. I felt stripped to my core integrity. But yes, my upright stability was wobbly. I felt exposed, shaken, and unable to function at first. It was like profound shock, yet I knew the experience was good news. I had been abruptly freed from a prison and found it both disconcerting and wonderful. "From [purgation] many are truly bewildered and greatly amazed."[48] I had to get my bearings and function.

I drove to work still feeling exposed and transparent, as though others could see my bones and soul. Nothing earthly could cover me enough to fix that. This was not a superficial change; it was deep purification. My life had changed. St. Hildegard says, "The Holy Spirit will pour forth the dew of Her grace among the people, together with prophecy, wisdom, and holiness, so that they will then seem to be changed into a different way—a better way—of life."[49] I was shaken in a good way. *I'm not sure I even look quite the same in the mirror. Maybe I don't look so tough. I don't know.* I gathered my courage to be in the world naked and revealing. "I have set all my hope and confidence in the mercy of God alone."[50]

I saw my spiritual director that evening. He said of my experience, "It's certainly not unheard of in spiritual development." I worried aloud about surviving the industrial workplace without toughness. Maybe I'd be eaten alive in a week. "Well," he said, "You could put on the armor of God; let faith be your shield." St. Hildegard says, "Fear is the beginning of a just intention."[51] My director's suggestion became my intention on the spot. He recommended I pray with Ephesians 6:10-17. He said, "We need committed Christians in the marketplace. Don't give up the ship. Keep praying. You said yourself that God knows what's best for you." So I did. Even so, I missed my familiar shield. I journaled, "God is asking for love, and it costs me."

How do you "put on the armor of God" or "hold faith as a shield"? St. Hildegard says, "Therefore I will have faith and confidence in God, and never blot out God's name from my heart."[52] I discovered that vulnerability did not mean weakness in confronting what was not of God. St. Hildegard says, "She perseveres faithfully and steadily . . . [and] trusts not in deceptive vanities but in God, and this . . . she declares about herself."[53] Ephesians 6:17 says, "Take the sword of the Spirit." I felt more capable of that after my stripping-away experience. I now realized that toughness, a "deceptive vanity," had clouded my spontaneous hearing of the Spirit. Staying attentive to the Holy Spirit had become far easier in a given moment. I could "hold the sword of God's strongest virtues."[54] Not perfectly, but better than before.

For days I felt the shock, bracing freshness, and fragile trembliness of the stripping away. Yet I could concentrate and function. I felt happy and new. St. Hildegard says, "Let that summer be in you which causes the roses and lilies and other spices of the Holy Spirit to grow."[55] I prayed that my newness was real and true. Deep inside I knew it was. "None of the works of God are in vain."[56] I felt un-bound as I might never have gotten to on my own, and it happened in what, a minute?

I poured out gratitude to God for this compassionate help. What mercy! At last I felt compassion and empathy for myself in all I'd endured that made me so tough. What a prison that became! God's activity had shaken me, but allowed me to be different and free. Inner silence during prayer was now more thorough. I realized that my past experiences and toughness had also affected my prayer.

"Shed some light on the feelings"

What do you feel when God has made you new?

"Shed some light on the feelings of your heart,"[57] says St. Hildegard. As the days went by I felt effervescent, thrilled, and free. I was not my old, bottled-up self. My awareness and feelings had new intensity and vividness. I wondered what might now be possible. "Stand in the valley, gradually learning what you are capable of."[58] In moments when I noted the finger of God in my work, joy bubbled up, an inner delight and richness beyond what I'd typically had. Self-control and steadiness in my demeanor were easier. St. Hildegard says, "Now, let your mind be at ease, and take peace unto yourself."[59]

I trusted myself more. Life was more fun. St. Hildegard says, "A compassionate, loving mind has been planted in you."[60] Indeed, I could more reliably and spontaneously "be mild and gentle in my spirit and my heart."[61] Colleagues commented that I was "different somehow." Then one day my young godson said, "Oh, Aunt Sue, you are such a marshmallow." I knew in my heart the change in me was real, lasting, and palpable.

The impact on my relationship with God was wonderful. I journaled, "I can now feel more in my relationship with God: excited, intrigued, happy, eager to learn more about God, closer, loved, confident of the future, trust, no need to worry." I found it easier to tell when I was spiritually attuned and when not. "Blessed is the person who clings ever to God in everything."[62] I wrote, "Life has become more complicated because I care so much about God, and yet it is ever simpler."

Gradually I felt less fragile, though not tough. St. Hildegard says, "God carries and strengthens all things."[63] I grew in touch with that. My thoughts returned to the armor of God, so different from my toughness shield. The Holy Spirit's gifts, especially fortitude, came to mind. St. Hildegard says, "Gird yourself with the mighty armor of the seven gifts of the Holy Spirit."[64] A new strength pervaded my being. I journaled, "A powerful sap makes all my cells firm so that I am sturdy in the wind. I think it is the Spirit within me." *Can it be I have acquired the armor of God, the sword of the Spirit?* I wrote, "I am closer to my true self, more a rock for God."

The Creator of the universe cared about me and invited me to intimacy. I wrote, "Intimacy begun is not to be backed away from. Preferring my fears once again would be such a betrayal." Deuteronomy 18:16 spoke to me: "This is exactly what you requested of the Lord, your God." Yes, it was. Intimacy with God required that no stone go unturned, no barriers be left intact. St. Hildegard says, "Persevere in good and live in holiness with God."[65] This tall order named my desire. I wrote, "That feeling of closeness, fulfillment, and permeation I experience when God's presence is unmistakable is like feeling I could die without fear, and being drawn to God is my inevitable future. This will be my kingdom attitude."

"Humbled in all things, she shows herself truly subject to God.... [Divine Love] wears shoes that reflect Her brightness like lightning, because all a person's journeys should be in the light of truth."[66]

This bright lightning strikes in the same place again. I would have been lost without God's help. Hard as it was, I had more stripping-away experiences. Always the starting point was my inability to change myself, no matter how hard I tried.

"In sorrow of heart you find weaknesses, and these in turn are multiplied in your mind. . . . But you must resign all these things to God and trust in God."[67] So, I did. I begged God for help. St. Hildegard says, "With the soul's full viridity she is to sigh strongly for God."[68] Next, I sensed the imminence of the stripping-away. Then, with greater ease than before, I trusted and gave myself over, holding still in prayer as the Surgeon worked.

Stripping, by definition, is the rapid, thorough removal of one's trappings. In other words, we lose nothing we actually need in the reign of God. Always, the process ruptured the way things were. Reintegration was repeatedly necessary. Eventually I journaled, "Life as I knew it has been over many times."

Each time, I became ever more my true self and a better, deeper friend of God. "Since God is good, God will make me good. . . . God will perfect all good things in me."[69] In all of us. The stripping-away, though intimate, is not what the great saints call "union with God," but it is a critical step in God's drawing us closer. Our desire remains "to arrive at the leaping fountain."[70]

"Attending God"

How do we accompany someone with whom God is working intensely?

Spiritual direction of a person drawn to deeper prayer requires our own trust and awareness of God's accompaniment and ways. St. Hildegard says, "Fear not, because God, by Whose grace you are endowed with wisdom and knowledge, will never abandon you."[71] At first it seems the directee hasn't much to say. Prayer is mainly time in solitude with God. How does the directee seem? Like herself, only quieter? We might gently ascertain whether the directee is lonely, depressed, unengaged, stuck, or tired. She will say no if the uptick in solitude is of God.

A director might worry the directee has ceased opening up to her and speculate about the reasons. Such thoughts are the director's own "stuff," to be discussed with a supervisor. The director is called to help the directee notice God's role in the shift to greater solitude and to encourage continual, trustful giving over to it. A director wisely anticipates the new places prayer may go next. She is prepared when the directee needs support, direction, and reassurance.

A directee of mine began spending more time in solitude with God. He hadn't typically relished silence in the past, but now surrendered to it consistently. I sensed as I prayed for him that this was a predecessor to something more. I asked the Holy Spirit to help me be an effective director for him. I was aware of some unfreedom in the directee that caused vacillation in his relationship with God.

For some months, as nothing shifted, I thought perhaps my perception was wrong. Then the directee went away for an extended work assignment. In his absence, I continued to pray for him.

While he was away, he stayed at a lodge where he didn't know anyone. In his spare time, he prayed. Suddenly, I received frantic emails and one lengthy phone call. The directee described "weird things" happening in prayer.

"Everything is dark here—the poverty, the sickness, the exploitation," he told me. "Is that why I'm confronting a dark scene in my prayer?"

"Maybe," I said, "but might this be God's doing? What is your sense of that?"

He admitted that God seemed to have changed his prayer.

"The main thing is to trust God," I counseled him. "To give yourself over to whatever God is up to, to be very courageous about that."

In subsequent emails, he said prayer was "awful and wonderful and freeing." Upon his return, he described moving through experiences similar to, but not exactly like, my descent into Mystery and stripping away. I supported his processing of prayer experiences and his reintegrating. I affirmed his courage to go wherever God took him and his willingness to endure whatever God deemed essential for his freedom.

"It's all God's goodness, Sue," he said. "I can see that."

Yes, "God is good and all things that come from God are good."[72]

REFLECTION QUESTIONS

What is your experience with being drawn into greater solitude and silence with God?

What experiences have you had of "descent into pitch-black Mystery" or nakedness before God or something analogous? How do you understand these?

What is your experience of God "stripping away" a false shield? Or in another way helping you to "full integrity"? How did you approach reintegration?

How do you "put on the armor of God" and "take the sword of the Spirit" as a committed Christian in challenging situations? How has "real, lasting, and palpable" change in yourself affected your relationship with God?

What is your prayer about directing a person called to deeper prayer? What is your prayer about becoming a better, deeper friend of God?

chapter thirteen

————•••————

MYSTICISM

"God reveals . . . hidden mysteries"

$\mathcal{A}$ re you a mystic?

"God reveals to humankind God's hidden mysteries."[1] Mysticism involves becoming privy to what was hidden. As I prayed about this mysticism section I experienced a locution, words from God spoken in my inner spiritual ear. The words were, "The relationship already exists." I understood God to mean that we are in intimate relationship with God from the moment we come into being. "For God lives and God gives life to God's own."[2] God dwells in each person, and not passively so. Mysticism means we become directly aware of God beyond our usual ways. The relationship that always existed becomes less hidden from our awareness.

Let us look at mysticism generally and then consider examples.

Humankind "shines in God and God in humankind."[3] Mysticism reveals relationship with God but also accelerates our growth and maturity in that relationship. We more seriously and consistently cultivate, take responsibility for, become deeply conscious of, draw strength from, trust, enjoy, find our identity in, and proclaim our relationship with God. We are in trusting relationship with God. "The works and wonders of God appear great and splendid above all things"[4]—in fact, we cannot ignore them.

Mysticism is on the continuum of graced experiences we all have. We customarily use *mystical* to name experiences that are toward one end of the continuum—experiences that are direct, less common, not subtle, and unusual. To call an experience of God "mystical" is to make an arbitrary distinction. That need not diminish our deep appreciation of the usual and less direct experiences of God along the continuum. All is grace. All is God.

Grace is God's self-giving and revealing. "For God's grace . . . appeared to give life in life . . . [and] is mysterious."[5] It shows God's mercy and "comes in great abundance and fruitfulness."[6] We are sustained in a graced process of deepening, developing a more conscious relationship with God. God grows relationship through the familiar moments of consolation, pangs of conscience, thuds of realization, shining inspiration, compassion, forgiveness, love, and awe. Mysticism accelerates that same growth and transformation into deeper friendship with God.

All along, we observe God's presence and action in our lives and learn what God is like. We know that "the Holy Divinity burns so brightly with every kind of goodness."[7] We grow in love and desire for God. We surrender to God in prayer and hear the call of Jesus to discipleship and God's agenda. We grow in faith, hope, joy, and love. The Holy Spirit dwelling within us forms us into the body of Christ helping with God's concerns. "This ascent," as St. Hildegard says, "is full of the righteous actions God works and perfects in humans."[8] In other words, grace.

An early desert monastic said, "If you will, you can become all flame." The time comes for us to be all afire. Can we simply will this? St. Hildegard also uses fire imagery, but she says, "The Holy Spirit is truly an inextinguishable fire."[9] She attributes becoming "all flame" to the Holy Spirit, not to our willing it.

The writings of mystics do not suggest that they willed themselves to be mystics, per se. They willed their deep commitment to God. They surrendered faithfully and regularly to God in prayer. They were increasingly conscious of God. These acts were in response to grace. "The human, who is all creature, seeks a kiss from God through the good will of her soul when she obtains grace, and she longs to be with the sweetness of God as she runs strenuously toward God."[10] Seeking a kiss from God, longing to be with the sweetness of God, great openness, and running toward God are ways we will ourselves to be "all flame."

God is free. St. Hildegard says, "I received [visions] . . . as God willed it."[11] Mysticism is God's doing and not something we can will. "Indeed, things are shown to me there which my mind does not desire and which my will does not seek."[12] God acts on our natural capacity for the hints, whiffs, and thuds of God, present and active, that we've always had, but now there is much more. Mystical grace is freely given by God if we are open to it. Surprise, intensity, transformation, powerful love and Presence, unimaginability, and knowing without active logical thought are all common in mystical experiences. Mystics describe a variety of experiences, but a common denominator is the enhanced ability to live Christian life in a deeper, more generous way. "In that faith many have performed great multitudes of wonders."[13]

Christians believe God cares about us personally. Mystics experience that directly. Love for God, self, and others grows as the loving touch of God is experienced with unmistakable vividness and brilliance. "This brightness is your condition."[14] Moments of consolation, inspiration, pangs of conscience, robust inner strength, surprising courage, and peace in the face of the unpeaceful—all the usual graced experiences—are now surpassed by extraordinary manifestations of Who God is and who we are to God. "I have seen the miracles of God in my soul . . . as God in God's grace has granted to me,"[15] says St. Hildegard.

What once was mildly and intermittently perceived becomes full-blown mystical experience. The silent, mysterious Life nourishing our being communicates more fully in experiences never known before, changing the mystic profoundly. God reveals in excruciating, intense intimacy. "Let a person understand God and let her take God into the innermost chamber of her heart,"[16] says St. Hildegard.

"The relationship already exists" and deepens. The signs were there in earlier, subtler experiences. The pre-mystic did not know the extent of the relationship, but the mystic is now aware, surprised, and amazed at all that occurs within. "God lives in her tabernacle and God's grace is not overshadowed there."[17] The mystic is personally addressed by the Greatest Love Who dwells in the center of her being, and she becomes more fully herself. "The fire of the Holy Spirit . . . blazes in her."[18] As a result, her faith tradition, the writings of the great saints, and Scripture make more sense than ever. Through visions, says St. Hildegard, "I understand the profundities of Scripture."[19] The relationship, celebrated in baptism, becomes the mystic's true reality with startling clarity.

Given mystical gifts, a person cannot respond to God casually, as though unaffected. Now she is sharply conscious of Love at the heart of her being, and loves back with greater concreteness. "She kisses God with the most worthy contemplation and she loves God with the strongest love."[20] Love is at last more mutual, as is God's agenda. Now baptism will be lived out with greater urgency and consistency. "Let God's gift to you inspire you . . . to carry God's light diligently,"[21] says St. Hildegard. What does Love ask? To follow Jesus in true spiritual freedom and zeal. To be the person of passion Presence emboldens. To be true to the Christ-life within, to the relationship that already exists. To be "all flame." To have the honesty and integrity of a mystic. To be a loving friend of God.

"*I hear as I heard*"

How does God speak to you?

"I did not perceive in dreams, or sleep, or delirium . . . or by the ears of the outer self . . . but I received [mystical gifts] while awake . . . [with the] ears of the inner self . . . as God willed it. How this might be is hard for mortal flesh to understand,"[22] says St. Hildegard. God is "[One] Who is not silent."[23] The phenomenon of locutions is hard to understand; the words themselves are not. "I hear as I heard."[24] They have clarity and power and deeply penetrate.

As my prayer and inner quiet deepened over time, I heard a voice in my prayer say, "I am with you always." It was distinct, slightly louder than a conversational voice, and registered deep within me. The voice repeated, "I am with you always." I was certain I heard it. I was startled, yet comforted beyond imagining. Jesus was with me. His words accomplished what they said. God promises, "So shall My word be that goes forth from My mouth. It shall not return to Me empty, but shall do what pleases Me, achieving the end for which I sent it" (Isa 55:11). The message was like the end of Matthew's gospel, "And behold, I am with you always, until the end of the age" (Matt 28:20). St. Hildegard says, "Divine Love is saying to you, I long to remain with you, and I want you to . . . love Me diligently."[25]

I was surprised to hear Jesus speak directly to me. His voice did not sound forth in the room; I did not hear it with my physical ears. I heard Him with inner spiritual ears alone. St. Hildegard says, "I do not hear these things with bodily ears, nor do I perceive them with the cogitations of my heart or the evidence of my five senses."[26] Descriptions like hers would one day be a great relief to me, but at the time I heard Jesus's words, I did not know of others' experiences.

This experience took place while I was facing significant life challenges. I felt Jesus's compassion deeply. St. Hildegard says, "My heart's knowledge recognizes a shining gem in the gentleness of Your sweetness."[27] For a time, Jesus repeated these words at random points in my prayer nearly every day—and soon, I began to believe Him. I recalled His words throughout my day and was strengthened and encouraged. "In [Jesus] charity burned so to enlighten the whole world,"[28] says St. Hildegard. I knew this truth.

And yet I also reacted with amazement and concern. St. Hildegard says, "God is beyond the mind and understanding of all creatures."[29] I journaled, "Who hears God's voice in prayer?? Right. Go ahead! Be utterly true to such an experience! Be the one to stand by this reality! Yet, what is God's gift is God's gift." St. Hildegard quotes God's invitation, "Let the one who . . . hears with attentive ears welcome with a kiss My mystical words which proceed from Me Who am life."[30] I treasured being spoken to by God. But to speak truthfully to another about my prayer gave me great pause.

I didn't want Jesus to stop speaking to me, odd as the experience was. I decided to simply receive His words with gratitude. He was not doing this to freak me out. As I pondered, I noted that the sound and its effect on me were radically different from my own self-talk. I wrote, "My battles with my ego illustrate how very different my ego is from the Source of the voice I hear in prayer. Clearly, the words in prayer are not words spoken by my own ego." Nor have my words to myself ever caused me to feel Jesus tenderly present or given me the urge to kneel.

Months later, a job opportunity came up in my workplace. Due to my background and experience, I was the most logical person to take on the role. In fact, colleagues assumed I'd soon make this career move. There were no women in those ranks; I could break new ground for women and the company.

In prayer, I asked God, "Should I do it, throw my hat in the ring?"

I expected subtle guidance unfolding over time. Instead, right then, God said, "What's the real question?"

I sprang to upright attention, zinged to my core with the bracing freshness of truth. St. Hildegard says, "Through the Holy Spirit's gifts the ears of her heart opened."[31] *Yes,* I thought, *what is the real question?*

With experience, I now can say that words spoken within me in prayer are the most readily taken into my heart. But, typically literal in my responses, I tried to get at the real question. *Can I do the job? Is the timing right? Will they hire a woman? Who would I supervise? Is management committed to this research long term? What's the salary?* I didn't feel I was zeroing in on the real question.

The next day, I returned to prayer, still pondering the real question. Finally, the realization dawned: *God is not calling me to this.* St. Hildegard says, "The Word of God is knowledge in you."[32] I knew this was the point—and, to my surprise, I felt greatly relieved.

I realized I would not be as happy as I was in my current role. I felt even more relieved. St. Hildegard, who counseled others on their choice of roles, says, "Choose from these two directions what is good for you . . . and God will not abandon you."[33] The real question, I now understood, was: *How am I called by God, Who desires my happiness?*

I then understood my sadness and dread over the alleged golden opportunity. I felt called and happy in my current role. I didn't want to leave it. I wasn't drawn to the new position. St. Hildegard says, "Be true to your calling, because this is what the grace of God wishes."[34] My deepest desires, my alignment with God Who calls me, had been temporarily hidden from me. God's "What's the real question?" was an epiphany. St. Hildegard says, "O human . . . these things [are] meant to manifest what is hidden, not in the disquiet of deception, but in the purity of simplicity."[35] A locution is a loving epiphany.

"The Mystic Breath and Voice of Wisdom thunders forth."[36] We are invited to ponder the real questions of our lives. God's golden opportunities are often countercultural. A Scripture verse—"Do not be conformed to this world, but be transformed by the renewing of your minds" (Rom 12:2)—now had new relevance for me. *I needn't go against the happiness God desires for me.* Sometimes we say, with the wisdom of hindsight, "Thank God I made the decision I did." St. Hildegard says, "Be careful not to leave the good paths, because God wants you and knows you."[37] Not leaving the good path I was on brought me wonder and joy in all that unfolded. Even now, I am renewed in gratitude that God spoke. I was free to choose, but God's words alerted me to the real question, and in doing so powerfully influenced my direction and happiness.

After I heard God's voice in prayer, I gained new insight into a rite for catechumens. The presider touches their ears and says, "Ephphatha, that is, be opened" (Mark 7:34). A new Christian must be open to hear the Word of God. St. Hildegard says, "Jesus put the Holy Spirit's gifts into her ears, so that the person could obtain a sense of hearing different from what she had before."[38] Like all sacramental gestures, the richness unfolds and deepens throughout life in Christ. "In holy baptism Heaven opens . . . so that the faithful person may receive the knowledge of how to worship the One God. . . . [And] through Christ the brightness of the blessed inheritance . . . is opened to them."[39] To hear God is our inheritance and our worship.

God speaks to us in many ways, including through Scripture. We hear the Word and try to keep it. Initially, I was surprised God spoke directly to me in prayer. I have since awakened to how often this occurs in Scripture. "The Lord said to Abram, 'Go forth'" (Gen 12:1); "The Lord said to Moses, 'Speak to the whole Israelite community'" (Lev 19:1); "Then I [Isaiah] heard the voice of the Lord saying, 'Whom shall I send'" (Isa 6:8); "He fell to the ground and heard a voice saying to him, 'Saul, Saul, why are you persecuting me?'" (Acts 9:4). St. Hildegard says, "God was speaking to them with God's mystical wonders."[40] We are prudent to be still, open, and listening in prayer.

We also encounter locutions in the saints' writings. The women declared Doctors of the Church all report them. The apostolic letter proclaiming St. Hildegard a Doctor of the Church states that her authority comes via "authentic human and theological experience," and her works "were born from a deep mystical experience."[41] She herself says, "I spoke and wrote these things not by the invention of my heart or that of any other person, but as by the secret mysteries of God I heard and received in the heavenly places."[42]

Pope Benedict XVI notes, "Precisely because God 'speaks,' man is called to listen ... to the sound the Word of God creates.... But man of course is the creature who can answer the voice of the Creator with his own voice."[43] St. Hildegard says, "A faithful person pays attention to these things and remembers them well."[44] She answered the voice of the Creator with her own voice, and we are the beneficiaries.

In critical moments, I recall God's words to me. St. Hildegard quotes God's admonition to "say those things you understand in the Spirit as I speak them through you."[45] I have, at times, with discretion and conviction, said to another, "We know God is with us always, even in this." I have also asked directees, "What is the real question?" These words from God are well worth repeating, and they make God's presence known. I feel the power of the gift and humbly recognize that it is not for me alone. St. Hildegard says, "These words, moreover, the faithful should receive with devout affection of the heart, for they have been revealed for the usefulness of believers by the One Who is the first and the last."[46] After all, "God speaks reasonable words."[47]

"Attending God"

How would you guide the person in the episode you just read?

Imagine me coming to you for spiritual direction before the locution. How would you help me discern my decision? What do my sadness and dread suggest to you? How is the locution a loving epiphany in my case? St. Hildegard writes, quoting God, "Let the one who sees with watchful eyes and hears with attentive ears welcome with a kiss My mystical words, which proceed from Me Who am Life."[48] How do these words inform your direction for this directee?

REFLECTION QUESTIONS

Describe how your internal voice or ego or self-talk sounds to you. How does it contrast with God's voice within you?

How do you understand locutions in Scripture, saints' writings, or your own experience?

What has prepared you to guide a directee who experiences locutions?

What is your prayer about being "the creature who can answer the voice of the Creator"?

"Your mind prays"

How do your thoughts become prayer?

"Your mind prays."[49] Prayer is dialogue. God, Who dwells within us, communicates through our intellect, reason, and understanding. St. Hildegard says, in her visual way, "The intellect is joined to the soul like an arm to the body."[50] Many of us have experienced a call that began as thoughts about our life's direction. Initially, these thoughts were unexpected—perhaps seemed absurd or not what we desired—and yet they were compelling. Isn't this the activity of God in our very thoughts? The intellect is a "power of the soul" that "understands the work [of the soul]."[51] God gets in our heads, so to speak. "The soul utters the sound of reason in the hearing and the understanding of humanity."[52]

St. Hildegard says, quoting God, "When a person's mind is touched by Me, I am her beginning. . . . I initiate good in her."[53] I experienced the initiation of good in this way. As I prayed one morning, the troubled face of one of our administrative assistants, whom I will call Marcie, came into my mind. I asked God to bless her. "If you cry out to God in proportion to the need of your sister . . . God does not stop fulfilling whatever petitions are just."[54] Marcie had undergone cancer treatment two years earlier and had not regained the work capacity she'd once had. To make matters worse, the new department head had heaped new responsibilities on her. Given time, she could do the work, but time wasn't being given, and she was struggling.

As I concluded prayer with the Sign of the Cross, an unexpected thought arrived: *You must stand up for her.* The thought came with intensity and a strong sense of God's presence. In my heart, I agreed, so I told God, "Okay." St. Hildegard says, "You should stretch out your hand . . . to those prostrated with troubles."[55] I was unsure what action I could take, but Marcie's distress was apparent and I wanted to help.

"You know good through evil, because when you have been scandalized by evil you turn toward the good."[56] I soon learned the truth of St. Hildegard's words. That very day, the department head and admin supervisor called the senior staff together and told us to document Marcie's failings, as they wished to fire her.

I was shocked. Without hesitation, I said, "No. I refuse."

There was quite a long silence. St. Hildegard says, "Stay calm and stand firm, relying on God and your fellow creatures and God will aid you in all your tribulations."[57]

One by one, each of my colleagues also said no. The department head and admin supervisor were stunned. The big boss was furious, momentarily foiled. "Anger is like a cloud full of hail."[58] I knew the troubles wouldn't end there. St. Hildegard says, "The Holy Spirit will not abandon you."[59] That was my hope. "In failing to speak out against the evil of those in your company, you are certainly not rejecting evil. Rather, you are kissing it."[60]

That night, I prayed for Marcie again. Suddenly a new thought came: *You can change this, Sue.* Again, it arrived with intensity, strength, and Presence. I felt directly addressed by God. I did not know how I could change the situation, but the thought was compelling. St. Hildegard says, "The Serene Light . . . gives words to ruminate upon."[61]

The next morning I returned to the subject in prayer. The next big thought arose, again with intensity and Presence: *She can work with you, Sue.* At the time, I was assisted by a superstar admin who was quite loyal to me and my project teams. No one in her right mind would give up such gold. St. Hildegard says, "Your mind prays and your desires are blazing in thirst for the justice of God, and you say, 'Where am I, and where will I go?'"[62]

During my pensive commute to work, I prayed as St. Hildegard did, "May God give me that sweetest Mother Mercy as my assistant."[63] That is exactly what happened. "God's will is bright and clear in the mystery of spiritual life,"[64] says St. Hildegard. True. I moved forward before I could chicken out. "Do not flee from the light . . . lest you be ashamed."[65]

First I asked my superstar, "What do you think Marcie needs right now?"

"A chance," she said. "She just needs a chance."

"Yes," I said. "And what might that mean for you and me?"

Mysteriously, instantly, she knew. "Uh-oh," she said. "But yes, yes we have to help her."

Truly, "Wisdom displays her brightness in good people."[66]

Next, I visited the admin supervisor and proposed a rearrangement that would bring Marcie to work with me and my teams. My coconspirator went to work with another director whose hot projects would more fully utilize her talents. "One hinders the progress of others when one neither seeks out nor examines justice."[67] The significance of that did not escape me. "God turned every evil . . . into something better."[68]

The superstar picked up some of the extra work from the department head. The deed was done by noon. Marcie was overcome with relief. St. Hildegard says, "The eye of God looks upon the felicity of humankind."[69]

The department head's punishing, unreasonable ways and other failings ironically led, in time, to his own dismissal. "True mercy answers hard-heartedness."[70] But when Marcie was in peril, it was radical for me to directly challenge my boss. St. Hildegard says, quoting God, "Look to Me with a courageous spirit."[71] I was afraid, but with bold grace I moved forward, for "God compels us to good."[72] Psalm 2:11 says, "Serve God with fear, with trembling." I served God with fear and trembling. I could not turn away from my awesome, daunting, Self-giving God. "A person makes herself weak and poor when she will not work justice, or avoid wickedness . . . remaining idle."[73] I rejoiced that I'd acted despite my fear.

"Reach out and grasp mercy, which comes not from you, but only from God; and so do not withhold it from those to whom it should be extended."[74] What right had I to withhold God's mercy from Marcie? The big thoughts that came in prayer were a surprising invitation to help God show mercy to her. They were a sign of God's love for her.

Remarkable also was my prayerful assistant's immediate comprehension of the mercy we were being called to extend. "God also created . . . in a person's living conscience the force and strength of clear-sighted justice."[75] Indeed, we shared in God's power and strength as we participated in God's justice.

"That person is blessed whom God listens to and who has a gift from God because that person seeks the things that should be sought after from God."[76] I reflected on my path of prayer. It began with simply seeking God's blessings for Marcie. I journaled, "One doesn't think of prayer as radical activity, but it is! It's dangerous. Yet perhaps it is more dangerous not to pray. Prayer has definitely become more powerful and radical for me." St. Hildegard agrees: "Prayer has great power with God, and as a result of it God throws down the wheel of captivity of souls."[77] What joy to share God's great compassion for Marcie! "I . . . choose to present a joyful face to Your justice, O God."[78] It all started with a big thought. "The first root was placed in me by God's gift and the fiery grace of the Holy Spirit."[79]

The big thoughts in my prayer did not flow from active thinking or reasoning. They were not like ordinary consciousness. They dropped into my mind with an unanticipated thud, and at first did not seem logical. They arrived with a strong sense of God's presence. They were more compelling than my usual thoughts and could not easily be dismissed. St. Hildegard writes, quoting God's words, "There is no one who can resist My will and justice."[80] These thoughts clearly had a "for others" purpose and were an irresistible gift from God.

The experience was similar to inspiration, a gift most of us experience. Inspiration, however, is often mediated by something, such as a book or speaker. It does not necessarily come during prayer or potently compel us to action. Commonly it is the outcome of thinking along certain lines until an idea hits. We may not attribute it to God, as it usually lacks a strong sense of Presence. In contrast, thoughts that are unmediated, direct, unexpected, life-changing, compelling toward action, and accompanied by a strong sense of God's presence are mystical in nature.

The thoughts that came to me in prayer were not trivial. They led to a manifestation of God's compassion. God's Word bears fruit in us. Faithful people "do not turn themselves away from [right desires], but with every devotion cling to them without pause."[81] I described the thoughts as *radical*, a departure from the usual with risk involved. But *radical* also means "proceeding directly from the root"—for example, from God Who dwells within. Jeremiah describes how I experienced the thoughts: "Within me there is something like a burning fire" (Jer 20:9). St. Hildegard says, "She will feel the change in her mind."[82] I gained new awareness of my relevance for God's labors, particularly in bringing justice for the vulnerable.

God invites "participation in the Spirit . . . completion of Christ's joy by being of the same mind, with the same love, united in heart, thinking one thing" and "humbly regarding others as more important" (Phil 2:1-3). Before this, I'd not reflected deeply on what it is to have "the mind of Christ" or the help from God I'd need for that. St. Paul encourages, "Let the same mind be in you that was in Christ Jesus"; then he says that Jesus "emptied Himself . . . humbled Himself and became obedient to the point of death—even death on a cross" (Phil 2:5-8). Selfless love—"Not wanting anything else than what God wants"[83]—is the call.

Having the mind of Christ is to live out what a situation truly demands of a good person, a person who has received "the Spirit that is from God" (1Cor 2:12). It is to mature in Christian life (Phil 3:15). It is to let the Spirit transform one's mind and thoughts for serving with God. It is to love God with all one's mind (Luke 10:27). Having the mind of Christ is to act as one made in God's image and likeness. St.

Hildegard says, "When a person's reason imitates God, she touches God."[84]

Whose thoughts dropped into my prayer? Were they Divine thoughts shared with me? I think so. I believe they were a step on the mystical path toward having the mind of Christ. A gracious, courageous *yes*—followed by taking action—was the proper response. Ultimately, clarity and direction came such that the reign of God was asserted.

I touched my forehead as I made the Sign of the Cross when the first unexpected thought of the sequence came. That gesture changed for me. I now see it as mutual. St. Hildegard writes that the grace of God will "touch a person's mind to warn her to begin to work justice."[85] God received my gesture as an invitation to touch my mind and warn me to work justice. Touching my mind in the Name of God now means a lot to me. I pray to have the mind of Christ. I pray that the signs of God's presence be apparent in how I think and act. I pray to go forward "in perseverance and . . . not look back in indecision."[86]

Now I reflect on that experience and shudder. How close I came to not being Marcie's advocate in a worker justice emergency. I am greatly humbled that God had to act so directly to awaken me. That is proof that mystical experiences are about the agenda of God, not one's preexisting holiness. Rather, mystical experiences are God's drawing us to greater holiness, God's sanctification of us. "God knows all things, and God gives full knowledge to no person, save as God foresees the need,"[87] says St. Hildegard. I am grateful that God shook me out of my oblivion and gave me a chance, too, as well as the courage to act. God's work with me helped others around me act according to their own values and sense of justice. The Spirit came to us as a community. "The all-surpassing goodness of Divinity, which is without beginning and end, brings aid and comfort to the faithful."[88]

"When heaven has touched you"

How have you been touched by God?

St. Hildegard relates God's words, "I choose, by My help and action, to be on a person's side in the struggle."[89] These words describe well God's deeds during a great struggle in my late thirties. My scientific career was on a wonderful trajectory, but my physical capacity for working in my laboratory had plummeted. My childhood injuries had caused my right lower leg to eventually deteriorate, and pain was now a constant.

One Sunday I arrived early for Mass at a chapel near my home. I had allowed extra time to maneuver on crutches. I sat with my leg propped up on a chair. A few weeks prior, I'd had a second surgery to resolve my leg issue. I had just learned that the surgeries had failed.

There was plenty of time before the liturgy was to start, and no one was around yet, so I began to pray. I needed God. St. Hildegard quotes God's promise: "Cry out and persevere in seeking Me, and I will help you."[90] I poured out my discouragement. My very leg cried out for mercy, its pain a plea to God. What a low point. How could I live like this? What would happen to my work? What could we try next? "I have set all my hope and confidence in the mercy of God alone."[91] I remained in silence and sorrow for a time.

St. Hildegard says, "God seeks you out."[92] In my misery, I felt the light touch of a hand placed gently on my shoulder, and then overwhelming love, tenderness, and compassion flooded my being. The sensation was beyond description. I knew it was God. Even so, I looked all around. No one was there. "God has aided us by stretching out God's hand in all our tribulations, and in my anguish, God is giving aid to me."[93] I felt lifted up, encouraged, and hopeful. "God watches over all things."[94] *God is aware of my plight, heard my prayer, and is with me,* I thought. "The Holy Spirit lifts the human spirit upward."[95]

Once home, I prayerfully savored the experience. I marveled at the palpable touch and how instantly different I felt. St. Hildegard says, "Divine Power . . . fortifies on every side the inner spirit of the person who joins herself to God. Moreover, a breath comes forth from it to cause the mystical gifts of the Holy Spirit to touch that person."[96] Yes, the physically perceived touch of God was a mystical gift that fortified my inner spirit. I'd joined myself to God in utterly honest prayer, and God responded in this way.

St. Hildegard says, "God Who is great and without flaw has now touched a humble dwelling, so that it might see a miracle."[97] My miracle was hope in the face of repeated medical failure. "God knowingly has compassion on human miseries, and is the hope by which people enter into salvation."[98] I felt less discouraged and more hopeful. There was no obvious reason for that change other than God's touch. "A human person extends trustful hope through the soul to God."[99]

St. Hildegard says, "God's grace touches and instructs you."[100] There was more to learn. As I savored, I journaled: "The touch on my shoulder; so real. I knew it was You. I felt a compassion that was deeply familiar. It was You." Deeply familiar. Why did I write that? I reflected on the familiarity of God's touch. Then I knew; I remembered. *God touched, embraced, and held me in the wood at the time of my original injuries. That, too, was quite physically palpable and saving. Decades later, God is still with me to help me with the same injuries. God has not abandoned me in my present difficulties or in my whole life. Such is God's track record.* St. Hildegard says, "Fear not, because God, by Whose grace you are endowed with wisdom and knowledge, will never abandon you."[101] *I know this God; in my inner wisdom, I perceive and recognize this God.* "The person's spirit quickly perceives the One Who sent it, and Who will never abandon the person who faithfully receives God."[102] *Yes, deep within my spirit I remember God's touch; the touch of God is unmistakable. God's constancy has been affirmed by the touch in the chapel.*

Trustful hope flowing from God's touch and track record carried me through weeks of tests and consultations. Then came a day when, my leg up on pillows, ice pack in place, I was praying about a big decision. St. Hildegard writes, quoting God, "When heaven has touched you, if you call on Me I will answer you."[103] Three different orthopedic specialists had determined that my lower leg was unsalvageable. Amputation was my only route to comfort and mobility. All that remained was my consent.

Such a drastic step. Yet I'd felt accompanied during the steady march toward it. "All things are in the view of the Seeing Eye, which is God."[104] In deep self-honesty, I'd long since concluded that God's hand on my shoulder was about what was coming as well as the misery of the moment. The experts had only confirmed what I already knew in my depths.

I was nearly ready to accept amputation. Yet I was saying goodbye to an old friend who'd tried hard to complete the journey with me but couldn't, and I was sad and scared. I needed grace. St. Hildegard says, "Look to God Who has touched you."[105] I prayed for God's help. Again I felt physically and spiritually touched by God. It was very like the long-ago embrace in the wood. I felt taken up in God's arms. "God will gather you to Her bosom like a book."[106] I gave myself over to Divine tenderness. Later I journaled, "God is present and close. God can be felt. How to describe this? A hug that permeates my entire being. Presence. Certainty." As St. Hildegard says, "God embraces with great love all things."[107]

More flowed from God's embrace than tenderness and compassion. I was deeply at peace and fully prepared. I faced how irreversible and final this surgery would be. Yet I knew I would not look back in regret. St. Hildegard quotes God's words, "The soul . . . goes forward in perseverance and does not look back in indecision. Therefore, blessed is the one who, confiding in Me, puts her hope."[108] I dared think that God supported what would be positive for me. Amputation wouldn't merely end pain and debility; it would bring new life. "God is good and all things that come from God are good."[109] This wasn't a glib notion. I embraced the Gospel message that pruning makes one "bear more fruit" (John 15:2). My change in perception surprised me.

"Cast away doubt and sadness and turn those into joy as you persevere with God in fortitude."[110] Joy came later when I walked comfortably and confidently with a prosthesis and began to play golf. Meanwhile, courage and strength were the great graces of God's embrace. St. Hildegard uses the phrase *forti fortitudine*. She says, "What is born in you is salvation . . . firm fortitude."[111] Firm fortitude was my salvation for months. "Through the hidden mysteries of God's secrets, God is in the strength of the soul, as from the top down to the soles of one's feet. . . . And the strength of the soul has . . . courage and firmness."[112] I needed all the firm fortitude and courage God gave me.

Recuperation provided time for reflection. I marveled that God's touch seemed new and yet recognizable from long ago. As an adult, I was more surprised than I had been in my innocence as a child. God was the same. Had I become more skeptical, less a child before God? The common denominators were that I was in trouble; I prayed for God's help; I was open; God touched me; I felt it physically and spiritually; I felt it throughout my being as loving, compassionate, caring Presence; I "just knew" this was God; I couldn't bring on the experience myself; the benefits persisted and unfolded well beyond the moment; and the memories of it were vivid. "God, Who rules every created being, imparts the power and strength of this blessedness by the great clarity of God's visitation."[113] How different from what Jesus says as He weeps over Jerusalem: "You did not recognize the time of your visitation from God" (Luke 19:44).

If God touched me, I realized, *I touched God. True, God initiated the touch and embrace, but the experiences were mutual and intimate.* St. Hildegard says, "A person cannot see God with the outer eyes, but touches God by faith inwardly in the soul."[114] Of course I believe that God is everywhere and Jesus is present in the Eucharist, and so I inevitably touch God. The difference in this case, the mystical aspect, was directly feeling God's touch, the concurrence of deepened faith, and God's uniquely personal initiative. St. Hildegard says, quoting God, "O My flowers, who when they feel My presence, rejoice in Me and I in them! . . . When they feel My touch, they hasten to Me like the hart to the water-brook."[115]

I rejoiced in God's tender concern for my whole being and life, and that this was always so. God understood this wasn't just about my leg. My whole self, my entire life, was afflicted, and God graced my whole self and life. My trouble was bodily, emotional, vocational, and spiritual, and God perfectly addressed all. St. Hildegard expressed my sentiments in song: "Fiery Spirit, fount of courage . . . balm flooding the heart . . . armor of the heart and hope of the integral body."[116]

The Gospel stories of Jesus taking people by the hand (Matt 9:25), touching them (Matt 9:29), and lifting up a sufferer (Mark 9:27), took on new potency. I especially cherished the story of the woman who merely touched the fringe of Jesus's cloak and was made well after years of suffering (Matt 9:20). She knew she'd touched God. St. Hildegard says, "Show God your wounds and seek medicine from God."[117] I now knew the power of Jesus's touch and the transformation it brings. "Humans could not endure . . . if God's grace and mercy did not first come upon them."[118] Amen.

The significance of the senses and physical gestures in my faith tradition came alive for me as I mulled over this experience, especially the laying on of hands and anointing with oil. In sacraments, we celebrate the fact that God touches us and we, in turn, touch God. "The

Spirit of God . . . rubs oil into wounds."[119] God's touch is our true anointing. We believe that and celebrate it, just as we have for centuries, because it is still happening today.

God's touch, embrace, and tender concern; the hope, strength, and fortitude I received; the remembering of Scripture and sacraments—all transformed me. I sought to follow Jesus in all I endured. I remained prayerful, patient, real, strong, courageous, uncomplaining, and open to support. I understood and forgave those who turned away, either unable to find words or to accept amputation as a right choice. "That Lofty Strength never fails that founded all the sources of strength."[120] God embraces us and imbues us with grace. In response, we receive and live out that embrace. "So too our strength is God's praise, for through God we have overcome."[121] We must "grow therefore in vigor and fortitude . . . [and] follow the footsteps of Him Who taught you the Way."[122] All is easier when we know we are "in the sweet embrace of God."[123]

REFLECTION QUESTIONS

Describe a time when hearing God led you to bold action on behalf of another. How was justice done?

"Mystical experiences are not about one's preexisting holiness." How is this statement consistent with or different from your own understanding?

Reflect on touching God and what that means to you.

What is your prayer about God's touch and embrace?

"By some other experiential means"

What is your experience with "thin places"?

Religious traditions use shrines, pilgrimages, and meditations called exercises to aid spiritual experience and growth in passion for God. These aids involve vivid imagining, remembering, and engagement of heart, mind, and senses. Jesus and the saints are prominent in Catholic practices and devotions. St. Hildegard says, "Do not desert the devotion that God gave and gives to you in the embrace of God's love."[124] We engage the Stations of the Cross or spiritual exercises inspired by Sts. Francis, Mary, Ignatius, or others. These help us to "Remember our faithful Creator, Who redeemed us."[125] We also use religious art in remembering God. "For a human being, who is earth and born of earth, it is impossible to look upon heavenly things save as she is able to grasp them by faith. Therefore, God does not expect her to have any knowledge that she cannot learn from her own self or from any earthly phenomenon, either by hearing or seeing, or by some other experiential means."[126]

Mystical experiences may come about during the enhanced availability to God fostered by these traditions. The Irish describe shrines and wells as "thin places." They refer to a Celtic saying, "Heaven and earth are only three feet apart, but in thin places that distance is even shorter." The expression declares the mystical character of people's experiences in spots where "a veil slipped away." Such places foster the "other experiential means" St. Hildegard mentions.

I prayed *The Spiritual Exercises of St. Ignatius* in a thirty-day directed retreat, and discovered that they are rich with experiential means and thin places. One exercise is to pray with the Visitation, Mary's visit to Elizabeth (Luke 1:39–56). I prayerfully read the passage twice and then, as instructed, imagined myself in the story. At first, I pictured Mary asking around for a group to travel with, feeling excited to see

Elizabeth, and making preparations. I envisioned the story until Mary's arrival at Elizabeth's house, and then my imagination was taken over. Without effort on my part, the events unfolded. The scene was now more vision than visualized. The powerful moment of Mary encountering Elizabeth, tears streaming down their faces, their love for each other and for God pouring out, was an experience, not an imagining. I will never forget it. St. Hildegard says, "My seeing, hearing, and knowing are simultaneous, so that I learn and know at the same instant."[127] I was so engaged in this encounter of the two women of prayer and faith that I felt I'd invaded their privacy.

The Spiritual Exercises of St. Ignatius provided many experiences of imaginative prayer taken over and made mystical in character. I had anticipated that the exercises would be hard work for a scientific, nonfiction type like me who is more reliant on data than imagination. But God, in great generosity, did most of the work, gifting me with powerful graced experiences beyond imagining. Therein is a characteristic of mysticism: what occurs is beyond our imagining. St. Hildegard says, "Imbue your perception with streams of water from the Scriptures and with the calling and way of life of the saints."[128] In doing so, we make ourselves available for all else God brings. Thin places abound.

"Attending God"

How do spiritual directors honor God's creativity?

I have directed others in *The Spiritual Exercises of St. Ignatius.* Some have been like me in their tendency to be fact-oriented and less inclined to imaginative prayer. In one case, the directee was simultaneously taking a Scripture class and found it difficult to disengage from study mode and approach the Scriptures differently. He also struggled to focus on the graces he was to be praying for—he couldn't imagine God interacting with him in the ways St. Ignatius suggested. I invited him to trust God and St. Ignatius and to keep praying.

I assumed he would sit quietly, imagining the Scripture scenes. "Be peaceable and devout in God, so that you may flourish in God's garden,"[129] as St. Hildegard says. Instead, I learned that he began reading the Scriptures and then literally running with them, allowing them to come alive within him as he ran along Lake Michigan. When he returned from his runs, he grabbed his journal and wrote down everything he experienced. God was "shining in goodness and wondrous in God's works."[130] It would not have occurred to me to suggest this process to him, but as he described his experiences, it was evident the retreat graces were flowing. His imagination was alive and well. Running functioned as a thin place that opened him to God.

One of St. Ignatius's admonitions is that directors "leave the creature alone with the Creator." In this example, I realized his wisdom, for "in it, God is faithfully recognized."[131]

"I see as I saw"

How do you understand St. Hildegard's visionary experiences?

Regarding visions, St. Hildegard boldly says, "I see as I saw."[132] She repeats a locution expressing God's validation of visions: "I again heard the voice from the Living Light say to me: 'These things that you see are true and as you see them, so they are, and there are more.'"[133] She says God became human in Jesus precisely because God desires to be seen and heard. "For even as God is seen by the celestial spirits, so too God wanted to be witnessed by creation in human nature."[134] She describes the unbidden nature of her visions, "Indeed, things are shown to me there [in the Living Light] which my mind does not desire and which my will does not seek."[135] What is shown to her "confirms her faith" and helps her know "how to worship."[136]

I do not know how common visions are among Catholic Christians or any group. I have thousands of hours of experience accompanying Catholics in spiritual direction at a parish. Only 6 percent have revealed "seeing" something in prayer. Other "beyond the ordinary" experiences, such as locutions, have been described by 15 percent. I assume the percentages may be higher among retreat directees and contemplative religious.

From the experiences shared with me, the writings of visionaries such as St. Hildegard, and my own experience, it seems that visions usually occur more than once for a given person. The writings of saints and Scripture suggest human beings have received visions as an outpouring of the Holy Spirit throughout history. St. Hildegard says, "The Fire that appeared to Moses from the middle of the bush—flaming but not burning—should be believed to be the Holy Spirit."[137] In general, then, visions are expected in humankind, but unexpected for a given person; they are not unusual in human experience, but they are not common.

One day, after a little spiritual reading, I set my book aside and began centering prayer. By this point in my journey, I moved with ease into inner quiet. After a few moments of being present to God in stillness, a shift occurred. The shift was effortless on my part—quite different than the conscious surrender in prayer described earlier. The analogy that comes to mind is that I was driving a car and it spontaneously began to drive itself, and I trustingly let that occur. St. Hildegard says, "I will skip over the mountains and hills, and bypass the sweet weakness of this transitory life, and with pure heart regard only the Fountain of living water."[138] She is certainly more eloquent than I about a shift in prayer.

I had no idea what was to transpire. Without conscious imagining, I found myself in a scene with darkness all around. I was kneeling, though there was nothing to kneel upon. I felt I was waiting expectantly, as if in a spontaneous, vivid Advent. I felt deep peace and God's loving presence. I remained thus for a time, in great serenity. St. Hildegard says, "The Holy Spirit Itself is a burning and shining serenity which cannot be nullified."[139]

Then a cloud of golden light appeared above me. Though it was light, it had thickness, a substance and texture that ordinary light does not have. As I looked up, the cloud of light descended toward me. Gradually I was covered with this light as if it were a garment. "God's grace clothes me like a garment."[140] When I lifted my arms, the thick light moved with them like sleeves. The light was beautiful, bright but not glaring, a flawless, perfect fit. "The True Light . . . has no imperfection."[141]

St. Hildegard says, "I looked and I learned, seeing in the True Light—certainly not through my own cogitation."[142] Once completely covered with light, I was given to understand it was a great gift. I had done nothing to deserve it, and knew I could never repay it. In the vision, I regarded myself with wonder and amazement. Never had I been clothed in so rich a garment. I trembled in awe. St. Hildegard says, "A true vision of the unfailing light had [been] shown to me. . . . I saw a vision of such mystery and power that I trembled through and through."[143]

It sounds strange, but I felt like God had personally dressed me. I felt treasured and beloved. St. Hildegard says, "God values the human being."[144] Yes, valued. I sensed God looking at the result with great satisfaction, as if saying, "There. That's it. Much better, don't you think?" Wisdom "looked upon Her work, which She had set in order and right proportion . . . [and] revealed . . . certain other profound mysteries."[145] I felt cherished by a wonderfully tender and personal God.

I wanted to wear what God wanted me to wear. Nothing else

would do. St. Hildegard says, "God, Who, without beginning, flaw, or change, is the day whose brightness comes from no other light, for God is the Light over all God's creation. . . . God is an inextinguishable Light, which will never fade, or vanish, or grow dim . . . Whose glory continues undiminished by any darkness of night, and never wanes."[146] I trusted God's judgment. There was no more perfect garment. "So the faithful ought to look to God in the mirror of faith with the soul's inner sight, and trust that they are saved by God Who can do all things."[147] The garment of light adhered to me. It was not light I could step out of or away from. It would go where I would go, a persistent, integral part of me.

The vision abruptly ended. I felt like the disciples at Emmaus, whose "eyes were opened, and they recognized Him; and He vanished from their sight" (Luke 24:3). *Poof*, the Divine experience was over. I dropped back into my ordinary little prayer space in astonishment and some embarrassment, thinking, *Who am I to be covered in light?* St. Hildegard says, "In these visions my spirit rises, as God wills, to the heights of heaven."[148] *Absolutely I didn't deserve that.* I was relieved that none of it was my own imagining—that it was all God's doing. "God reveals to humankind God's hidden mysteries."[149]

I felt claimed by God, which was exhilarating, breathtaking. My poor scientific mind was rattled, struggling to reconcile the experience with the known facts of the universe. Yet I believed; I trusted my experience as God-given. St. Hildegard says, "A person who sees by her knowledge, which is her inner eye, what is hidden from her outer sight, and does not doubt it, most certainly believes; and this is faith. For what a person perceives outwardly, she knows outwardly, and what she sees inwardly, she understands inwardly."[150] I hastily jotted in my journal, "My prayer experience frankly seems very odd."

I didn't know what to make of the content or the process. Driving to work, I thought, *It was like having a dream in broad daylight while full of coffee and wide awake.* "The visions I saw I did not perceive in dreams, or sleep, or delirium, or by the eyes of the body . . . but I received them while awake."[151] *I watched and yet was in the scene simultaneously. But wait, all went on within me; it was not external. Who knew prayer could be like this?* St. Hildegard says, "Still I cannot fully understand those things I see."[152] *I felt fantastic, like I was glowing inside.* "When my spirit sees and tastes [visions], I am so transformed . . . that I consign all my sorrow and tribulation to oblivion."[153] *What does it all mean?* I walked around all day with an incredible secret and amazing energy. I did not speak of it to anyone.

St. Hildegard says, "Temporal things cannot understand eternal things unless God in God's mercy wants to reveal such things to them for God's own glory and for the perfection of God's faithful ones."[154] When I finally could process and reflect, it hit me: *I am inseparable from the Light. Jesus tells me often, "I am with you always." Now I am given to see as well as hear this reality in prayer.* As the reinforced message swept over me in unmistakable truth, I wept in profound gratitude and consolation. *I live inseparable from the Light of Christ. I cannot step out of Jesus's Light.* St. Hildegard says, "Live and rise up in the Light."[155] *Yes—live this way, this truth.*

I recalled the verse we sing when a person is baptized, "You have put on Christ. Alleluia" (Rom 13:14). A verse shortly before it says, "Put on the armor of light" (Rom 13:12). St. Hildegard says God "is the brightest Light that cannot in any way be extinguished."[156] *God clothed me in the Light of Christ. It cannot be extinguished. I cannot be separated from it.* "A person who is anointed by God's grace with the chrism and oil, and enkindled with the fire of the Holy Spirit, is born anew and is sanctified through baptism."[157] Never had my baptism into the life, passion, death, and resurrection of Jesus seemed so vivid and relevant. "Through Christ the brightness of the blessed inheritance . . . is opened to them."[158]

I reflected on my sense that God had personally dressed me and had reacted to the result with great satisfaction. *Is this how God worked and reacted at my creation?* I imagined my coming into being at God's hands to God's delight. St. Hildegard says, "God indeed had created the human being with complete brightness so that she could see the light of the purest air and could know the songs of the angels. And God clothed her with such brightness that she shone with great splendor."[159] The vision reminded me I was created in the image of God (Gen 1:27), that I had such promise in the eyes of God just as "God once clothed the first person in the whiteness of light."[160]

I so imperfectly lived out that promise. Even so, as for Adam and Eve, God "made garments" and "clothed" me (Gen 3:20). God always provided. Now I was reminded that my failings need not separate me from the Light of Christ, to God's great satisfaction and my amazement and joy. St. Hildegard says, "God is indeed the Living Light from Whom all lights shine; and so it is through God that a person remains a light alive, and fire too."[161] I wanted to wear what God wanted me to wear. My desire to be an image of God, to live inseparable from the Light, and to reflect this Light was powerfully strengthened. God awakened and deepened my desire and showed me this is my truth, my possibility.

I'd glimpsed eternal light, the hope of my ultimate destiny. The vision was so loaded with realizations that I was challenged to bring them all to my journal pages. St. Hildegard says, "Omnipotent God [is] incomprehensible in . . . majesty and inestimable in . . . mysteries and the hope of all the faithful."[162] I didn't read into the vision. I simply tried to keep up with the brilliant Professor who'd filled the board with extraordinary insights. St. Hildegard says, "My spirit drinks up those things I see and hear in that vision, as from an inexhaustible fountain, which remains ever full."[163] I agree with her that "the Holy Spirit reveals eternity."[164] She relates God's advice on what to do with a vision: "If you will diligently contemplate Me with your inner vision, as in faith you have been taught, I will receive you into My kingdom."[165] Diligently contemplate God.

In God's great goodness, I had been granted a wonderful vision. I'd done nothing to deserve it, nor had I known beforehand what a vision was like. I cannot reimagine it with the same quality and impact, but I shall not forget it. St. Hildegard says, "Whatever I see or learn in this vision I retain for a long period of time, and store it away in my memory."[166] To know myself covered with Light, to know this as my desire, to embrace the potent truth of it, to trust that nothing can separate me from the Light, and to be called to live out of this Light—all were transformative.

I often call to mind and take strength from this vivid, unforgettable experience of God's love. Surely, to be a friend of God is to be clothed in the Light of Christ and to keep that desire warm in one's heart. St. Hildegard prays, "May your soul be in the embrace of the Living Light."[167] That is the path of the baptized. "May the light of God's grace cover you."[168] My friendship with God was enhanced by my awareness that God not only clothes me but also delights in doing so. May I always live in this friendship.

Weeks later, I was confident I'd had the one and only vision of my spiritual life. But then a new scene involving light came during prayer. In this vision I stood in darkness and in trust, for "it is for You, O God, that I wait" (Ps 38:15). A bright light appeared before me, lightening the scene. The light was beautiful and stirred my heart, even though it lacked detail. St. Hildegard says, "Let the Fiery Illuminator enkindle your heart."[169]

As I gazed, a shape emerged. The pure white light streamed from five discrete places. The shape became distinct. I knew this was Jesus. Light shined in stunning beauty from the wounds in His hands, feet, and side and lit the entire space. I was awed and amazed. Light and

Love were one and the same in the vision. St. Hildegard says, "In [Jesus] charity burned so to enlighten the whole world."[170] In this moment, my world was all Light and all Love.

I stood before Jesus, gazing at the light from His wounds and feeling the Love pouring out with it. He said, "Look at your wounds." I looked at my body's old injuries. Red-orange flames burned in them. My wounds were not as beautiful as Jesus's wounds, but they did not lack beauty. The flames in my wounds were active and flaring like a log fire. I knew these flames to be of God. "God is that fire from which every fire . . . is kindled, as sparks come forth from fire."[171] In the vision I, too, spoke, but not with the conscious volition of ordinary life. I said to Jesus, "Can my wounds be like Yours?" Jesus replied, "Yes. They will be. I will change them. You will see." And the vision ended.

Again the return to my ordinary little spot was harshly sudden. Even so, I remained amazed by the sheer beauty I'd seen, the love experienced, and the message received. So much had been conveyed. Of her visions, St. Hildegard says, "My seeing, hearing, and knowing are simultaneous, so that I learn and know at the same instant."[172] *How can light itself be so spectacularly beautiful?* I asked myself. The fire in my wounds was so real that I half expected pain and smoldering—but no, all was ordinary.

Or was it? I felt abashed by my audacity in the vision, asking if my wounds could be like Jesus's wounds. *How forward! I wasn't thinking about wounds before prayer. So where did all this come from?* I wondered. Yet what had Jesus said to me? "Yes. They will be. I will change them. You will see." Now? In this life? Or did He mean in the afterlife? I felt powerful hope in Jesus's help in any case. "I heard these words from the mystical light of a true vision."[173]

I sensed that more had happened deep within me than I was aware of, but I trusted Jesus to help me know. St. Hildegard says, "The Lord of all and the God of all creatures will give you the grace necessary. . . . Jesus will fill your soul with heavenly joy and light. . . . He will free you."[174] I felt such hope and confidence in Jesus's help. I was ready for whatever would change the burning fire in my wounds to beautiful light. Jesus was committed to my healing, and I was committed to Him. I will "call upon the living God, that God might lead me into the path of light and cure my [wounds]."[175]

But now, I realized, I must be off to work. "Dear Jesus," I said, "whatever You are going to do, can You do it without making me late for work in the future?" Then I hurriedly journaled, "I'm in new territory spiritually, not in the same place anymore. I might have traveled far. I have felt like I've left more ordinary ways behind, operating on a different plane."

Oh golly, I thought as I drove. *What is happening to me? This is God's doing, I know that. In my wildest imaginings I couldn't think this up. I can tell God from me any day, and this was definitely God. I feel like my normal self, only different. Why would God do this? Where are we going here? I was just bobbing along as one of God's paradoxically prayerful scientists, and look what's happened to me.* St. Hildegard says, "Indeed things are shown to me there which my mind does not desire and which my will does not seek."[176] *How could I know I should desire this?*

I thought of spiritual direction. My spiritual director had recently been missioned to another country. *Time to get serious about finding a new one,* I told myself. *There's that Jesuit whose homilies I like so much. He's sweet and humble. I could probably trust him. I will ask. He may say no, but I will ask.* I felt relief. That seemed right. *This, too, is grace.* St. Hildegard says, "For the love of God . . . that I may be assured."[177] *Please tell me I am on the right track in prayer, yet I do know . . .*

"In Your light we see light" (Ps 36:9). The psalm is true. I prayerfully mulled over the events in the vision, still awed by the incredible beauty of the light streaming from Jesus's wounds and the love He had continuously poured out. *How easy it is to believe that He is God!* St. Hildegard says, "I have . . . seen great marvels which my tongue has no power to express, but which the Spirit of God has taught me that I may believe."[178] *Jesus's wounds were once a bloody mess, but look what they became.* I was a modern-day Thomas, getting a close look and believing deeply.

Jesus's wounds did not disappear upon His resurrection. They were utterly transformed and became a source of faith. St. Hildegard says, "That person is blessed who is awakened to heavenly things through a miracle of God."[179] Had the vision ended there, I would still have been more spiritually rich than I'd thought possible before. I'd experienced an intensity of love "incomprehensible in the mystical greatness of God's mysteries and incalculable in the might of God's divine power."[180] Even so, there was more.

I had looked at my wounds in the Light and Love of Jesus's wounds, and seen an active, red-orange, purifying fire in them. What was that fire? St. Hildegard says, "Sparkling fire signifies the Holy Spirit . . . [and] gives light to dark places by burning what it touches."[181] She says, "God is fire."[182] Her words helped me see, as I reflected further, that the fire in my wounds was the Holy Spirit's vivifying, loving power. "Fire . . . is Divine power, which vivifies and sustains all things. This fire is sweet and mild, and . . . does not consume (although it is mighty) but sets hearts ablaze with love."[183]

St. Hildegard says, "I say to you in the love of Christ that in the vision of my soul I see many miracles of God, and through God's grace, I understand the profundities of Scripture."[184] As I pondered the flames in my wounds, Scripture's description of God as "like a refiner's fire," as One Who "will sit as a refiner and purifier of silver" (Mal 3:2-3), came to mind. Malachi says this refining enhances relationship with God and causes blessings to flow.

"This blazing fire that you see symbolizes the Omnipotent and

Living God . . . that Fullness that no limit ever touched . . . for there is nothing that is hidden from God or that God does not know."[185] My wounds were not hidden from God or from me in the prayer vision. I understood God would transform them to be more like Jesus's wounds. St. Hildegard says, "God does not stop doing God's work until God has brought it to perfection."[186] My attitude toward my wounds shifted. I received the grace of reverence and felt deep respect for them as the dwelling place of the Transforming God. "God has imbued humans, along with all creatures, with God's Spirit, just as a potter makes all her vessels beautiful with fire."[187] My wounds would be made beautiful by God.

I recalled the confident voice of Jesus, "my Light and my salvation" (Ps 27:1). St. Hildegard says, "I saw a great splendor in which resounded a voice from Heaven."[188] The previous vision unfolded in deep silence, but in this vision I saw, heard, and spoke as Mary did at the Annunciation (Luke 1:26–38).

I rejoiced in the wondrous hope of the vision and desired the fulfillment of Jesus's promise. St. Hildegard says, "So all beings that live by You praise Your outpouring like a priceless salve upon festering sores, upon fractured limbs. You convert them into priceless gems."[189] She relates God's promise, "I do not refuse to close [wounds] gently up . . . by touching them with the mild fire of the breath of the Holy Spirit."[190] May it be so. I prayed her prayer: "Cause me to be always aflame with the fire of the Holy Spirit."[191]

I reflected on the Light at the start of the vision when Jesus lit up the darkness. St. Hildegard says, quoting Jesus's words, "I am the Living Light Who illuminates the darkness."[192] Jesus as light in darkness is scriptural: "The Life was the Light of all people. The Light shines in darkness, and the darkness does not overcome it" (John 1:4–5). In the vision, the Light seemed so "in charge," as though darkness and all else were powerless against it. The effect of the Light was inevitable.

God is "the perfection of beauty" (Ps 50:2). The sheer beauty of the Light had captivated me. "The splendor of God shone forth."[193] I believed that I had glimpsed this splendor as far as my meager capacity could allow. The psalm prayer is, "To behold the beauty of the Lord" (Ps 27:4). That is possible only if God grants it. I praised God for the brief experience of such splendor. St. Hildegard says of a bright light in her vision, "It was beyond human understanding. . . . I knew there was every type of delight . . . all the joys of the happy, and the greatness of all gladness . . . infinite joy in the joys of this brightness."[194] Such eloquence.

Her declarations about God say what I hadn't words for: "The Savior is grand and kind;"[195] the Spirit "is Blazing Love;"[196] "God will make you burn yet more for love of God;"[197] God "will transform all creatures into the eternity of steadfastness."[198] Some inner transformation was already apparent. I felt great hope, loved beyond imagining, and committed to Jesus, Who was committed to me. I desired to be steadfast and unwavering as He exerted His healing ways. I wanted to consistently reflect the Light and Love I received. St. Hildegard says, "Let God's gift to you inspire you, my daughter, to carry God's light diligently."[199]

My experiences were inner spiritual events, and not external phenomena like apparitions. "Let your adornment be the inner self with the lasting beauty of a gentle and quiet spirit, which is very precious in God's sight" (1Pet 3:4). I prayed to retain lasting beauty and gentleness in my inner self and spirit.

Soon after the visions involving light, I encountered 1 Corinthians 2:11: "Among human beings, who knows what pertains to a person except the spirit of the person that is within?" The verse called me to trust my experience and God's work within me. St. Hildegard says, "Carefully guard that beautiful form in your heart."[200] I required a spiritual director who could go where I needed to go. I would not return to a director who could not. I must be true to Jesus's promises.

St. Hildegard says, "Blessed soul, maintain your temple with discretion, so that the fruitfulness with which you embrace God does not wither, because God greatly loves your soul."[201] I worried about revealing my experiences, but like St. Hildegard, "I see as I saw, and I hear as I heard."[202] I was obliged to be loyal to my true self and to my revealing God. A friend of God lives in God's truth, however odd it seems to others.

REFLECTION QUESTIONS

St. Hildegard says that God wishes to be seen. What is your experience or awareness of visions?

How has God's activity challenged your view of what's possible in spiritual life?

How do you handle the reality of profound prayer directly followed by a rush of daily activities?

What is your prayer about mystical visions?

"You nevertheless question . . . as if you do not know what to do" and "Attending God"

How did you learn about mysticism?

For years I was unfamiliar with the name and phenomenon of

mysticism. It was well hidden in my faith tradition. I do not recall mention of it in my faith education. I knew the stories of Mary's appearances at Lourdes and Fatima. However, no one mentioned that "words are uttered by the Mysteries of God."[203] I did not learn that one might be "compelled by a spiritual vision."[204] I thought the saints worked harder at goodness than most of us. I had no idea how much God directly helped them, or that this help was available to me.

Since Vatican II I'd become more informed about Scripture, but I did not know how spiritually accurate the stories of God's interactions with human beings were. St. Hildegard says, "The Scriptures were revealing God eagerly."[205] *Eagerly*; not with the reluctance I felt. I also did not anticipate how significant the sacramental life of my faith tradition would become to me, or how much I would come to treasure the saints. St. Hildegard says, "God is the light from which the mysteries proceed that have the life of the miracles in them. This life is in God."[206]

I grew intent on speaking to someone wise regarding this mysterious life in God for which I lacked vocabulary and instruction. I sought out the Jesuit I admired as a homilist. I prayed to be honest, open, and revealing. St. Hildegard says, "God in God's wisdom seeks the sacrifice of your heart offered up in simplicity."[207] I did not yet feel such grace. Fr. C. said that he had never directed a scientist and looked forward to it. St. Hildegard says, "Those who should be assenting totally to the Spirit" experience persuasions that "becloud" them. [208] That was me.

Partway into the session, the tension between my reluctance to speak of my prayer experiences and my need to open up about them grew unbearable. My new director looked at me with kindly eyes and said, "Why have you come? What has caused you to seek spiritual direction now?"

Desperate to name my experience, for some reason I chose the word *metaphors*. I said, "Metaphors are happening in my prayer. I'm wide awake, but I have these metaphors." I related that I couldn't control these prayer events, and that it was hard for me as a scientist to understand what was going on.

Somehow, my director picked up on what I was trying to reveal. "Sometimes what you refer to as 'metaphors' are like 'waking dreams' or 'vignettes,'" he said.

I nodded.

"These are true prayer experiences and should be taken seriously," he said. "One can see things or have visions or hear things, and these are legitimate." He pointed out that similar events are related in Scripture, and "Such experiences can bring clarity and direction."

St. Hildegard says, "God is good and all things that come from God are good."[209]

I felt understood and relieved, and yet concerned about what taking the events "seriously" involved. "It's been a little confusing, even a little frightening for me," I told him. "I don't think I'm crazy. I'm doing fine at work. But when I pray, I seem to be playing with fire. I know it's God. I never know what to expect, what will happen. I could never come up with this stuff on my own."

"That's the beauty of it," Fr. C. said. "It's God's doing and you know that and can trust that."

As we wrapped up, Fr. C. said, "My job will be to watch for the Gospel authenticity of your path. Your job will be to write things down as best you can."

My immediate thought was that I didn't want to do that. St. Hildegard says of obedience, "I touch nothing, I wish for nothing, I desire nothing unless it is in God."[210] How far I was from her obedient attitude.

I sat in my car and wrote down everything I remembered of my conversation with Fr. C. When I got to "Write things down as best you can," I thought, *In ink? On paper? Where someone might read it?* I lived alone and loved to journal, but at this I panicked. St. Hildegard had been there: "This [vision], however, I showed to no one except a few religious persons."[211]

For a time, I was a spiritual direction rebel. At work, I wrote up research findings with absolute detail and thoroughness. At home, I captured prayer events in code—a few words that helped me remember but gave away nothing. St. Hildegard says, "Never . . . am I wont to speak in undisguised words."[212] The closest I came to compliance was to write, "I must overcome my reluctance to write about my experiences in prayer."

At our next session, I revealed a few specifics about my prayer. I said I truly believed that something was happening, that I was learning what prayer could be and it was changing my life. "Yes," Fr. C. said. "A bright scientific mind is no match for Mystery. You seem a little more acceptant."

"Why me?" I asked. "Why not some other good person?"

"This is how God has chosen to work with you," he said. "God is very trustable, don't you think?"

Although I agreed, I was still adjusting to God's surprises. "God is very interesting," I responded. I did not yet share the exuberance of St. Hildegard, who says, "God is fire and living Spirit."[213] Mysticism had unexpectedly disrupted the ordinariness of my life, and it was disconcerting.

At the end of the session, Fr. C. affirmed my path and reminded me, "Keep writing things down as best you can."

I felt so guilty. "Is there something I can read to help me with this path?" I asked.

He recommended the autobiography of St. Teresa of Ávila.[214]

In the bookstore, Carol Flinders' *Enduring Grace*,[215] a book about seven women mystics, caught my eye, so I bought that too. "All saints in Paradise cheered God's name."[216]

I read with interest fueled by experience. The women mystics, who spanned centuries, were quite credible to me. "God shows various miracles to God's holy ones . . . in every age of the world."[217] Their experience affirmed mine, and mine theirs. My vocabulary about mysticism grew. Some shared my reluctance to write things down.

Finally, I boldly journaled, "Based on what I have read, I have to say I believe I am a mystic and visionary. I just haven't dared to write much so far. . . . There is a good match between my experiences and those I've read about." Yet I was far behind these women in other ways. They brought me a sizable dose of humility. It is one thing to say one is a mystic, but quite another to live a saintly life, to respond to the gift with all one's being.

I noted the different forms God's activity could take and felt reassured. St. Hildegard says, "I saw a multitude of people who sighed to God, each according to ability, like a garden filled with every kind of plant."[218] Like a scientist interpreting data, I deemed it significant that I found out about mystics when I did. I wrote, "First I had the experiences. Then I read about mystics. . . . It was not the other way around, and I am glad for that aspect of my credibility." The sequence was scientifically sound. I trusted my experience as fresh, original, and unique, but grounded in and supported by a long tradition of prior data.

I was impressed with the open, vulnerable revealing of the women I read about. *Why am I not journaling as I ought? I asked myself. In truth, I'm not really risking exposure in my little home where I live alone. Yes, it is daunting to express these events in words. But the real problem is that I have not fully accepted these events as my reality.*

That began to change. St. Hildegard says, "Although you sometimes scale the mountain of assured faith . . . you nevertheless ques-tion . . . as if you do not know what to do. . . . But I say to you, walk in pure faith."[219] I wrote, "How God works with me works for me. How mysticism works is all in the part God does. The inner events are real. Mysticism is real. So I must deal with it as a real thing. I must make time for prayer, which is to return for more. I can't betray the gifts of God."

I returned to my spiritual director and tried out the word *mystic* in reference to myself. I said, "I'm embracing the truth of my experi-ence and my identity. Also, I don't think we should say 'waking dreams.' I am not dreaming. I am presented with what I 'see.' I think it's better to be bold and say 'visions.'"

Fr. C. agreed.

St. Hildegard says, "I had sensed in myself wonderfully the power and mystery of secret and admirable visions."[220] I had visions. I felt like I'd just been accurately diagnosed.

"With mysticism, one has experiences one would not otherwise have," Fr. C. said.

I understood him to mean that in ordinary life, there certainly wouldn't be flames in my wounds. I also could not imagine such a scene with the force, Presence, and grace the vision had brought. Fr. C. confirmed that what one "hears" in prayer is called "locutions."

After our conversation, I journaled, "I was confirmed in being a mystic by my spiritual director. God was affirmed as the Source of all that goes on." St. Hildegard says her visions were "Implanted in my soul by God, the great Artisan."[221]

Usually, I reserve my revealing about mysticism for "those with eyes to see and ears to hear" (Matt 13:16). Such a gift from God is not for my own glory. It is not to be cast before people—even spiritual directors—who are unlikely to treat the gift with respect and perspec-tive. Mysticism is often misinterpreted, disbelieved, misattributed (e.g., to migraine), or explained away. Some directors overreact and regard one as saintly. Such reactions, though quite human, are uninformed, unhelpful, and disheartening to a mystic. "Truth has none of falsehood's shadow."[222] The focus must always be on God and God's purposes. A spiritual director who is well-informed and well-read on mysticism or who has personal experience with it is a great gift and someone with whom I can truly be myself. St. Hildegard says, "That person is blessed who is awakened to heavenly things."[223]

When genuinely called to reveal, as in spiritual writing, I trust that God's grace will be given to the reader. St. Hildegard says, "God alone knows all things and holds all things together. And God preserves all things according to the plan of God's grace."[224] I keep focused on God's desires and not my fears. Then I can boldly share what God has brought. "With the soul's full viridity I am to sigh strongly for God."[225]

St. Hildegard describes her angst about revealing her mystical life. "I am terribly afraid to speak or write to my male superiors about those things which I see in my spirit in the True Light, in my spirit only, unaided by my corporeal eyes."[226] She owns her mysticism "by the fortitude God gives."[227] Through "great virtue arising from God's Divinity," others take the leap with her; for "it is by great fortitude that people believe . . . what they cannot see with their bodily sight."[228] She responds to a classic misinterpretation of her mystical gifts in writing to an inquirer, "God reveals matters to me about the correction of sins and the salvation of souls, but nothing about how to find treasure."[229] Material treasure, that is.

"Heavenly inspiration appears in secret quiet,"[230] says St. Hildegard. Early in my wrestling with the call to reveal mysticism, I journaled, "Birds are not shy about their singing. They instinctively do it. It flows straight from being a bird. Can there be a flow straight from being a mystic? I'll have to be myself. I'll have to reveal. I feel as though I am trying to cross a personal boundary of revealing, and I'm very daunted by it. I'm getting worn out by the effort to protect this part of myself. I'm holding back from God's radical ways. I cannot be my true self with overly much reticence." Later I wrote, "A mystic gives God's Word a place to live, especially if we write, like St. Hildegard or St. Teresa of Ávila. God needs mystics. Mysticism is part of God's larger agenda and not just for me." Mysticism is part of the practical reality of furthering the reign of God on earth. "God is . . . concerned with the salvation of humankind."[231]

In spiritual direction and in journaling, I embraced the word *mystic* as a self-descriptor. Yet it is not wholly self-defining, any more than naming myself an "amputee" or a "writer" is. Being a mystic is a normal part of being Christian. (Note: other faiths have mystics, too.) I seek to take it in stride. "God works God's will for the glory of God's name, not for the glory of any earthly person."[232] Mystical experiences are God's mercy and efficiency in action. "Set ablaze with the Holy Spirit's fire to multiply . . . like the sparks of a fire"[233] to change me.

I have needed much transformation to become a proper friend to God and to serve God as I do. My director points to my openness as key to my mystical experiences, and that is true, but God also adapts God's activity to each in our need and according to God's desires. St. Hildegard says, "God gives full knowledge to no person, save as God foresees the need."[234] I treasure and practice many forms of prayer fruitfully and leave to God what God chooses to do. St. Hildegard says, if God "sees her reaching out towards the light . . . it will be present for her in all things and inspire in her what is just and holy."[235]

REFLECTION QUESTIONS

What experiences of God have been hard for you to articulate and share?

How have you struggled to accept your experiences and to name your identity as the one who has them?

What did you learn from Fr. C.'s modeling of spiritual direction?

What is your prayer about embracing, naming, articulating, and revealing your most profound spiritual experiences?

"As God foresees the need"

Why is there mysticism?

Never have I read about a mystic who believed the experiences were deserved or resulted from being unusually holy. While deeper modes of prayer are conducive to mystical experience, one's prayer style does not guarantee mystical experience. Most mystics, like me, wonder about what has occurred, but wondering can distract from purpose. I learned to read beyond the prayer experiences of mystics to what happened next.

To continually wonder is to "stand looking up" (Acts 1:11) when one is to get on with discipleship. St. Hildegard advises, "Look zealously after the things God has entrusted to you so that you may bring your talent back to God doubled in value."[236] One must, with gratitude and humility, accept, embrace, and seek to fulfill what God asks through these experiences. St. Hildegard says her experiences occurred "so that God could reveal what God could do through a thing [herself] which would not presume anything of itself."[237] She says they occurred "that I may believe."[238]

Without presuming anything of myself, I explore God's reasons for mystical experiences. St. Hildegard says, "Weak, mortal thought cannot grasp God's purpose."[239] However, we can observe and draw conclusions as any good scientist would do. Through Jesus, we know God's desires: to speak to us; to be seen/revealed/known; to touch us; to call us disciples and friends; to teach and inspire us; to share Divine Life with us; to bring truth, light, fullness of life, and freedom to us; and to raise us to eternal life with God.

Jesus reveals that God wants us to know how to pray; to understand Scripture; to be healed; to believe; to love God, self, and others; to know we are loved by God; to be forgiven and to forgive; to remain on the vine; to not offend; to be faithful; and to live in the joy of resurrection even now. Mystical experiences are in service to all God's purposes as revealed by Jesus. Above all, mystical experiences are encounters with God, Who "is here," as St. Hildegard says, and is "an effective fire" and "not a hidden fire nor a silent fire."[240]

In mystical experience, God is not abstract but personal. We directly experience God. Presence and great love are intensely palpable in authentic mysticism. "God embraces with great love all things."[241] We are transformed by Love and desire to love back more generously in concrete actions. We experience God intensely and intimately and seek ever-deeper relationship with God. We try to understand God for Who God is, as well as what God desires. Our focus is purified. St. Hildegard says, "You gave me to act following You."[242]

One reason for mystical experience is that "God gives . . . as God foresees the need,"[243] in St. Hildegard's words. We see this in God's desire for justice for Marcie, my spiritual director's statement that "we need committed Christians in the marketplace," and more personally in Jesus's request that I look at my wounds in the light of His. More broadly, God works to bring about God's reign and eternal life with God. St. Hildegard writes, quoting God's promise, "I will transform all creatures into the eternity of steadfastness."[244] Mysticism occurs because "God foresees the need."[245] That is the umbrella for all else.

Jesus emerged from His wilderness experience (Mark 1:12–13) and soon called disciples (Mark 1:16–20; 2:14; 3:13–19). The disciples required transformation to fruitfully function as such. Their direct, personal experiences of Jesus transformed them. Their transformation continued when they encountered the resurrected Jesus (Mark 16; Luke 24; Matt 28; John 20–21), the Holy Spirit (Acts 2), and "many wonders and signs" (Acts 2:43). St. Paul was converted from a persecutor to a stunningly effective apostle through mystical experience (Acts 9). There are examples throughout Scripture of persons encountering God, then working with God.

The four women Doctors of the Church were mystics. Sts. Teresa of Ávila, Catherine of Siena, Thérèse of Lisieux, and Hildegard of Bingen were transformed into powerful disciples, convincing witnesses, and inspiring writers working for God. All developed intimate relationships with God. Their holy lives and ultimately their sainthood and status as Church Doctors flowed from prayer and mystical experiences. Their inspiring witness and teaching continue to assist us through the centuries. St. Hildegard says, "God shows various miracles . . . so that humankind's soul does not completely stray from heavenly desires."[246]

Mysticism deepens faith and love. St. Hildegard says, "I have from earliest childhood seen great marvels which my tongue has no power to express, but which the Spirit of God has taught me that I may believe."[247] Mystical experiences of powerful, intimate love change us deeply. "In this is love, not that we loved God, but that God loved us... . So we have known and believe the love that God has for us. God is love, and those who abide in love abide in God, and God abides in them" (1John 4:10,16). St. Hildegard says, "Love is an inextinguishable fire, the love which enkindles the sparks of true faith."[248]

How can we turn away from such love? Wouldn't we desire to love back, to share in such love? To believe in it with all our hearts and live as the beloved of God? St. Hildegard says, "Sparks burn in the hearts of the faithful, who are enkindled to the faith through the love of God, faith which they could never have unless they loved God in their hearts first. And so love has been ordained in us."[249] I told my spiritual director, "I feel as though I have cheated, for mystical experience makes faith and love come more easily."

God's power "sets hearts ablaze with love."[250] We feel greatly valued by God. "The more one recognizes the good in oneself, the more one loves God."[251] I know the lengths to which God goes in response to our seeking. Profound and intimate interactions with God help women feel treasured within a Church still struggling to embrace our equality with men. From experience, I know that God loves, respects, is committed to, and invites me to full discipleship. No person or institution or other experience can negate what God has done. "The words of the Holy Spirit cannot be altered."[252]

I am true to my experience and unshakable in my belief that God manifests in ways we might perceive as feminine, despite all the male imagery and vocabulary of the Church. St. Hildegard sings, "Sophia! You of the whirling wings, circling, encompassing energy of God; You quicken the world in Your clasp."[253] Mysticism expresses God's freedom to manifest beyond static, male-dominated imagery and language. In this, too, "God foresees the need."[254]

Through mysticism, God develops our passion for God and God's agenda. St. Hildegard writes, quoting God, "You are . . . touched by My Light, which kindles in you an inner fire like a burning sun."[255] After one experience I journaled, "I have a feeling of having flown too close to the sun . . . I feel as though I have fallen hopelessly in love . . . I have the sense I may never be the same . . . I cannot leave this path." Mysticism helps us to love not the God of our projections but the God we have directly experienced. "I, the Fiery Force, lie hidden within these things [body and soul], and they burn because of Me."[256]

Growth in love and passion for God makes it ever more painful to offend God. St. Hildegard says, "If I had not known You, I would sorrow more lightly! . . . So with great care I will seek the narrow ways."[257] God helps this cause. "The true Light strengthens [us] in the fear and love of God."[258]

Scripture opens in new ways for mystics. One understands Moses hearing God speak from a burning bush (Exod 3), Jeremiah seeing what God shows him (Jer 1), Mary receiving an announcement from God (Luke 1:26–38), the disciples' witness of a transfigured Jesus (Mark 9:2–8), and Paul not knowing whether he is in his body or out of his body (2 Cor 12:2) and stating that we are to be stewards of God's mysteries (1 Cor 4:1). St. Hildegard says, "I say to you in the love of Christ that in the vision of my soul I see many miracles of God, and through God's grace, I understand the profundities of the Scripture."[259]

I now see myself and my journey in Scripture and I relate to the biblical characters who experienced God mystically. St. Hildegard says, "I sensed . . . the deep profundity of scriptural exposition."[260] Scripture writers express the human experience of God in a variety of ways. I have not experienced anything beyond what they have described. I often say, "Yes. Like that."

Mysticism is a way to know God better. "God reveals to humankind God's hidden mysteries."[261] God reveals through Scripture and through mystical experiences. St. Hildegard says of herself,

"Through the lens of the rational soul she sees spiritually certain mystical things of God."[262] Awareness that God isn't so hidden from us brings hope. "God lives and God gives life to God's own."[263] We see God as the Life within our own lives. "God is truthful and without illusion."[264] God is willing to let me in on things through mystical experience: that I will lose my leg, but thrive. There is truth and no illusion in that, but also God's caring, loving, and mercy, as well as God's pushing away darkness. St. Hildegard quotes God, "I am the Living Light, Who illuminates the darkness."[265] God pulls out all the stops in mystical experience to make God's self known. The God I address in prayer is the God I know more deeply and desire to know eternally.

"The work of God, which is the human being, will endure and not be ended."[266] Mysticism brings glimpses of and confidence in eternity. "The Holy Spirit reveals eternity."[267] Jesus not only spoke of this destiny for Himself and for us but also appeared after His resurrection to reveal this truth. The wonder, beauty, Presence, and intense love in mystical experience, as well as the extraordinary character of it, give the mystic a strong sense of eternal life. St. Hildegard says, "You will live in eternity, and your soul will be praiseworthy before God, despite your doubt, for a victorious person is loved by her Lord."[268]

We are so loved as to be desired in God's eternity. Jesus's presence in mystical visions brings today's disciples their own upper-room experience and confidence in resurrection. We need such hope so as not to forget or despair about our destiny and worth to God. "God shows various miracles to God's holy ones and prophets in every age of the world . . . so that through faith human beings might remember eternal life."[269]

God intends our personal transformation through mysticism. St. Hildegard quotes God's words, "I will prepare many hearts according to My Own heart."[270] Joy, strength of spirit, indomitability, freedom, boldness, sense of abundance, confidence in God, and love, desire, and intimacy with God become more consistent. St. Hildegard speaks of the spirit acquired by "those who have drunk deeply of God's wisdom in elevation of spirit,"[271] and of her own experience: "I am so transformed, as I said before, that I consign all my sorrow and tribulation to oblivion. And my spirit drinks up those things I see and hear in that vision, as from an inexhaustible fountain, which remains ever full."[272]

We are not spared the slings and arrows of human life and all its pain, but we can weather them well spiritually. St. Hildegard says of St. Paul, "Because he had seen God's wonders in the spirit, he also had in his own spirit the mightiest strength."[273] She adds, "He received such great fortitude from God that he could never again doubt."[274] How could St. Hildegard know that unless through experience?

"I see you terribly bound up and hence you ought to be freed in this life."[275] Spiritual freedom is our ability to respond to God's call without false restraints, to use our gifts as God intended, and, above all, to love God, self, and others with all our heart, soul, mind, and strength. We acquire spiritual freedom in small steps, grace by grace. "God does not stop doing God's work until God has brought it to perfection."[276]

For some of us, spiritual freedom has been compromised by trauma or other issues. Through mystical experience, we take big, not small, steps toward the spiritual freedom we have been unable to achieve through lengthy self-work. God helps us catch up with the pack, so to speak, and brings the "singular justice" discussed earlier. St. Hildegard shares God's words: "I choose, by My help and action, to be on her side in the struggle. I start by gently touching . . . and from henceforward discharge her as free. She will no longer be troubled."[277] St. Hildegard says, "God has made her a new person, with a life in her different from what she had had before."[278] We can then "look to the One Who established [us] in freedom,"[279] with the joy and loyalty spiritual freedom allows. St. Hildegard says, "I breathe in the love of God. . . . How do I deserve to share in the highest of joys?"[280]

Transformation via mystical experience improves our effectiveness as disciples. "On account of the good deeds you are going to perform you will be turned toward the comprehension of the heavenly Jerusalem."[281] Mysticism imbues us with a deep desire to give back to God as disciples. This becomes a prominent part of our identity. "The Holy Spirit . . . stirs up all good things . . . and assigns speech to human beings with Divine flames."[282] Mysticism works like the tongues of fire the early disciples received (Acts 2:3). "God enkindles you with the fire of the Holy Spirit to do good works."[283]

Despite our limitations, we trust that "God will perfect all good things in us."[284] Our real work changes. "Because God is full life without beginning and without end, so a person's work is also life in God."[285]

Mysticism is not for self alone. There is an impact on others. St. Hildegard says, "When a person does a good work through wisdom, that work shines forth to others, and they apprehend with joy the sweet scent and taste it has."[286] As disciples, we are "branches [that] grow out from a root"[287] and we are to "let God's gift to [us] inspire [us] . . . to carry God's light diligently."[288]

"They will heed My voice because they proceeded from Me in true incarnation,"[289] says God to St. Hildegard. Since mystical experiences are inner, we grow to see ourselves as incarnate; we know God dwells within. St. Hildegard says, "God lives in your tabernacle and God's grace is not overshadowed there."[290] The Holy Spirit makes you "a tabernacle of sanctification so that in the joys of supreme bliss you may live always with God."[291] She says, "The shadow of the Living Light is always present to my spirit."[292]

Seeing ourselves as incarnations of God deepens our appreciation and understanding of the sacraments—especially baptism, confirmation, and Eucharist—and all the gifts that flow from them. "The
creature was kissed by the Creator when God gave it all the things it
needed."[293] Through the indwelling Spirit, we possess the courage
and wisdom we need in a given situation—providing that we are
open to them. "All of God's good things are sufficient."[294] The mystic knows that the Spirit within simultaneously has and knows about
all she experiences. The Spirit remembers all, even when she does not.
Truth dwells within, awaiting our appropriation. St. Hildegard says,
"Be a mirror of truth in your spirit."[295]

I am fortunate to be in a faith tradition that values its mystics,
and has even named some Saints and Doctors of the Church. The
Church recognizes that "God foresees the need,"[296] even for the
mystics themselves. They are a treasure trove, historic and yet ever
refreshing the people of God. Mystics witness to God's revealing and
to the human capacity to experience God. "Whoever is touched by a
spark from the Holy Spirit is so infused and filled up that she can
never cease from constantly and continually giving voice to new miracles of the mysteries of God through the inspiration of the Holy
Spirit."[297] Some of their experiences are subtle, others anything but.
The Church's saintly mystics reveal that mystical experiences bring
both personal transformation and a call to share God's work in specific, unique ways. I articulated this when I journaled, "Mystical experiences are important for my knowing. . . . I find that some things are
made possible by them."

What can a mystic do for God and us? Their writings influence
our prayer, spiritual life, faith, ministries, and work. They give hope,
inspiration, and insight. We learn, "Clearly there will be miracles in
faith and human knowledge and human understanding."[298] A
mystic, as St. Hildegard illustrates, can live out and give witness to

everyone's call to God's life and ways. She says, "God is glorified through the mystery of God's creatures, just as a person is honored for her work on a garment."[299] St. Hildegard underlines the fact that we can see God's reflection in a mystic, an ordinary human being who is the work of God.

Mystics challenge images of God as wholly external, remote, indirect, impersonal, or exclusively male. They illuminate Christian life, Scripture, sacramental life, and Church teachings through their experiences of God. The soul "understands God through the taste of holiness."[300] That taste makes the mystic a living witness of our baptismal initiation into mystical life and Spirit-filled personhood. The mystic illustrates how personally rich prayer can be. "Set on fire by the Holy Spirit . . . spiritual people . . . with the heart's every devotion and in contemplation, gaze often upon God. . . . They continue in their praise of God and never grow weary, for they can never reach the end of God's praise."[301] As the story of Marcie shows, mystical experience can be local in its impact, helping a person to insight, courage, a sense of justice, and the will to act in a situation. "In the beauty of God's justice no injustice can be found."[302]

For the Christian mystic, direct experiences of God energize following Jesus, including a willingness to share in His passion for the sake of others. The mystic confidently affirms God's love and compassion, giving hope to us. St. Hildegard says, "The Creator loved the creature greatly" and gives us "all the things . . . needed."[303] The mystic, with new eyes, points to God's presence and actions as well as God's willingness to bring light in our struggles and be with us when we most need God. St. Hildegard writes, quoting God's promise, "I embrace you, and I will warm you with the fire of the Holy Spirit."[304] The mystic, confident that God will be discovered, inspires others to seek God with open hearts and humility.

In their time and through their timeless writings, mystics guide others on their spiritual journeys. Mystics illustrate the uniqueness of each path. Yet they also reveal what mystics have in common: a consistent, robust commitment to prayer, growth in self-knowledge, many conversions, the stripping away of what is not the true self, steadfast obedience to God, great openness, and the determination to be trustable to God. St. Hildegard says, "I want to embrace God always with pure and joyous face, and rejoice in all God's judgments. And I do not want to change, but to remain always in one mind and praise God continually."[305]

As this book shows, a modern-day mystic relates to and renews the experiences of mystics who have gone before. We apply their wisdom to our lives and narratives, giving historic mystics a contemporary, relevant context. We refresh their credibility in relating our own experiences credibly. We affirm that "God was speaking to them with God's mystical wonders."[306] We confirm their words as "revealed for the usefulness of believers by the One Who is the first and the last."[307]

A mystic identifies with Mary, "she who believed that there would be a fulfillment of what was spoken to her by God" (Luke 1:45). A modern-day mystic reveals the consistency of God, Who gifted human beings with mystical experiences in ancient times, all through recorded history, and into the present. What a mystic does in response to God's overtures is a matter for the mystic and God. But mystics have made contributions to the faith tradition, awakened sparks of faith in others and helped them walk the same path, vividly shown us the nearness of God, and given us glimpses of fuller humanity. It seems regrettable, therefore, that many mystics today are known as such only to their spiritual directors and we know nothing of their paths.

"Holy Love . . . will, in purest humility, kiss your heart."[308] We come now to the most intimate purpose of mysticism: friendship with God. St. Hildegard writes, quoting God's request, "Hold Me earnestly in your strength, not as your overseer, but as your dearest

Friend."[309] God moves the mystic, experience by experience, toward a new capacity for freedom and a new identity as the beloved friend of God. "Since God is good, God will make me good . . . [and] perfect all good things in me,"[310] says St. Hildegard. "The more [a person] recognizes the good in herself, the more she loves God."[311]

"I kiss the sun when I hold God with joy; I embrace the moon when I hold God in love."[312] Is this not the very path of the disciples? "I burn with so great a desire in love for God that I can never be satisfied."[313] Jesus says, "I do not call you servants any longer, because the servant does not know what the master is doing; but I have called you friends" (John 15:15). St. Hildegard says, "I will have faith and confidence in God, and never blot out God's name from my heart."[314] The love a mystic experiences in friendship with God is a love that is available to all.

REFLECTION QUESTIONS

What has God done in your life because "God foresees the need"?

What do mystics do for others? For you?

St. Hildegard says, "Love has been ordained in us." How so?

What is your prayer about the purpose of mysticism?

"Attending God"

How does mystical experience change a directee's image of God and life direction?

One of my directees was a woman of substantial means. Though quite generous to others, she nevertheless thought her wealth was a problem in her relationship with God. She said, "God must think I'm like the rich man who turns away from Jesus (Mark 10:17–22)." I invited her to pray with Mark 10:17–31, which includes the topic of wealth, and to talk with Jesus about her perceptions.

During our next session, she described praying with the Scripture, and then, while reflecting with her eyes closed, seeing Jesus standing beside her. She said, "He knew everything about me, like the woman at the well (John 4:29). He knew all about my excesses and that I have more than I need. I thought for sure He'd ask me to give everything up, and somehow I felt willing to do that when I was with Him. But instead, He asked me for my heart and told me to be a trustworthy steward."

God, says St. Hildegard, "is miraculously even and without roughness."[315] The directee's image of Jesus changed radically after this experience. She began to view her wealth as belonging to God—as something to be stewarded with discernment. "What is the life God gives?"[316] Is it not a life of greater freedom and service?

"Never let Me go"

Why do mystics feel so responsible, and what do they do about that?

"Mortals . . . should not neglect to love God above all things and to humble themselves in all things."[317] Mystical experience brings feelings of great responsibility in this regard. The mystic must be attentive to and responsible for a new and deeper relationship with God. The mystic is so aware she is loved and provided for by God that casualness or intermittency in the relationship is dishonorable. St. Hildegard writes, quoting God, "Many seek Me with a devout, pure, and simple heart, and having found Me, never let Me go."[318] God trusts the mystic to honorably embrace God's revealing and actions, to believe in what is happening, to return trust, and to keep balance. God's call is to relate to God in a new way and to undergo transformation. Life seems difficult if the mystic does not say yes to God's call in all these aspects. "Faithful people devoutly acknowledge God with ardent desire and embrace God eagerly in the very depths of their souls."[319]

One responsibility of the mystic is continued prayer, openness, and availability to God. "God wants you. See to it, therefore, that you do not withdraw from God,"[320] says St. Hildegard. How often does a directee describe a profound experience of God and then a month later confess that she hasn't been praying? I recognize the pattern from my own life. The experience of God is so intense, so daunting and overwhelming, that we run the other way for a time. Instinctively we know that in prayer, "God will make you burn yet more for love of God."[321] We feel stretched beyond capacity. In truth, we are wise not to press for more—loving the experience more than God, so to speak. For the sake of the relationship, though, we could simply remain available and open. "After desiring to reach for God, one lives again for God."[322] We must learn to remain on the vine. "Steady souls remain fixed in their good and honest ways and do not consider changing."[323]

A second responsibility of the mystic is to assimilate her experiences with humility and gratitude. "In God's sublimity I know the sweetest good, which is humility, and feel the sweetness of the unfailing balsam, and rejoice in the delightfulness of God, as if I were amid the fragrance of all perfumes,"[324] says St. Hildegard. A mystic sees the love, compassion, and generosity of God and responds in kind. "People should . . . wrap God around their minds in pure love, and embrace God in joy and gladness."[325] The mystic is honest with herself about what transpires in prayer and assimilates it "not in pride, but in humility, the joy of the soul."[326] She appreciates that such abundance is undeserved. In humility, she asks herself, *Could I have efficiently developed into a friend of God without mystical encounters?*

"Humility opens heaven to those who imitate it and closes it to those who neglect it."[327] The mystic embraces new growth in and responsibility for the relationship with God. She humbly acknowledges her incomplete understanding of the experience, but also that God loves her even in her inadequate comprehension. The person "who perpetually looks in the mirror of her heart at God from Whom she has her body and soul, is wise,"[328] says St. Hildegard. If she focuses on and rejoices in God and God's great goodness, rather than on herself, she reinforces humility, gratitude, and wisdom. However daunting the experience, it is Good News she embraces and remembers. "Let a person understand God and let her take God into the innermost chamber of her heart. . . . Let her always remember God well."[329]

Another responsibility of the mystic is to reflect on this Good News alongside Scripture, sacramental rites, or Church teachings and find the connection to faith tradition, for an authentic mystical experience will have one. St. Hildegard says, "Why will a person chew on a grape and still wish to remain ignorant of the nature of that grape? . . . A person who acts like this wants merely to chew and gratify her own appetite."[330] Mystical experience brings fuller life in Christ, and this is further enriched via the lens of faith tradition. Mystics are "spiritual people who, with the heart's every devotion and in contemplation, gaze often upon God."[331]

"God's Word will enlighten your spirit."[332] The converse is also true. Mystical experience shines new light on teachings held to all along and makes for a more robust, living, deeply embraced faith. The mystic understands teachings more fully. "If you will diligently contemplate Me with your inner vision, as in faith you have been taught, I will receive you into My kingdom,"[333] says God to St. Hildegard. A spirit of loyal discipleship grows through reflection, as does the responsibility to live accordingly. Mystical experience helps us become more insightful, enthusiastic, and credible teachers of the faith.

A fourth responsibility of the mystic is to probe the authenticity of her experience. The purpose is not to doubt God but to grow in clarity and conviction. St. Hildegard says, "The faith that one has before God in her blazing heart through the inspiration of the Holy Spirit is very glorious when she embraces with the embrace of true love the things she cannot see as if they were the visible things she prizes."[334] A glorious faith and an embrace in true love certainly are signs of authenticity. Self-knowledge and self-honesty are also critical. What makes us so sure the experience is of God? Did surprise, change, challenge, and awe occur? Could it have been imagined? Or reimagined with the same impact? Was it uniquely God's doing? Did it unfold without volition?

St. Hildegard says, "I had sensed in myself wonderfully the power and mystery."[335] She writes, quoting God, "For I have closed up the cracks in her heart that her mind may not exalt itself in pride."[336] Was the experience humbling? Does God sound like our own inner voice or a new voice? What was the sense of God's presence? What was the spiritual consciousness like? Was there an intensity, uniqueness, or shift from an ordinary spiritual state? Were we fully awake? What did we receive by way of truth, love, and hope? How was God personal, intimate, and direct? Did a compelling, unplanned action result? St. Hildegard says, "Acknowledge that you have no power except in God and through God."[337] Like her, have we "seen great marvels which the tongue has no power to express"?[338] In other words, is there difficulty in describing the ineffable? Lastly, if we are deeply honest and unwilling to betray God, what sense of the experience's authenticity are we left with? In truth, people know what is of God.

A fifth responsibility of the mystic is to speak with a spiritually wise person, such as a spiritual director, about her experience. The conversation aids in safe articulation of the experience, allows for assimilation and authentication, ensures that we are not ignoring it or treating it too casually, keeps the focus on God and the relationship with God, and helps bring the faith tradition into reflection on it. St. Hildegard says, "Watch over that garden which the Divine gift has planted. . . . Do not overshadow your garden with the weariness of silence."[339]

St. Hildegard says that she "searched in her mind as to where she could find someone who would run in the path of salvation. And she found such a one . . . knowing he was a faithful man, working like herself on another part of the work that leads to God."[340] This was the monk, Volmar, in whom she confided and who became her secretary. She also wrote to Bernard of Clairvaux, saying, "I lay my claim before you," and requested that she "may be assured."[341] Bernard responded, "We rejoice in the grace of God which is in you. And further, we most earnestly urge and beseech you to recognize this gift as grace and to respond eagerly to it with all humility and devotion."[342]

A wise spiritual director reassures, informs, helps keep perspective, and encourages us to take responsibility for the gift of mysticism. Ideally, our director neither downplays the gift nor blows it out of proportion. St. Hildegard advises directors, "Prevent them from snuffing out their spirits, which have many merits."[343] Not all directors we encounter serve mystics well, but some are extraordinarily helpful. We pray to be guided to the right one, someone who affirms what is of God, someone "instructed by the inspiration of the Holy

Spirit."[344] The mystic's spiritual director has, "Ears to hear" (Mark 4:9) from the One "Who planted the ear" (Ps 94:9)—that is, has the needed spiritual comprehension.

A sixth responsibility of the mystic is to be trustable to God, aligning with God's larger agenda and the "for others" purpose of her deepest spiritual gifts. "A person who wants to be subject to Divine Love cherishes what is in God, looks upon God in the purity of faith, and does not set any . . . thing ahead of God . . . for God has foreseen that she should come to such a place."[345] We respond in willingness and courage. A mystic is a steward of God's mysteries and must "be found trustworthy" (1 Cor 4:1–2). Discernment is usually in order, yet often the explicit request within the mystical experience is trustable, not debatable, and compels. "God compels us to good."[346] Feeling compelled is a hallmark of mysticism. It brings an inspired, overwhelming conviction to do as God has asked. The Marcie story, for example, illustrates God's compelling request to advocate for another and to take a stance for justice.

A compelling call comes directly "from God, watered by the rain of the Holy Spirit."[347] The mystic, to be trustable to God, rejects temptations to resist or doubt or postpone. The God Who asks provides the grace to respond. St. Hildegard says, "Indeed I always tremble in fear, since I know I cannot safely rely on my own innate capacity. But I stretch out my hands to God."[348] If a cross is involved, with grace it can be shouldered. In doing as asked, the mystic discovers that more was imparted in the mystical experience than imagined, and this further authenticates it. Each response brings growth in her trustworthiness to God. The mystic also expects herself to be a trustworthy friend and disciple.

St. Hildegard prays, "Prove me, Lord, through faith and hope, so that my faith may be an eye to see, and my hope, a mirror of life. And try me in righteous obedience like Abraham, so that I may not work according to my own will, but may abandon it for Your sake . . . and thus become Your loving friend."[349] A seventh responsibility of the mystic is to be the friend and disciple God seeks in the long term. "The Holy Spirit, by Its power, draws the human mind . . . that it may share in the vision of the Spirit . . . that it may clearly see the works to be done in the Spirit, the great works of God."[350] Mysticism disrupts both inner status quo and outer habits, and causes fundamental change. The mystic is "burning with love of God and not wanting anything else than what God wants."[351]

Through mysticism, God gains a disciple and friend, someone more capable of loving with all her "heart, soul, mind, and strength" (Mark 12:30)—that is, with her whole being and all that she has. "She loves God with the strongest love."[352] Reintegration and change occur in who the mystic thinks she is and what she is about. She grows in communion with God, in the ability to find God in all things and to see God in others. Mysterious prayer insights become very clear when lived out. The courage and strength to act increase. "God enkindles you with the fire of the Holy Spirit to do good works."[353] Spiritual freedom, deep joy, and inner peace are palpable. "Contemplate the charity with which God freed you."[354]

Focus on God becomes the priority. St. Hildegard says "God is like a head of a household who entrusts his goods to a close friend."[355] The mystic is the friend of God, Who is All Truth, and dwells within her. Thus, she experiences painful recoil from and abhorrence of falseness. An everyday mystic is but a spark relative to the flames that are the great mystics of the faith tradition. Even so, she can embrace the way God has given her, and, no longer a servant (John 15:15), be God's friend and disciple. A consequence is healthy solidity in self-esteem and humble awareness of who she is to God.

An eighth responsibility of the mystic, as with all disciples and friends of Jesus, is to bear witness. To God goes the credit and glory, we boldly say. St. Paul writes, "Such is the confidence that we have through Christ toward God. Not that we are competent of ourselves to claim anything as coming from us; our competence is from God" (2 Cor 3:4–5). With St. Hildegard, a mystic declares, "I see as I saw and I hear as I heard"[356] and seeks to "carry God's light diligently."[357] A mystic affirms that mysticism is real and of God.

How can a mystic be so personally aware of God's love and compassion and keep mum? How can she know God intimately, yet refuse God's urging to reveal and share? Caution, judgment, discretion, and not running ahead of grace are prudent. Yet it seems a universal experience of mystics that God's persistence wears away their reluctance to reveal and bear witness. "What flows from the fountain of eternal life cannot be obstructed or hidden."[358]

St. Hildegard expressed initial caution about disclosing mystical experiences: "This, however, I showed to no one except a few religious persons who were living in the same manner as I."[359] At first I resisted writing of my experiences even in my journal, despite the urgings of my spiritual director and God. I had doubts and fears. I felt my undeservedness, the improbability that I, who knew nothing of mysticism and had no special holiness, would nonetheless experience it. St. Hildegard described her feeling: "Puny little woman that I am, who have seen and heard these words, as You alone know. . . . Preserve me, body and soul, from every doubt that arises from my ignorance."[360] *If the experiences are a new phenomenon to me*, I thought, *why would anyone to whom I reveal them understand?* St. Hildegard says, "I am terribly afraid to speak or write to my male superiors about those things which I see in my spirit in the True Light, in my spirit only, unaided by my corporeal eyes."[361]

Finally, I journaled, "I was reminded by God of what my lot would be if people like St. Julian of Norwich had refused God's request. That thought fills me with awe for what they did, the saints who wrote, especially the mystics and visionaries. . . . I have to give up my resistance to have any peace. I also have to stop filtering and do my best to write about everything I experience. As St. Julian said, these become one's strength. It is good to be able to return to a vivid record."

Later, I saw that more had been revealed and understood than I initially captured in my journal. I realized that writing helps me see more deeply. St. Hildegard reports God urging her to write: "There happened a voice from heaven, saying to me: 'Daughter of very many labors . . . flooded by the depth of God's mysteries . . . entrust to fixed writing these things that you see with the inner eyes and perceive with the inner ears of the soul, to be useful for humankind.'"[362] How could St. Hildegard then believe her writing was for her alone?

"Obedience is indeed a fire."[363] I began consistently journaling about my prayer. I wrote, "I have been surprised by God's use of my scientific skills of observation, description, and even logic. I note details and am led to conclusions that surprise, enlighten, and fulfill my ever present quest for truth. Prayer should become more open, not narrowed by preconceived notions about who can participate and how." God said to St. Hildegard, "I Am also rationality, possessing the breath of the resonating Word."[364] More resonated in me as I obeyed God's request to write.

One day, I chanced upon God's words to the prophet Habakkuk: "Write the vision; make it plain on tablets, so that a runner may read it. For there is still a vision for the appointed time" (Hab 2:2–3). I suddenly felt the powerful Presence of the Great Underliner and the force of obligation in my spirit and realized, *Oh no, this too has a for others purpose.* I so did not want to write that others "may read it," but now I felt compelled to consider and embrace that. "[Rationality] is set ablaze with the Holy Spirit's fire to multiply its praises like the sparks of a fire."[365] I did not yet know the entirety of God's purpose in what I experienced.

St. Hildegard says, "By a vision, which was implanted in my soul by God the Great Artisan . . . I have been compelled to write."[366] She also says of her experience, "I concealed it in quiet silence" and "refused to write for a long time."[367] Her resistance caused her to fall "upon a bed of sickness."[368] For an embarrassing length of time I, too, resisted writing for a reader. My resistance made me feel sick at heart; I was aware I was disappointing God. But I didn't want the exposure, to be subjected to the negative things written about mysticism. I journaled:

> Sometimes what I read about mysticism is a challenge. Some write so confusedly about it, presumably because they do not have such experiences and/or have not found the way to take up responsibility for them, and/or never look at Scripture as containing both experience and the responsibility. . . . One has to come to grips with the reality that many do not understand, and some even write in negation of mysticism. But, God will not be denied! If God wants mystics, God shall have them. . . . I find detractors hard because it's like an attack on my identity, but ironically, that too is a Jesus-like experience.

St. Hildegard counsels, "Make your God known by your honorable way of life and magnify God."[369] Life must change. "Run courageously in God's commands."[370] Being afraid and resisting are temptations, not proper motives for our behavior. "A faithful person glorifies her Creator with every effort of her mind and body, with a spirit of humility."[371] At last I journaled, "I am a mystic; I must be a credible, solid one, acting in ways consistent with the beautiful graces received." St. Hildegard reinforces these conclusions: "Be true to your calling because this is what the grace of God wishes."[372]

Ultimately, of course, St. Hildegard capitulated. She says, "I set my hand to the writing."[373] Life is harder when one is not aligned with God, and God is insistent. She reports several messages from God on the topic: "Cry out therefore, and write thus!"[374] "Relate and write these My mysteries."[375] "Explain these things."[376] "Write them and speak."[377] "Explain these things in such a way that the hearer, receiving the words of her instructor, may expound them in those words."[378] Indeed, as her hearer, I expound her messages extensively in these pages as well as in guiding others.

For me as well, writing seemed the spiritually healthy, obedient, and appropriate response to God's call. What could I do? I, too, capitulated.

I sought to make my experiences understandable and relevant to others. I began with short talks and brief articles showing the application of mystical insights. St. Hildegard writes, "From time to time I resound a little, like the dim sound of a trumpet from the Living Light. May God help me, therefore, to remain in God's service."[379] I am a collaborator with God, the women Doctors of the Church, and the Scripture writers. St. Hildegard says, "It is Another Who breathes into [the trumpet] that it might give forth a sound."[380]

"Gird yourself for this task with sincere love, humility, and patience, then you will not fall."[381] Keeping focus on God's revealing, God's message, and God's call, rather than on my fears and reluctance, is critical. God says, per St. Hildegard, "Speak and write, therefore, now according to Me and not according to yourself."[382] The task is all about responding to God. St. Hildegard says, "The words I speak are not my own, nor any human being's. I merely report those things I received."[383] The lens of humility is key. "In the descent of true humility, [the soul] attributes whatever good it has done to the One Who is the Highest Good and through Whom it possesses the good."[384]

And so, with grace, I reveal. What is a mystic if not someone who gives the Word and all the teachings of our rich tradition a place to live? As I write, the Holy Spirit deepens my understanding and love.

St. Hildegard says, "Whoever is touched by a spark from the Holy Spirit is so infused and filled up that she can never cease from constantly and continually giving voice to new miracles of the mysteries of God through the inspiration of the Holy Spirit."[385] What better confirmation of the discernment to write could there be? God "must not be concealed, but made manifest."[386] I, like mystics, disciples, and friends of God before me, have a responsibility to bear witness. I pray with St. Hildegard, "Watch over and take care of the great and small who have written about Your Spirit, and over me, a puny little woman who, animated by the breath of Your Spirit, has labored over this writing."[387]

REFLECTION QUESTIONS

Have you ever run the other way after an experience of God? What happened?

St. Hildegard says, "Why will a person chew on a grape and still wish to remain ignorant of the nature of that grape . . . [wanting] merely to chew and gratify her own appetite?" How do you understand these words in the context of your relationship with God?

How have you grown in availability, trustworthiness, and bearing witness to God?

What is your prayer about your responsibility for God's gifts?

"*Look sharply to the work in hand*"

What goes through your mind when prayer seems ordinary or dull? There are breaks in the action from the more exuberant forms of mysticism. Prayer resumes its ordinary character. I did not cause the experiences, but I wondered if I caused the breaks. Often my job required international travel, and praying peacefully during those trips was hard. I was not as available and open to God as usual. Mystical experiences were rare at these times. Even so, I was aware of God's presence and action in my life and work. I knew from experience that God "holds all things together. And God preserves all things according to the plan of God's grace."[388] God said to St. Hildegard, "I am life indeed pure and whole . . . every living thing has taken root in Me."[389]

As time went on, long stretches of peaceful prayer remained ordinary and yet fruitful. I assumed that God had ceased interacting with me in a mystical way. I struggled a little. I journaled, "Visions helped me learn to love God. Now I must be true to God when I can't 'see' anything. I am to be faithful with and without visions." I saw a call to humility in the shift. I wrote, "One must not push or imagine or clamor for these. One must humbly wait, even assume they may never happen again. It's all up to God and God's pace."

Breaks in the action were proof I was not in control; all was God's doing. St. Paul says, "We have this treasure in clay jars, so that it may be made clear that this extraordinary power belongs to God and does not come from us" (2 Cor 4:7). God is our "omnipotent God, incomprehensible in majesty and inestimable in mysteries and the hope of all the faithful."[390] Breaks in the action reminded me that I am a clay jar, and God is the Source of all things mystical.

My prayer was nevertheless rich. "The grace of God shines like the sun and sends its gifts in various ways: in wisdom, in viridity, in moisture."[391] With grace, I was at peace with whatever God desired in prayer. I named feeling abandoned, though I knew I was not. I moved on humbly and fruitfully. St. Hildegard says, "Fear not, because God, by Whose grace you are endowed with wisdom and knowledge, will never abandon you."[392] I wrote, "I feel more peaceful, God, more confident Your silence is not my abandonment." I appreciated the break from continual transformation and reintegration, and sensed God knew I required rest. St. Hildegard says, "God seeks you out, and God will rest in you."[393]

God is present in rest. Genesis tells us that God rests from creating, and blesses and hallows rest (Gen 2:2–3). I wrote, "I can sit in silence with God without expectation. Be humble enough to realize that whatever happens or does not happen is fine. Be satisfied with a few moments of complete quiet as a great gift. I mustn't be so eager to hear God say something, for it is with words that God creates! Am I so sure I'm ready for what God would create within me if I hear God's word? Maybe silence is ok right now. Maybe God lets me rest sometimes."

Like other aspects of mysticism, breaks in the action are worthy of reflection. I believe they reveal God's loving purposefulness. I noted that we must be available to God in peaceful prayer. Breaks remind us that our lack of availability works against mystical experience. At the same time, breaks keep us aware of the fruitfulness of other forms of prayer. God guards us from becoming spoiled and dependent on fireworks in our relationship with God. Breaks grow humility, trust, maturity, and faithfulness. Breaks confirm that mystical experiences are not in our control. They help us confront the false notion that God would abandon us. Breaks allow us to rest. St. Hildegard reminds us that "God wishes from the beginning to the end of the world to take pleasure in God's elect."[394] How else might God's desire be revealed in breaks?

I grew to appreciate my opportunities during breaks to give back to God by doing my part in prayer again. The space to give praise and thanks on my own initiative felt so right, given all God had done for me. "Neither angel nor human being can set a limit or boundary to the glory which is God."[395] A break provides time to praise God for that truth.

Mystical experiences are sizable perturbations and cause spiritual flux. St. Hildegard says, "Clearly there will be miracles in faith and human knowledge and human understanding."[396] One must process, reflect, and seek to understand. St. Paul says, "Now we have received not the spirit of the world, but the Spirit that is from God, so that we may understand the gifts bestowed on us by God" (1 Cor 2:12). During breaks, the Spirit works differently, growing our understanding of our mystical experiences. To steward the mysteries of God, we must first understand them as best we can. St. Hildegard and other mystics reflected on their mystical experiences and reported the fruits. Reflection is a deeper response than simply receiving.

Spiritual homeostasis is critical for discernment. We cannot discern without a stable inner environment in which we notice subtle movements of the Spirit. Trying out our options and noting our inner state is the essence of the method, as described earlier. We will not easily arrive at the correct decision when in the glow of a profound experience. In fact, we should not trust that glow as indicative of our direction; it is a reaction to what went before, not an indicator of what is to come. In discernment, it is not the amazing Fire or Great Light sense of God we need; rather, as St. Hildegard says, "The likeness of the Dove teaches you."[397] Breaks in the action of mystical experience help us discern and notice the Spirit's subtle guiding of ordinary life.

St. Hildegard says, "Look sharply to the work in hand."[398] Breaks help me feel integrated, ordinary, and able to focus on service to God and others. Just as we are to "speak and write . . . now accord-ing to [God] and not according to [ourselves],"[399] all our work is to be thus. Our ordinary, integrated, practical self is the instrument for God's work, more so than the self who knows not whether she is "in the body or out of the body" (2 Cor 12:3).

St. Hildegard describes "the true visions which I . . . labored over for ten years" and being "weighed down with a lot of work" after her visions, "so that I might explain them."[400] She says of a vision she had at age sixty-five, "After seven years, I have finally brought this vision almost to completion by writing it down."[401] Much would be lost if mystics did not write about their experiences. After capturing them immediately, mystics follow up with prayer, written reflection, and writing for readers about them. Writing also requires spiritual homeostasis. The mystics of our tradition have left voluminous writ-ings behind. To do so, they spent most of their time in ordinariness, down from the mountaintop, laboring to fulfill what God asked of them.

Locutions and visions are intermittent in my prayer, according to God's loving purposefulness. I do not yet know what will happen for me in the long term—for example, in advanced age. At seventy-seven St. Hildegard wrote, "I was possessed of this visionary gift in my soul, and it abides with me still up to the present day. In these visions, my spirit rises, as God wills to the heights of heaven."[402] Visions are mere glimpses compared to the eternity we are all meant to enjoy. All I need know is, "God has neither a beginning nor an end."[403]

"Attending God"

Are any of your directees mystics? Aren't they all?

Many of my spiritual directees seem unaware of mysticism,

whether through reading or experience. Some do note it in their spiritual reading, the lives of the saints, and Scripture. Often, they are skeptical about it. Others assume mysticism flows from the holiness of the saints. The rare person is excited about and desires mystical experience. In every case, "they should not neglect to love God above all things and to humble themselves in all things."[404]

I once guided some parishioners through St. Thérèse's *Story of a Soul.* Now and again, I was pulled aside by participants who revealed mystical experiences. Often their first words were, "I've never told anyone about this," and they ended with, "It's changed my life." They desired to talk to someone about their experience and sought validation and reassurance. Each was utterly convinced the experience was of God. They were ordinary, unassuming, prayerful persons taken by surprise and greatly humbled by their experiences. Each insisted she or he wasn't as holy as St. Thérèse. They spoke "not in pride but in humility, the joy of the soul."[405]

In learning about St. Thérèse's experience, these persons no longer felt alone. Why trust me? I had taken the saint's experiences seriously, provided background on mysticism, and characterized it as a normal spiritual development. My role in these conversations was to "hear the mysteries of God."[406] To have someone to talk to, and to be believed, affirmed, reassured, and encouraged to take their experiences seriously, brought relief, gratitude, and renewed wonder to the sharers. I could see the inner strength and faith these people had acquired through their experiences. "Through the hidden mysteries of God's secrets, God is in the strength of the soul."[407] Each was known in the parish for good works. St. Hildegard says, "When a human begins to know God she afterwards works for the good and then embraces God."[408]

A woman who participated in the book discussion came for spiritual direction. Her opening statement was, "From everything you said about St. Thérèse, I know you're not going to think I'm crazy." She spoke about mystical experiences and how her relationship with God had grown, such that she was now willing "to do big things for God." St. Hildegard says, "God compels us to good,"[409] and indeed this woman now ministers to those who need a new start in life. She takes responsibility for and fruitfully lives out her experiences of God. Now that she has read about mysticism, she feels less alone. She prays with Scripture daily. She insists she is "very ordinary" and "never knew God would do all this." She said she would never have re-arranged her life to serve others, "were it not for God." She considers it "a great privilege" to share in God's love and compassion for others. "I know the love is from God," she says, "because some are a challenge to love, but I never give up on them; I can't." St. Hildegard says, "One way of justice is . . . burning with love of God and not wanting any-thing else than what God wants."[410]

This woman has become a person of great courage, faith, and self-sacrifice. She holds God "not as her overseer, but as her dearest friend."[411] Her work illustrates the loving, radical agenda of God that might be unrealized if mystical experiences were rejected by the directee or mishandled by the director. Her experiences are a sign of God's love for those she serves.

"Help her as much as you can, so that the vineyard in this daugh-ter may not be destroyed,"[412] says St. Hildegard. Whether or not we spiritual directors have mystical experiences ourselves, we must be aware that they are normal and not unusual, albeit uncommon. If we are well informed and prepared, we can journey with people re-sponding to direct interactions with God. The spiritual director helps the directee to fully assimilate and take responsibility for such gifts. "Faith always looks to God through obedience, and thus carries out what has been commanded."[413]

Another directee reported locutions that did not seem genuine to me. Within myself I felt a desolating sense of their falseness as I listened. I struggled; I was reluctant to disbelieve the directee. Later, I reflected at length on what I noticed. The locutions seemed to come from the directee's own power. Why did I think that? I did not observe the humility, surprise, wonderment, and reluctance to disclose typical of mystics. Mystical experience is difficult to describe, and yet the directee didn't even mention the unusual way of hearing with inner spiritual ears that is universal to mystics. The locutions lacked insight, originality, and freshness and asked nothing of the directee. There was, as St. Hildegard says, "the name of sanctity without the substance."[414]

The locutions were obvious and predictable. In contrast, my own experience is that they involve surprising insight. The locutions seemed to have little impact on the directee. The directee reported receiving them on the spot, as though "channeled" in brief silences during spiritual direction, and yet my impression was they were simply her own thoughts. The truth was, I myself was not surprised or inspired by the content, and I found that unusual compared to other directees' reports.

What should a spiritual director do in this situation? St. Hildegard's words help: "Imitate the gentlest God in humility, patience, and mercy."[415] I kept the focus on God and gave the directee the benefit of the doubt. I invited her to reflect on what she'd learned about God and to notice the fruits of her experience, for the great mystics tell us that greater love for God and others flows from mysticism. St. Hildegard counsels, "God in God's wisdom seeks the sacrifice of your heart offered up in simplicity, for God is true,"[416] so I gently reminded her that God desires our sincerity and simplicity in response to grace. "Commend the sincerity of your mind again and again to the omnipotent God."[417]

I also said, "We are always wise to confirm the authenticity of our experiences for ourselves, so do that prayerfully. God will help you." I encouraged her to pray for grace to see her experiences as God sees them. That is always a spiritual director's best bet. "Take care to see . . . what is of God, and what of man."[418] I simply set the bar where our mystic predecessors set it.

I reflected further. *What am I listening for?* Hallmarks of authentic mystical experience are deepening faith, hope, love, enlightenment, and courage to follow the Way of Jesus. Surprise is a hallmark to which St. Teresa of Ávila points. Mystical experience is hard, not easy, to imagine. Locutions are not trite or predictable. Instead, they bring unexpected light and truth. They are bracing, make us think, shake us up a little, and humble us. And yet they are consistent with the ways of God in Scripture and tradition. Ears don't hear in their normal way; the hearing is with inner spiritual ears. God's involvement is clear from the powerful sense of Presence and love. A person feels undeserving and a compelling desire to respond authentically. St. Hildegard advises, "Walk in Christ's footsteps lest you deceive yourself."[419]

I journeyed many years with a directee whose mystical experiences were primarily of Mary. She figures in the mystical experiences of some saints, including St. Hildegard and St. Thérèse. St. Hildegard says, "By following the example of the saints, and by observing their character you will learn the nature of the righteous God."[420] The directee was a simple, straightforward, unassuming, and consistently prayerful man. He was at first stunned that these experiences were happening to him and took his time accepting them. With each spiritual direction session, however, I observed that he questioned less and assimilated more.

When it came down to it, this man could not turn his back on Mary. Instead, he was on fire to respond to her. His love for her and all she stood for grew and grew. He would have appreciated St. Hildegard speaking of her as the "Mother of Love."[421] He never missed a feast-day Mass, visited all Marian churches and shrines in driving distance, and developed solidarity with our Latinx community, whose love for Mary he shared. St. Hildegard describes Mary as a "Life-giving source," "Unclouded Brightness," and one who "opened to us the door" and carries our souls "on the wings of Your call."[422] We could add "Sponsor of Transformation" to her list.

The transformation of this directee was thorough, beautiful, and notable to the community, though he did not reveal to others his inner path. He abandoned relative inactivity to become greatly involved in the work of God. At his wake, I learned that many lay ministers, particularly the young, had received notes of support and encouragement from him. His service to the poor was legendary; the entire archdiocese was touched by it. He attributed all his work to God working through Mary, a "Self-Portrait of the Maker" who "lifts us frail ones out of our old bad ways."[423] And on his deathbed, he thanked Mary for being present even then to help him.

All I did for this directee was affirm him, reassure him, marvel with him, and share his joy. St. Hildegard says, "God Who is fire and light, vivifies the human person through the soul and moves him."[424] Mary is certainly a light made bright by God, who, in turn, helped this man become a vital light to people in need.

REFLECTION QUESTIONS

Have you ever felt a tinge of abandonment when God's activity in your prayer seemed less pronounced? How did you handle it?

What is "spiritual homeostasis"? Why is it important in your spiritual life?

What are your thoughts and feelings about directing those reporting mystical experiences?

What is your prayer about the ordinary and not-so-ordinary experiences of God that come up in spiritual direction?

chapter fourteen

————•••————

DEEP HEALING

"The God of all creatures will give you the grace necessary"

*H*ave you ever said, "Where was God?"
"You endure tribulation and fear and grief in the tumult
of life. Nevertheless, in this way many saints, like the martyrs, come to
God. And so you also, trust God because God will not desert you, and
the Holy Spirit will diminish your grief."[1] God will not desert you.
And yet when tragic events strike, we often question, "Where was
God?" Tragedy and trauma threaten our friendship with God. Where
was God when this happened? We struggle to believe that God is with
us when this question seems unanswered. The experiences that shout
this question the loudest are unhealed. Where was God? Is this not
Jesus's question, too, when He prays Psalm 22 on the cross, "My God,
my God, why have You forsaken me" (Mark 15:34)?

Much Scripture was written years after threatening events in
human experience: exodus, exile, and crucifixion. The events were
remembered and recorded as our ancestors worked out the question
of where God was. They gained a deeper understanding of God's revealing, redeeming, liberating actions: God did not prevent these
events, but dwelled among those enduring them. Through Scripture

we share the age-old question: where was God? Faith traditions that hold Scriptures sacred are religions of remembrance. What we call salvation history was remembered and written down under the guidance of the Holy Spirit, and has been commemorated liturgically ever since.

Through meditation, reflection, and study of Scripture we find some answers to the "Where was God?" question. We grow in our understanding of the spiritual realities and truth in our heritage. We notice God acting, revealing, guiding, inspiring, helping, and dwelling with God's people when their existence, faith, and fullness of life are threatened. St. Hildegard says, "In the perfection of the works of God there was an ancient plan for the salvation of the human being."[2] We read that human trauma was not isolated from faith and God's presence and action. Scripture is the Word of God, and yet it contains stories of murder, rape, beheading, deadly disease, assault, abandonment, and crucifixion. Scripture is a bloody business. Horrific truth is told, and the question, "Where was God?" is repeatedly posed and pondered.

Healthy spirituality does not separate personal trauma from other soul work. "For the spirit without the bloody material of the body is not the living person, and the bloody material of the body without the soul is not the living person."[3] At its best, spirituality deals in the truth of our experience and brings us into a right and holy relationship with our truth. "The God of all creatures will give you the grace necessary. . . . God will fill your soul with heavenly joy and light . . . and free you."[4] Freedom is at stake. Faith and joy are at stake. Friendship with God is at stake.

Salvation history is also personal, a story of God with each of us. We, too, remember events after the fact. We, too, cannot forget them. We, too, pose the "Where was God?" question. We want to know how God revealed, acted, helped, and was present in our traumatic events.

In faith, we assume it is a matter of discovery and not that God did nothing. We desire meaning and purpose. We want to heal. We find that "God alone and no one else is able to free us."[5]

Salvation means deliverance, freedom, true possibility, fullness of life, abundance, and participation in the life of God. For a Christian, it also means fullness of identity with Christ, God incarnate, doing the work of God, and suffering, dying, and rising to new life.

Deep healing in prayer is difficult. Our brokenness must be unmasked. Trauma reconfigures our inner lives, even the way our minds function. A resulting isolation is not unusual. In severe trauma we are in fact given more than we can handle, platitudes aside. We are dealt a terrible blow that is not of God and are left different than we were before. Our capacity to cope, respond, and be resilient and heroic may be remarkable, even admirable, but it does not save us or restore us to fullness of life. Coping and resilience are not *healing*, per se. "God's power restores."[6] For true healing, we need God.

"In the darkness I . . . call instead upon the living God, that God might lead me into the path of light and cure my sores, so that . . . the cords of my captivity will be burst,"[7] says St. Hildegard. In her spirituality, "The soul is diffused throughout the entire body."[8] For her, healing involves body, soul, and God. "A person's body is strengthened and sustained by the soul."[9] There is no separation. "Soul and body cannot be disjoined but work together."[10] In fact, "Body and soul are joined together in twofold love by the unction of the Holy Spirit."[11] The soul and the Holy Spirit have an impact throughout the body. "The soul, which was sent by God's Spirit into the body, floods it entirely with its powers."[12]

St. Hildegard says, "The soul is a breath of God's Spirit that exists as life through the Life that is God."[13] This matters in human life and healing. "The human . . . is strengthened and preserved with God's grace through the soul . . . like a medicine."[14] The promise related by

St. Hildegard is that "God does not hide God's face from you.... A great light of consolation will soon come into your soul and into the joy of your body, in God's own good time. For God lives in your tabernacle [body], and God's grace is not overshadowed there."[15] From her experience she prays, "With Your medicine You touch my flesh, and with Your greenness You heal with discretion."[16]

How does God respond to our need for healing? Through St. Hildegard, God says, "For I the Living and true Witness of Truth, the speaking and not silent God, say ... My tabernacle is the place where the Holy Spirit pours forth Her overflowing waters. What does this mean? I am in the midst.... I am that Charity which ... a fall into the depths cannot dash to pieces and the wide expanse of evils cannot crush."[17] God is in the midst of it all.

Our realization that God is the "true Witness of Truth" and knows more about what happened than we do reassures. Our discovery that God is "the speaking and not silent God" on the topic of our pain opens up new intimacy. Finding God truly "in the midst" and "pouring forth" what we most need heals and transforms. Gradually, with healing, our life story changes to be like Scripture, the story of God with us. For the Christian, the significance of Jesus's passion becomes our significance, too. Passion leads to our raising up and greater fullness of life. "Healing will come forth from the heart when the dawn appears like the splendor of the first sunrise."[18]

What flows from deep healing in prayer? Jesus's psalm prayer on the cross begins with "My God, my God, why have You forsaken me?" and ends with the proclamation that "God has not spurned or disdained the misery of this poor wretch, and did not turn away from me, but heard me when I cried out"; "May your hearts enjoy life forever"; and "Proclaim to a people yet unborn the deliverance You have brought" (Ps. 22: 1, 25, 27, 32). What do deliverance and deep healing look like?

"New redemption has come about for human beings who live in physical bodies as in their houses,"[19] says St. Hildegard. In healing, we know God's presence in our experience and God's compassion and love. We can look at our worst moments and see love manifested. Crucifixion and resurrection become one event. We are freer; our wounds no longer dominate and haunt our lives as they once did. We are not isolated, bitter, angry, or unforgiving, nor are we estranged from any aspect of self or experience. We are able to be available and compassionate toward others in their experiences. St. Hildegard says, "Reach out and grasp mercy, which comes not from you, but only from God; and so do not withhold it from those to whom it should be extended."[20] When we have experienced "that sweetest Mother Mercy as our assistant,"[21] we are able to offer mercy to others.

Our wounds do not disappear as though nothing happened; they remain part of our experience of God with us. But they are transformed and have the potential to inspire belief, just as with Jesus and Thomas (John 20: 24-29). Our wounds are the locus of Good News. We grow stronger in the very places where we once were weak. We become more patient and acceptant, more forthright, creative, fruitful, and open in how we live. We grow in solidarity with Jesus and the suffering body of Christ. We return "wholly to God's service"[22] and give praise to God.

Some forms of prayer open us, our minds especially, to deep healing. If trauma can reconfigure our inner life, God can certainly reshape it with extraordinary creativity, sensitivity, gentleness, tenderness, timeliness, mercy, and love. "Let the faithful person walk to God in her faith and seek God's mercy and it will be given to her."[23]

"Such are the thoughts of your mind"

Are you haunted or triggered by "bad" memories?

Sometimes during prayer difficult memories are recalled. We are invited to find God in these so that healing may come. For example, the severe injuries of my childhood created memories I did not prefer to dwell on, and yet they did not cease coming to mind at times. When they came during prayer, I learned to address them in prayer. "Healing will come forth from the heart."[24] As a prayerful adult, I could see God in my experiences in ways I could not as a child.

One morning in prayer I abruptly, for no apparent reason, remembered being weak and unable to walk despite two surgeries. I stayed at my grandparents' home during my early recovery, and had no wheelchair or crutches, so I got around by crawling—and even that was difficult, because my right leg was paralyzed and I had to drag it forward. Whenever this memory came, I felt humiliation and indignity. I felt shame that the adults in my life had failed to have a better plan to provide for me. I easily believed that I had been neglected, even rejected, in that experience. St. Hildegard says, "Such are the thoughts of your mind, troubled as it is over the matter you have embraced in the core of your heart."[25] Embraced, but never examined. The memory of crawling like an infant, though I was seven at the time, was also disconnected from any positive outcome. "Creatures are little but the power of God is great and incomprehensible,"[26] as I soon learned.

Now, with Jesus, I examined the experience. "God in God's wisdom seeks the sacrifice of your heart offered up in simplicity."[27] Jesus seemed to point out my bravery and sacrifice in my effort to get moving again. I had not considered these before. I felt a touch of admiration for my determined young self. What a contrast to shame! I sensed that Jesus also admired my effort. "A faithful person glorifies her Creator with every effort of her mind and body."[28]

Jesus invited me to notice that I always knew I would walk again. This is true; I never doubted it. In my little head, it was just a matter of time and effort, like getting to third grade. I *would* walk again one day. Now, for the first time, I pondered the Source of that awareness. "God's grace pointed out, 'Do not doubt.'"[29] No one had dared tell me walking was possible. How did I know it was? "The human spirit is the certain cause of the knowledge granted a person by God, and permeates everything else God gives her,"[30] says St. Hildegard.

From my first moment of post-injury consciousness, I'd had an unshakable vision of walking again and felt compelled to live toward it. That vision was within me. It had not been an external message. Now I felt grateful that the adults around me had not suggested that walking was impossible, though their silence implied it. The spark within me was not quenched. "What flows from the fountain of eternal life cannot be obstructed or hidden."[31]

Next, Jesus invited me to reflect on the benefits of crawling. For this I put on my physiologist hat. How can crawling help an injured child? The list was impressive: redevelopment of motor skills, balance, strength, and coordination; restoration of neural connections; and reestablishment of sensory integration. A child has growth factors that aid healing, potent signals for regeneration of damaged tissue. Crawling and growth factors helped me rewire and gain strength. Why had I not realized this before? Was it possible the adults had known this? St. Hildegard says, "As the knees carry a person and the calves give strength to her feet, so also God carries and strengthens all things."[32] This was literally true.

Then I remembered the day I stood again, shaky and thrilled. I remembered my grandmother's surprise when I took steps. Now the once-humiliating crawling transformed to be the essential precursor to joyful accomplishment. "For the grace of God, in its strength and piety, bends down to the faithful and lifts them."[33] The wonder of it all amazed me. St. Hildegard says, "God's eye sees God's wonders in this person."[34] At last, I did too. God shared God's view with me. "The one whom God sustains will stand, because God is her staff."[35] I saw myself as the recipient of a miracle, "the result of the miracles of God."[36] The science added to, rather than subtracted from, my sense of the miraculous. "God established humankind as the mirror of God's glory and of God's miracles."[37]

Crawling was redeemed. "God created the human being from the mud of the earth, living in soul and body. . . . The human being is thus exceedingly dear to God, Who made her truly in God's own image and likeness."[38] Now it seemed natural and holy to have returned on my knees to the earth that I might live more fully again. It wasn't humiliating; it was logical and right. I was, after all, "made in a wondrous way with great glory from the dust of the earth."[39] There is no shame in intimacy with earth. There I received anew what I needed. "No form of creature walks or stands or is able to be seen unless it has been created and quickened by the water of growth and the life-giving Spirit."[40]

The next day, in prayer, I marveled that my story had itself been healed, made whole and new. My encounter with Jesus, like that of the man at the pool (John 5:1-18), had accomplished what nothing else had. My healing, too, proclaimed Jesus's identity and God's reign. I now remembered the story as God remembered it; I saw it as it really was. I now could imagine the shock, fears, uncertainties, and prayers of the adults who'd been around me, and see that they'd trusted in God's mercy. "People know in their heads that God will help them."[41] I felt compassion for them. I was grateful beyond words that I'd been allowed to crawl, stand, and walk at the pace my healing required.

As I prayed, my attention was drawn again to the fact that I always knew I'd walk again. Was this merely an assumption born of innocence? If so, it would surely have eroded in the harsh reality of the lengthy period of crawling and the numerous failures to stand. *Naive* means "lacking experience." I wasn't naive. I fully experienced my inability to walk.

I prayed to see more deeply into how I always knew. "God is the light from which the mysteries proceed that have the life of the miracles in them. This life is in God,"[42] says St. Hildegard. *Where did my miracle start? How did God help me?*

Spirit was the word that swept into my prayer. *Spirit* was used by others to describe me as a child, and still is even now. I experienced the Holy Spirit. Spirit pervades my journals as wonderfully positive energy, hope, irresistible inspiration, fiery determination, lifting up, vitality, courage, conviction, strength of will and desire, resilience, persistence, and trust in my direction. I experience Spirit as bigger than me and yet imbued in my whole being. As a seven-year-old, I could not have described or understood the Spirit's actions, but I remember being moved forward from within by conviction, determination, and the inner fire I now name as the Spirit. St. Hildegard says, "The human spirit is spiritual; it does not come from the blood, nor is it born out of the flesh, but it emerges from the secret places of God."[43]

So where was God? God graced my own will, desire, determination, and agency to help me rise up and walk. "The soul, burning with a fire ... gives strength to the heart and rules the whole body ... for it gives vitality to the marrow and veins and members of the whole body, as the tree from its root gives sap and greenness to all the branches."[44] God was in my forthright determination, my never giving up, my paradoxical hope.

Jesus asks the man at the pool, "Do you want to be made well?" (John 5:6). The man explains that because of his slow progress —his crawling—others get ahead of him (John 5:7). Jesus says, "Stand up, take your mat and walk" (John 5:8). The man is made well after all his crawling and his encounter with Jesus. He goes to the temple and proclaims Jesus's role in his healing (John 5:9–15). I now saw the man's story as a movement from crawling to standing and walking via Divine collaboration and the strengthening of his own desire, a desire that had not diminished in his lengthy struggle. My story was like this Scripture story.

"The Creator is present to the creature when God gives it green-ness and strength."[45] As a physiologist, I acknowledged the roles of youth, the instinct to crawl out of necessity, and growth factors. I was most fortunate in these. But "God is in the strength of the soul."[46] The part of me that focused on God's actions rejoiced also in Spirit and desire. St. Hildegard quotes God as saying, "In a human body I place the life by which I raised them up."[47] She says, "Whatever lives is first aroused to life invisibly before it moves itself bodily. Hence what is born is called, as it were, aroused by the Spirit."[48] Her idea that "what is born is called" expresses that primordial drawing within us toward fullness of life. We already have inside ourselves the Life by which we are raised up. "What is born is called" is an incarnational and sacramental view of healing.

"The will arises and imparts its taste to the soul, and its lamp is desire."[49] St. Hildegard helps us see the spirituality of will and de-sire. "The soul has breath and desire and will and it is joined to the flesh."[50] She situates these in our soul. Deep desire is "heavenly" and comes "to each and every creature with grace"; it is "the jewel of all the virtues" and "the psalter and harp of God's joy."[51] The Cre-ator can reorder creation through a powerful desire in the heart of a little girl crawling on earth to "lift up her head and learn to walk up-right."[52] We may not realize how it is all working in the moment. "No person can fully know how the soul permeates the human body and blood to make up one life."[53] There is Mystery. "The human spirit in itself testifies to [God] . . . [and] it rises again through [God]."[54]

A few days later, I prayed Psalm 119. My story was rounded out by some of the verses. "My soul clings to the dust; revive me according to Your word." Was that not my unspoken prayer? "You enlarge my understanding. . . Your word is a lamp to my feet and a light to my path" (Ps 119:25, 32, 105). My desire was also God's desire, of this I am certain. To this day, walking is my joy.

REFLECTION QUESTIONS

What is healing?

How do you describe your inner spirit? When has it mattered greatly for you?

"What is born is called." How do you resonate with St. Hildegard's idea?

What is your prayer about God working through your desire, will, inner spirit, and memories to bring healing?

"Attending God"

How do we accompany a directee who has painful memories?

An older woman came for spiritual direction for the first time in her life.[55] She announced, "I need to know where God was in the worst experience of my life. Also, I need to know how to let go of control in prayer." We reviewed a variety of ways to pray and the importance of sharing her story with God. Bit by bit, over the course of a year, she revealed her story to God and to me. The pieces came person by person: first, I learned her father had been killed in a car crash; the following month, I learned she had been in the car; next, she revealed that her mother had been seriously injured; and lastly, she told me her baby brother had also been killed.

I was primarily a compassionate listener for this directee. I encouraged her to pray with each memory of the event and to ask God to reveal God's presence. She also prayed with the psalms to help process her grief.

When she felt ready, the directee specifically asked God to take control of her prayer. When she did this, she experienced a flashback to being a little girl standing by the roadside, her dress covered in blood. Then she remembered that a beloved aunt helped her out of that dress and cared for her in the aftermath of the crash. She felt gratitude for the kindness she had experienced and saw this as God's presence.

As time went on, the directee also recalled her mother's resilience and all she'd done to help her. They had never talked about the story with one another, however, so it was important to her now that she get the chance to talk about it in spiritual direction. She could see the tragedy's impact on her life, but could also see that God was with her to help her. "I believed I had to achieve so much because I lived and my father and brother didn't," she told me. "I thought God expected so much of me. Now I realize God isn't that way." She said she felt more free, comforted by God, and closer to God than ever before. "A new sun came forth, and a new light shone out."[56]

"The mercy of God bends down"

How does God show mercy in our trauma? My childhood injuries threatened my life and caused me to suffer post-traumatic stress disorder (PTSD) in adulthood. I had vivid flashbacks to the most traumatic moments of my experience. Flashbacks are like reliving horrific moments and are difficult to endure. They cause an outpouring of adrenaline, powerful emotions, and shakiness. Great effort is required to regain concentration, focus, and peace, and to be fully in present reality. Therapy provided me with a diagnosis and coping skills but did not eliminate the flashbacks. I learned to live with the flashbacks and nightmares, moving on as best I could after each occurrence.

I had a great job at the time, and despite having PTSD, I was highly functional. "As for you, live, and cause your talent to grow in your Lord,"[57] writes St. Hildegard. This I sought to do; I always prayed about my work and grew ever closer to God.

St. Hildegard writes, quoting God, "I Who am present everywhere also sometimes raise [people] to true health."[58] That was my sense of God, too, and I believed as our saint believed that "my God, through Whom I was created and through Whom I live and to Whom I reach out when I sigh and from Whom I ask for all good things because I know that God is my God and . . . is my Helper in all good things."[59] So, with my love for and trust of God now well established, I asked God for help with my flashbacks. My therapist had said they could be permanent, as PTSD is notoriously difficult to treat. At minimum, I wanted God with me when I experienced them. "O soul, although you are pressed hard by tribulation, the grace of God will see to you, and the storm that afflicts you will not be strong; and when the summer comes, there will be joy,"[60] as St. Hildegard says. I prayed not to lose my joy even as my PTSD flared more than usual and worried me.

"The mercy of God bends down to humans and has compassion on their miseries, and so is available to those who seek it."[61] Mercy came first in the inspiration to treat my flashbacks differently. For days I had brief flashbacks—always the same, reliving the moment of being a terrified seven-year-old lying in the woods, hoping help would come before I died. Over and over again I relived the terror and the feeling of my life ebbing away. Despite their brevity, the flashbacks left me shuddering in horror, then flooded with sadness. One morning in prayer, I came to know I should not turn immediately away from the flashback scene and instead should look at it with God. Where was God in this? Only God could show me.

The flashback scene was vivid and stuck with me, so I prayed with it. I was determined not to turn away. I'd long been hurrying away from this experience. It seemed to me I was therefore inclined to turn away from the suffering of others. As I prayed, I realized the flashback was persisting because its time of healing had arrived. "Knowledge is the breath of life in the soul that has been rewarded with grace."[62]

A feature of PTSD is that the horrific events that caused it are dissociated from a person's present reality. The events have not been integrated into one's overall story, in part because the overwhelming shock was injurious to one's mind. As I prayed, I noted that I knew the rest of the story. I was alive and well and doing great due to God's grace. Logic told me God was in this flashback moment, too, and I wanted to know how God manifested. I became confident that not turning away would truly lead to good. I was ready. St. Hildegard relates God's words: "I wish to wipe away the thick clouds from my daughters."[63] That was my trust.

At first as I stayed with the scene, I felt horror and then sadness about all I'd lost in that one moment, all I would face, and how alone I was. As I looked, however, I sensed God's grief also. "God, Who created you, does not wish to lose you,"[64] says St. Hildegard. Then I understood my stillness and waiting in the scene as the very prayer of my young self. It is hard to describe, but I comprehended a certain beautiful preciousness to God of my seven-year-old self lying there in stillness and waiting. The words of a psalm came to mind: "Precious in the sight of the Lord is the death of God's faithful ones" (Ps 116:15). A great tenderness and Presence filled the scene. I had looked anew at a moment when I assumed I was dying, and it was filled with Love, not fear. I had been loved into life, not death, and I dwelled in that Love still.

The next day's gospel was about the rich man and Lazarus (Luke 16:19–31). In the story, the rich man repeatedly ignored the plight of Lazarus, "who longed to satisfy his hunger with what fell from the rich man's table." Eventually, "a great chasm" was eternally fixed between the rich man and Lazarus. Then and there I resolved not to go to my grave with a great chasm between the self that suffered trauma and the self that quickly moved on. I would be present to my experiences and with God's help find grace, meaning, and healing. I would choose a deeper, more courageous response in hope of the spiritual and psychological freedom for which I greatly hungered.

As I write this today with St. Hildegard, who loves the topic of salvation, I see more in the above decision. To my amazement, she describes the rich man as "sluggish in both fear and honor of God" and as one who does not "look within" or recognize himself "as a human being."[65] In contrast, she describes Lazarus as in touch with his "soul's appetite," "humbled at revealed understanding," and "longing to be filled by the smallest gifts of wisdom."[66] St. Hildegard defines the hell of the rich man as remaining "in great weariness, in despair, without the assurance of complete hope."[67] In her unique exegesis, the rich man's request for Lazarus's help in eternity is an acknowledgment that he lacked the poverty of spirit Lazarus possessed.[68] Within the "great chasm" between them is "the obscurity of God's mysteries."[69]

Susan Garthwaite

St. Hildegard points to "looking within" and recognizing one's humanness as ways to honor God. Indeed, it is hell to lack hope—for example, the hope that PTSD can be healed. I feel gratitude anew for the appetite and longing for whatever God might reveal, for understanding and wisdom. God's mysteries could easily have been left in the gap, had I continued moving on quickly at the slightest glimpse of my trauma. May God be honored by my decision to remain where God could be found, and by the poverty of spirit I embraced in response to grace.

Turning toward, rather than away from, this flashback awakened painful grief over what happened to me as a little girl and how it changed my entire life. One thing led to another in the complexity of healing. That is our fear, right? We may open a giant Pandora's box of troubles if we don't move on quickly. St. Hildegard describes a woman "who has not yet completely shown her hidden wounds."[70] I could not turn away from the hidden wound of grief. At last I was doing what Jesus asked of me in an earlier mystical vision; I was looking at my own wounds.

"Jesus," I prayed, "my heart breaks. It is hard to see the promise in this, to in any way embrace or welcome it."

Jesus responded, "The Abba wastes nothing. The Abba's grief is great. I am with you always."

His confirmation that God shared my grief was so comforting. I was not alone with the big knot below my diaphragm.

Jesus said, "Be not afraid of your own feelings, your own grief."

"How does one grieve?" I asked.

And He said, "With oil on your wounds."

St. Hildegard says, "The Son of God Almighty, descending in true humility . . . came to wash, anoint, and cure our festering wounds with true compassion."[71] The very mention of oil immediately and mysteriously soothed me. I reflected on Jesus's anointing with nard

276

(Mark 14:3–9) and His gratitude for that "good service" performed for Him. He said this act was to be included in the "good news" proclaimed. Could my own anointing be good news? I was baptized, anointed with oil, into the life, passion, death, and resurrection of Christ. St. Hildegard says, "The faithful soul is betrothed through Baptism . . . to Wisdom."[72]

I journaled, "Maybe it's time to re-choose and live out my Baptism, to renew my belief that a cross leads to resurrection." St. Hildegard says, "God will demand that the human be resurrected."[73] Did I expect the life of Christ to be otherwise? I believed my life had become good news. My grief lifted a little. "A person who is anointed by God's grace with the chrism and oil and enkindled with the fire of the Holy Spirit, is born anew and is sanctified through Baptism."[74]

I remembered that in the hospital after my injuries, I was also anointed with oil in the sacraments of confirmation and anointing of the sick (then called *extreme unction*). Did I believe these sacraments had an impact? Yes, I believed they did. St. Hildegard says, "The gentle Creator will rejoice over you and God's word will enlighten your spirit, and the Fiery Lover will shed the ointment of salvation and the invigoration of the flower of wisdom upon you."[75] Anointing with oil meant that God anointed me into a new life, a new way, and a marvelous raising up.

As I journaled I noted the sacramental impact. The Holy Spirit granted me great fortitude for my journey. I felt it powerfully every day. St. Hildegard says, "The dove will anoint you and make you a simple tower before the face of God."[76] Yes, a simple tower, not a person of false, ego-based bravery, seeking to prove something. Instead, I had deep courage and resilience that persisted through trial after trial. Where did these come from, if not the Holy Spirit? I was anointed to the Way of Jesus. The words of the psalms entered my prayer: "Now I know that God will help God's anointed" (Ps 20:6), and

"God is the saving refuge of God's anointed" (Ps 28:8). St. Hildegard says, "We do not perish who have hope in You."[77]

Traditionally, oil was valuable and pervaded life. If one had a lot of it, one was rich. The Church uses oil to symbolize the presence and action of the Holy Spirit. I had so much sacramental oil in my life. I was, indeed, rich with it. St. Hildegard speaks of oil as a "superabundance of fullness," as well as transcendence since "oil floats above other liquids."[78] To her, oil symbolizes what is "beyond measure."[79] The Holy Spirit was the true oil to her as well. She says, "You are the ointment beyond price for open, festering wounds and You transform them into rarest gems."[80] She wrote to an abbess in distress, "May the light of God's grace cover you, and may God anoint you with the ointment of God's mercy. . . . May God anoint you with the viridity of the Holy Spirit."[81] The Holy Spirit is "She Who rubs oil into wounds."[82]

The flashback taken to prayer required processing my grief and meditation on oil and anointing. The work of healing had begun, but was incomplete. "People are vessels which God has fashioned . . . [and] has imbued with God's inspiration so that God might complete all God's works in them."[83] I now knew that I must never turn away from my flashbacks. Instead, I must bring them to prayer, find God with me in the experience, and develop my faith story in its full meaning and purpose, that is, my own scripture. St. Hildegard quotes God's words, "In both the brightness of the day and the darkness of the whirlwind, look to Me, and always seek out the ointment which heals, and you will live forever."[84]

The above scene never returned as a flashback, nor did any flashback that I took to prayer. One by one, they were no longer dissociated events but rather were integrated into the story of God with me. They indeed became "the rarest of gems." The severity of my PTSD declined to a mere whiff—just enough for remembrance that it, too, is part of my story.

Gradually, the difficult process not only healed me but also raised me up and made me a credible witness that good news comes of trauma and suffering. I can convincingly encourage more than superficial prayer for others who desire healing. I turn toward, rather than away from, others in their suffering. These capacities are in great demand in the human situation.

To help others we must be healthy spiritually, for we must give of ourselves. While it may be true that someone with wounds can help another with wounds, it is best to minister from transformed wounds, from awareness of the Good News, and from the ability to focus on another without one's own woundedness unduly stirred. Is this not the way of the Risen One? Restoration gives strength, perspective, and deep faith. "God will give you that life which God looked upon on the first day,"[85] says St. Hildegard.

Yes, only deeper.

"The Son of God endured the same things"

How does Jesus's suffering save us?

When we pray with Jesus in His suffering, we do not feel so alone or diminished in our own. Such prayer can intensify and result in healing. For example, in praying with the gospels or the Stations of the Cross, we realize that Jesus knows what our suffering is like. "Do not be afraid, because you are the vessel of the fiery Spirit. Sometimes you endure tribulation and affliction, but do not be afraid, because the Son of God endured the same things,"[86] says St. Hildegard.

One time, as I prayed the Stations of the Cross, I entered the scenes more fully by imagining details. At the seventh station, "Jesus Falls the Second Time," I pictured Jesus, who had already been tortured, struggling with a cross that grew heavier with each step.

"Christ ... willed to be subject to suffering, for if He had not been able to die as a mortal person, humankind could not have been liberated, and so He would have remained God alone,"[87] says St. Hildegard. In fact, I imagined only His humanness as I visualized Jesus falling under the weight of the cross a second time. In my mind, He hit the ground hard, the heavy cross pressing Him into the dirt. A leg amputee falls more often than nonamputees, so I knew well the sudden stunning of a hard fall. My heart ached for Jesus. How could He get up? Yet Jesus got to His knees, then stood. He persevered, moving forward slowly.

I did not enter this prayer with expectations of Jesus. I wanted only to be with Him in His suffering. But "He came to earth for humankind's deliverance,"[88] and my prayer was mysteriously taken over. As I watched, Jesus turned and looked directly at me. St. Hildegard says, "The Savior's humanity is in the Divinity's Majesty"[89] and "no human can understand fully the profound mystery of the Divinity."[90] I clearly sensed Divine presence as Jesus's look pierced me. He could see all within me—my horror, sorrow, helplessness, and compassion for Him. Yet in His look were also His own distress, anguish, pain, and utter vulnerability. I was deeply moved.

Jesus conveyed that He fully understood my dread and terror, my sense of life ebbing away, my helplessness, the all-out effort I'd made to stay alive, all that was at the heart of my early trauma and haunted me still. "For He knowingly has compassion on human miseries, and is the hope by which people enter into salvation."[91] Jesus understood my every setback and fall. And in this scene, now a vision, where He was my intended focus, He focused on me. "The Son of God will never be exhausted, but will always give the drink of life to those who thirst. For He is the Savior of Life. And we ... now are strengthened by the manifestation."[92] I experienced Jesus's generous love firsthand. "The abundance of Love is of so great an excellence in the flashing gleam of its gifts, that it surpasses all human understanding."[93]

In that mystical moment of extraordinary mutuality, I understood Jesus's experience and He mine. *This, I thought, is truly communion.* St. Hildegard writes, quoting Jesus, "You will endure many tribulations, and I will endure them with you."[94] I offered Jesus my understanding and compassion from experience; He offered the same to me from His experience. The high cost of such intimacy was worth it. In Jesus's look was also healing. "The wounds of humankind . . . may be healed in the wounds and blood of Christ,"[95] writes St. Hildegard. I realized this truth as the weeks wore on and I was no longer haunted by certain parts of my trauma. The truth of Scripture became my truth: "For we do not have a high priest who is unable to sympathize with our weaknesses, but one who in every respect has been tested as we are" (Heb 4:15).

"The true and ardent lamp of Charity was lighted when God so loved humanity that for its love God sent God's Only-Begotten to take a human body,"[96] says St. Hildegard. That Jesus had a body and experienced terrible trauma was a "true and ardent lamp of Charity" for me. I appreciated that more than ever before. I was filled with gratitude for my healing, and for Jesus's incarnation and passion. "We recognize His incarnation through ourselves."[97] In our humanity we recognize His humanity. In our passion we know His passion and He ours. St. Hildegard says Jesus's passion is like an inn where He brings us to be cured.[98] As Scripture says, "He took on our infirmities" (Matt 8:17; Isa 53:4). My healing proclaims Jesus's true identity as God incarnate. How significant my wounds were to Jesus and His to me!

To identify with Jesus's passion is to identify with His raising up. "In the Passion of Jesus, this virtue [salvation] became the strong heart of the believing people,"[99] says St. Hildegard. In a mystical way, I was present at Jesus's passion as one who could both see and be seen. I was befriended by the One I sought to befriend. I was not alone with my struggles. Such intimacy was my salvation and healing. Our relationship was imperishable, made deeper by the very experience that could have distanced me from God. "And why is Jesus beloved? Because He treads underfoot whatever obstructs the faithful soul."[100]

"The great brightness, the Son of God, appeared for the health and salvation of humanity, taking on the poverty of a human body, but shining like a burning star amid shadowy clouds."[101] Gentle healing power, not failure, shines "like a burning star" in Jesus's passion. I was amazed. "He exuded the sweetest balm from which flows all good things for salvation."[102] Balm—soothing, comforting, healing, restorative grace—flowed in abundance.

To glimpse Jesus's dread helped me with mine. Over time, prayer with different aspects of Jesus's suffering touched on more experiences we shared, and brought intense communion and deep healing. Jesus invited me to turn my gaze toward experiences I was loathe to confront, drawing me to do so and yet honoring my choice. Gradually, I felt only reluctance—not loathing, not the overpowering dread that had once blocked my healing. My urge to turn away, to give up the mission of healing and to remain pressed to the earth by my own cross, was gone. Jesus had chosen the perfect beginning for a lengthy process. Steadily, He "turned every evil . . . into something better."[103]

The more I realized that healing would be the outcome, the more willing I was. I sometimes asked for healing of specific things that troubled me. I marveled at my seeking because it required confronting. "The Savior has power in you greater than the frailty of your flesh. In the impossibility and powerlessness of your flesh you are seeking Jesus of Nazareth, Who will be sanctified in your flesh. He was crucified, and is crucified in you, as it is written: 'Truly He bore our weaknesses' (Isa 53:4), because He suffered for us. He is risen in your holiness to run the course,"[104] says St. Hildegard. Is deeper love and intimacy with Jesus what she means by "your holiness"? The "powerlessness" of my wounds sought Jesus. I was now bold about that. "Let us therefore approach the throne of grace with boldness, so that we may receive mercy and find grace to help in time of need" (Heb 4:16). He is crucified in me and rises in me.

What occurred in the depths of prayer was so different than I'd expected. I reflected on old messages now challenged by new faith. "Offer it up," a persistent message in Catholic mentality, made me cringe. I could not fathom a God Who desired my suffering or was pleased by it. Yet the sacrifice of the cross was now a less objectionable message. St. Hildegard says, "The voice of a person's outpoured blood rises up through her soul to cry out and lament that it has been driven from the seal of the body in which God had placed it."[105] What happened to me was contrary to God's intent. I desired to cry out and lament, not to passively offer it up as though God demanded such sacrifice of me or of Jesus. The damage to my very being, to my fullness of life, already rested upon the altar of the human condition. God had already received it and was doing something new with it. I merely offered my openness to God's activity.

Sacrifice comes from *sacra*, "holy or sacred," and *facere*, "to make or do." God made my experience holy. My personal sacrifice—what I'd given up—had initiated a different life, and now God called me to fully embrace it as a life made holy by God. I had not intentionally made this covenant, but there it was. "Blessed is the person who clings ever to God in everything."[106] God responded to my offer of self and my openness in a way that brought fruitfulness. God acted first, taking my situation very seriously, creating something new. I could see God's will to save, to make holy. "For God was moved by great mercy over God's own work."[107]

Mystical moments of deep healing in prayer with Jesus suffering accumulated. I noted the sheer volume of Scriptures, liturgical time, and devotions given to the theme of Jesus's passion and crucifixion. "The good Physician is not slow to mercifully anoint the wounds of humankind."[108] These events still save and free us today if we are open, willing, and praying deeply. "He took on humanity in order to liberate."[109] We are healed by Jesus's wounds (1 Pet 2:24), that through His blood we could be brought near to God (Eph 2:13). The cup of His blood poured out is truly a covenant (Luke 22:20). I carry in my own body Jesus's experience (2 Cor 4:8–12).

Insofar as much of my sinfulness was driven by my woundedness, healing and forgiveness were linked (Luke 5:23). Jesus includes forgiveness in healing a paralyzed man, then says, "Which is easier, to say, 'Your sins are forgiven you,' or to say, 'Stand up and walk'?" Being forgiven requires of us that we forgive others. Those of us who have suffered much from our disabilities have people, institutions, and cultures to forgive. So, yes, the path of forgiveness is hard. But if we receive healing and a new ability to stand up and walk, we can also forgive. If our sins are forgiven, we can show great love (Luke 7:36–50). Being able to show great love is to not be disabled.

I now knew Jesus as the Great Foreshadower. I remembered the mystical conversation about light in my wounds. I'd said to Jesus, "Can my wounds be like Yours?" Jesus replied, "Yes. They will be. I will change them. You will see." And He did so. I journaled, "In healing I came to appreciate that the self, a person, is the pearl of great price." As St. Hildegard says, "God has mercifully remembered God's great work and God's precious pearl."[110]

REFLECTION QUESTIONS

How does God share in your grief?

In what way has a transformed wound become your "rarest gem"?

Does it matter that Jesus was "tested as we are"? How so?

What is your prayer about healing what is difficult to heal in your life?

"Everything is . . . life in God"

When you struggle to accept something, what behaviors do you tend toward?

"She is continually racked with pain. . . . She has often been shaken by a deep weariness because of it. . . . But sometimes, with the great force of Her loving kindness, God's Spirit lifts her up out of this infirmity . . . so that she can continue to live in the world and function under the Holy Spirit's inspiration."[111] St. Hildegard describes her own path, her own call to acceptance of all that vexes her. She describes having "many grave infirmities of the body, yet also flooded by the depth of God's mysteries."[112] Acceptance means we say yes to receiving or undertaking what comes; we assent to our present reality. St. Hildegard points to a deeper acceptance, one in which we live as instruments of service, privy to God's mysteries.

At a workshop I encountered someone who, with every opportunity, spoke of wanting her life to be different. Much of her energy seemed taken up with protesting and battling against whatever she did not like about herself or her experiences, none of which seemed particularly awful to me. The constant return to these topics wore on me and sparked a little anger within me. In my mind I prayed, *God have mercy on us.* "When a person fights against God without any moderation, she brings about the destruction of her soul. She refuses to be with God."[113] Where was God? Better yet, where was the search for God?

That evening I read two contrasting stories in a magazine devoted to limb loss. In one story, the amputee wrote of many woes and struggles, dwelling on how hard it is to live without a limb, how intact people don't understand, and so on. The writer was honest but did not inspire. In the other story, the amputee was a self-proclaimed hero who took on risky endeavors, including the motorcycle riding that had resulted in his leg loss in the first place. I felt shocked and disturbed, and certainly not inspired, by his words.

Perhaps the editor set these stories side by side on purpose. I felt sparks of anger in response to both. I acknowledged that the authors had no duty to inspire me. Purely secular writing about human tragedy often strikes me as an incomplete story. "Everything . . . is life in God. . . . God gave us the life of the Spirit,"[114] says St. Hildegard, and so say I. She suggests that our desire to "Escape [life's] punishments" is best handled by "turning to the spiritual life,"[115] for "the soul is the headmistress of its house, the body."[116]

The next morning, in prayer, I gently probed my anger. By then in my life I had learned that anger often alerts me to what is important to me or tells me I am near to a truth I have not yet accepted. St. Hildegard writes, "When anger tries to burn up my tabernacle, I will look to the goodness of God."[117] I prayed with a poem that reminded me of my creaturehood and of God's arms around me. I prayed to know my feelings, to let them come, to be honest about them with God, and to see my struggles as God sees them. "The Holy Spirit, by Its power, draws the human mind . . . that it may share in the vision of the Spirit, Whose eyes are not obscured . . . and Who sees the inner things."[118]

I admitted to myself and to God that I felt anger at both sob stories and hero stories, even though these were common reactions to life's major disruptions. I was judging and labeling, impatient and annoyed, and feeling desolation. As I recalled the workshop woman's words, I felt anger anew. I did not believe it fruitful to pine for a life different than what one has. Out of my mouth came, "Where, dear God, was gratitude or acceptance?"

Aha! Where was *my own* gratitude and acceptance? "Not that any virtue is a living form in itself, but a brilliant star given by God that shines forth in human deeds. For humanity is perfected by virtues, which are the deeds of people working in God."[119] I knew the virtues of patience, gratitude, and acceptance were not shining forth from me.

Three weeks of international travel had exacerbated my disability. I'd endured long, grueling airplane rides, lengthy lines, luggage handling, problems getting accessible hotel rooms, and prolonged sitting in conference rooms. I was still tired and uncomfortable. "O soul, you are exceedingly weary, caught up as you are in the ceaseless turning of the mill wheel, but God loves you,"[120] says St. Hildegard. Now, in the loving arms of God, my anger readily bubbled up. I was angry that my limitations would never cease making things more difficult for me than for my able-bodied colleagues. "For concerning every matter that cannot be recuperated or restored, it is necessary that a human . . . have consolation when nothing else can be done,"[121] says St. Hildegard.

Usually I avoided comparing myself to others, but there it was. I was on a roll in my complaints to God. I told God that the situations, the culture, the importance of the work—and, most of all, I myself— demanded that I heroically press on, keep up, and never let my health challenges be an issue in my work. I wasn't telling God anything new. "Almighty God—Who truly recognizes this person's very wearied suffering—deigns to perfect God's grace in her,"[122] says St. Hildegard. If this was the grace of self-honesty, we were definitely getting somewhere. I admitted to God that I kept my story and my challenges tucked within brackets at work and often in prayer.

St. Hildegard, in her preaching, reminded listeners that we are tempted into deceptions, vanities, idols, and delusions. We do not comprehend that we have thrown ourselves into a trap.[123] As I prayed, my eyes were opened. *How unrealistic is my endless pressing on!* My false heroism had backfired. A false self collapsed with an inner clatter. My attitudes toward others were distorted by my entrapment. "The envious do not love the good that they see and find in others."[124] I had not seen the good. I now prayed in solidarity with the workshop woman and the amputee writers, "God have mercy; help us to patience, gratitude, acceptance, and balance." St. Hildegard rightly says that "afflictions fight against pride."[125] I was in a different place spiritually. My anger was gone.

The next day, I prayerfully reflected on gratitude. *How ironic that my path through life is actually quite successful. I am alive and walking. I have a great job with financial security and benefits. I find research to be fascinating and am doing well in it. I am generally happy and optimistic. I am able to do so much, even golf. I've grown spiritually and rejoice that God is my true richness.* "God gave human beings the ability to work; God also divided up their knowledge so that they could discern what is honest and what is dishonest,"[126] says St. Hildegard. I concluded that my heroic pressing on was dishonest; it thwarted my true gratitude.

I could support my disabled self better, not ignore my needs, and engage in self-advocacy. I could pry the brackets off this aspect of my life and let its reality speak. I felt grateful. A sense of freedom arrived in my heart. Possibility loomed. *My life need not be so hard. God loves me as I am and will help me.* "How could any creation of Mine be void and useless,"[127] says God to St. Hildegard. "As long as she desires help, . . . help will be given her, for if she calls upon God, God will help her."[128] I prayed for help to love myself in concrete ways.

St. Hildegard writes, quoting God, "I think about what is needed and I do that."[129] *What does mercy toward self look like?* I asked myself.

At work, I opened up about my challenges. I visited the occupational health department and got support for things I needed. Remember Marcie? By now she had become an office ergonomics assistant. She fitted me for a more appropriate office chair. She began to demand faxed confirmations for accessible rooms at my destinations to ensure accountability. She was delighted and enthused about helping me. All it had required was humility and openness on my part. "Choose for yourself humility, mercy, and temperance, along with all the other holy virtues,"[130] says St. Hildegard. That it was virtuous to love myself concretely was a new thought.

Confronting my needs did, however, underline my loss. "She will beat her breast as she remembers her younger life, the younger life she can no longer have,"[131] says St. Hildegard. In prayer I sensed God sharing my sorrow and helping me to see that others who loved me shared that as well. A feeling of mutuality swept over me and heartened me. I felt less isolated and more accepting of my loss. "And what consolation do I have? That which pilgrims have."[132] I was on a pilgrimage of acceptance, God was on it with me, and I desired to be faithful to it. "This is better for you than pilgrimages to foreign lands, because God has the same power . . . in all places."[133] St. Hildegard says "sorrow of the heart" reduces our resistance to God. [134] It is healthy to process it. She says, "God reminds us often to pray to God and inwardly lament and weep that God may deliver us."[135]

After time and space for gratitude and sorrow, my prayer shifted to God dwelling within me. "When the Word of God resounded, that

Word appeared in all creation, and its sound was life in all creation."[136] It dawned on me: *Everything that happens to me happens to God within me.* "God lives in your tabernacle [body], and God's grace is not overshadowed there,"[137] says St. Hildegard. *God experiences everything with me.* "Therefore I will endure [miseries] with you, since you are in Me and I am in you."[138] *Not only does God accept me as I am, God accepts all my challenges as God's own.* "I choose to share in and pity your pains,"[139] says God to St. Hildegard. *God accepts it all, and I desire to as well. What God embraces, I embrace. God and I are covenant partners. God is right here within me.*

Now I felt a sense of, "Where have I been?" I wrote, "Yes. Yes. My yes is my commitment to stick with it, to be with You, God, in full embrace of my challenges, to find a path of holiness." I recalled Mary's yes to whatever was ahead, to experiences and trials she could not predict. Her trusting yes brought light into the world. "The land of integrity flourished always in her."[140] I desired to be a person of integrity in covenant with God. In Mary's yes, says St. Hildegard, "a closed portal has opened."[141] I prayed, "May Your willingness be my willingness, Your acceptance my acceptance."

Christian life is shaped like a cross. Why should I be excused? Life is a cruciform adventure with God. Jesus is Truth (John 14:6). He told us the truth (John 18:37) about our lives, including that we will suffer (Matt 24:9). I could, like St. Paul, bear the marks of Christ on my body (Gal 6:17) and let that "mean fruitful labor for me" (Phil 1:22). St. Hildegard writes, quoting God, "Let her not doubt because she must struggle, for . . . I will help her most speedily and hold her as a friend; for patiently enduring, she has nobly conquered great misfortunes for love of Me."[142] Maybe this was the real truth my anger signaled. "You will frequently experience great tribulation—not like a prodigal son, but like the friend of God,"[143] says St. Hildegard.

What is my attitude toward my cross? I asked myself. *What does it mean in my friendship with God? I shall take it up and follow, carry it with patience, humility, gratitude, acceptance, love, and compassion for others carrying crosses.* "Make sure also that you bear your tribulations with patience, for through them, all the virtues are made more lovely in you,"[144] says St. Hildegard. I felt inspired and challenged by the call to discipleship instead of pulled down by my struggles.

Removing the brackets around my story and my challenges had an impact in prayer. My reality was opened to saving, healing grace. As promised—"I will help her most speedily and hold her as a friend"[145]—God befriended me in my struggle toward acceptance. My friendships at work also deepened as I grew more open, revealing, and vulnerable, as well as more sensitive to others' struggles. Gradually, I became a better witness to the grace of acceptance. "And thus the human being, having been delivered, shines in God, and God in the human being."[146]

Spiritual integrity means I must frequently go deeper. What is beyond or deeper than my present reality? How do I live in a more co-creative way, a way that is holy, right, and relational? "That person is blessed who is awakened to heavenly things."[147] My glimpse of God's wondrous presence in my struggles revealed that they were full of hope and worth the price. "I am present to every creature in true manifestation, never withdrawing My power from them,"[148] says God to St. Hildegard. My spirituality matured and became more authentic as I grew in right relationship with my physical limitations. "When the soul sustains the body, the body's works are lifted back up. . . . The soul strives for a measure of rightness, while the human body often races off into excess."[149]

What does a person who embraces acceptance and who has spiritual integrity look like? She seeks a deeper response to her situation and neither whines nor pretends to be unduly heroic. She does not seek more than her share of sympathy. She lives at the far reaches of her capability with creativity and zest; her life is right-sized, for "grace comes in great abundance and fruitfulness."[150] She lives out her awareness that God shares her experiences. She venerates her cross with sincerity and respect, boldly grateful for it as the locus of her raising up. She begins "to live in moral integrity . . . [and to] show that the good intention of her heart shines."[151] She knows joy and has a good spirit. "All viridity is of the Spirit."[152] In her journal is this prayer: "Dear God, I remain hopeful that You enjoy Your life in me."

Acceptance requires renewal. At times I tilt toward heroism or toward protest and complaint. New issues arise that I struggle to embrace and work with creatively. St. Hildegard says, "No one can have peace without anxiety in this present life, but only in life everlasting."[153] In these times, I seek balance and acceptance anew. I again seek a deeper response. Now, however, I know that deep inside I am still fine. "When a person [practices] patience, she ought to bear both prosperity and tribulation with equanimity."[154] I know my experience is God's experience, too. That is my strength and the heart of my renewed acceptance.

"Loving yourself in all this you shall also love your neighbor."[155] Our healing and acceptance make us authentic in helping others who seek healing and acceptance. We minister from a state of transformation. Our healing and acceptance are credible signs of God's presence, action, and will to heal us. "Do all things in moderation. Act in this way, lest you scatter Christ's flock."[156] Finding the sweet spot in our own capacity guards against distortions in how we see others. Our receipt of mercy inspires mercy for others. "For God is always merciful and lenient to that person who imitates God in mercy, for the holy and the elect, the poor and the weak, all are in need of mercy."[157]

Acceptance means embrace of Mystery. My medical science background became the backdrop for seeing more deeply into the mystery of healing. God did so much that medical science could not do. One day I journaled, "I am trying to open up to all sides of healing, to believe what I do not understand, to not be arrogant about my science. For I have felt over time that healing reverberates through me, eases my body's suffering, diminishes the frequency and severity of pain." Praying, especially for others, lightens my pain and brings me peace. "Humans, too, should lovingly desire Divine Love and embrace humility and hold also onto peace,"[158] says St. Hildegard. Praying returns me to my soul, the dwelling place of God throughout my being, and invites God's anointing anew. "Fiery Spirit, fount of courage, life within life of all that has being!"[159]

Our baptism calls us to work with God to alleviate suffering, including our own. However, we must also accept that some suffering is part of the human condition and cannot be escaped. In fact, attempts to escape via false comforts are not our deepest response. Only from the vantage point of our difficult condition can we grasp the wonder of our unconditional love for God. That same unconditional love is revealed by all who have been sorely tested and yet still turn to God—not just in need but also in love. In one lengthy locution, God said to me, "Imagine what it feels like, Sue, to be the God Who created a world that hurt you so much. Imagine My desire to embrace you, help you, bless you, heal you, to make it all count, to bless others with it. Be that wonderful blessing of compassion, healing, love, patience, appreciation, and humility today. Feed my sheep." And so we pray with St. Hildegard: "Cleanse Your children of their wounds with Your anointing oil, O Shepherd of souls, O Earliest Voice through which all creatures were created."[160]

"Attending God"

How can spiritual directors help those who have experienced trauma?

Practicing spiritual directors soon discover that trauma is common in the lives of directees. We have looked at one example above. Studies show that persons with firm spiritual grounding are more successful in healing. "The human . . . is strengthened and preserved with God's grace through the soul . . . like a medicine."[161] Spiritual directors therefore have a role in God's healing work. We are wise to learn more about it in our training, from our reading, and through mentors. Diagnosis and treatment are roles for health professionals, not spiritual directors, and we should refer people who need such professionals. If our own wounds await transformation, we should also refer to another spiritual director those directees whose experiences unduly awaken our own woundedness. If we are prepared, however, we can support and encourage deep healing through prayer. St. Hildegard says, "God's power sanctifies the faithful in the wonders of its grace."[162]

A fellow spiritual director and I noted what directors and directees may experience as God seeks to heal the directee.[163] For both, it becomes apparent that "God is in the strength of the soul. . . . And the strength of the soul has the courage and firmness of holiness."[164] The starting place is to help the directee feel safe and to begin integrating all experiences into the spiritual journey. As directors of people with trauma, we avoid pressing for details and mainly offer calm support, acceptance, reassurance, empathy, and gentle encouragement to bring all to prayer. St. Hildegard says, "Show God your wounds and seek medicine from God."[165] We express willingness to hear, but we do not probe.

A second feature of spiritual direction with these directees concerns the story of where God was in all that happened. Years may pass as the directee remembers and reveals fragments of the story. Each fragment must be faced, the feelings processed, God found in it, and then the piece integrated into a deepening story. The directee will not be the typical person, dwelling in the present; she will frequently return to the past. The director will be sustained by God in patient, compassionate listening as a new exodus story is woven into being, and will repeatedly reassure the directee, "God does not hide God's face from you."[166]

The directee may grapple mightily with the question of where God was in an otherwise hideous story. In spiritual direction, perhaps more so than any other space, we explicitly explore that question. As directors, we must be confident within ourselves of God's presence in the story, for we set God up as the One to Whom the directee poses that question. We may offer Jesus's Psalm 22 prayer and difficult stories from Scripture as aids for the directee's prayer, and point out that we are not alone with the question. Then we must prayerfully and trustingly wait for the directee's discovery.

The director must be cautious not to deny or minimize the evil of what has happened in favor of prematurely pushing a healing narrative or defending God from accusations that come God's way. "Although they each work in different ways, they all tend toward a single blessedness."[167] The process may be repetitious beyond imagining; even so, the directee is not so much stuck as still searching. The director should encourage openness, courage, and surrender to deep prayer. God sprinkles "heavenly grace upon God's people with the dew of divinity like a drop of honey."[168] Drips and drops are typical, for God does not move faster than the directee can handle, and the directee ought not run ahead of the grace, risking retraumatization.

"I am restored . . . and become a companion of God,"[169] says St. Hildegard. Another feature of the spiritual journey of deep healing is revision of beliefs. Ironically, as God and grace are discovered, the story of what happened requires the greatest revision. The story is no longer only a tragic human story. Now it is a drama of God's love for the directee, a story with deep meaning and connection to the larger story of God with us.

As new freedom and new encounters with God arrive, the directee can finally step back and consider, *What does this say about God, my images of God, my thoughts about Jesus, the sacraments and my faith tradition, and me as an incarnation of the Spirit? Where does my story fit in the community's story of God with us? Are God and good truly more powerful than traumatic experience? How do I tell my new story? What does my new freedom make possible?* "For it is through . . . distresses that a person often achieves spiritual wealth, and through that wealth gains entry into the heavenly kingdom."[170]

The spiritual director is not only a witness but also a midwife for the evolving story. We may safely pose the above questions when the moment seems right. For us there will be wondrous gratitude for the opportunity to participate with God in the directee's deep healing through prayer.

REFLECTION QUESTIONS

To what do your own sparks of anger alert you? How do you pray about them?

How does "prying the brackets off" your experience begin to change it?

What helps you feel safe with your spiritual director?

What is your prayer about acceptance and about directing those who seek deep healing in prayer?

———•••———

chapter fifteen

UNION WITH GOD

"O wholesome and upright desires"

W here is your spiritual journey taking you?

We know we are destined to be with God eternally. "God will greatly love you, and you will live with God in eternity."[1] But what is possible in our earthly life? Desire for God and what is of God can seem a persistent inner ache. I once journaled, "Desire is the best thing I can offer God. My will can simply be to align with God's will. I find my desires must sometimes be purified, letting go of those that are not of God and aligning with more vigor to those that are of God. To desire what God desires, that is a holy and pure-hearted life." St. Hildegard says, "O wholesome and upright desires, how resplendent you are when your sweet fragrance rises to God!"[2]

I learned from the great saints the spiritual advantages of recollecting God in prayer. I remember God's presence within me and the intimacy of our relationship. I pull myself away from distractions and think only of God. The practice eases that inner ache for God, Who is quietly present. I wrote, "To recollect God, I recollect my Friend. I appreciate what God is like. I remember key moments. I bask in God's fondness for me and mine for God, and think of how I can always count on God. I love the Mystery and Presence, the breathless adventure which is an experience in and of itself." Recollection deepens awareness of graces. St. Hildegard says, "A river from the Holy Spirit will flow into you, and will water all these things in you."[3]

Another time I wrote, "My memory is filled with God—all the ways that God saved me, loved me, challenged me, helped me, strengthened me, taught me, healed me, guided me, inspired me, gifted me, blessed me, sought me, found me, anointed me, called me, formed me, and befriended me." Could there be more?

St. Hildegard tells God, "When You created me, You gave me to act following You, as You also made me to be Yours."[4] I began to realize this, too, with God's help. God, perceived in Her feminine Sophia image, engaged me in playful, yet serious, banter in prayer to help me see what was missing in our life together:

Sophia: I am with you always.

Sue: I am at Your service.

Sophia: Oh, really?

Sue: I know, Sophia, Your work is not one of my jobs yet. I'm working on that.

Sophia: And yet, your work is my job, Sue.

Sue: Yes, I'm full of unawareness, lack of understanding, and even arrogance. Can you help me get clear in myself?

Sophia: You are My work, Sue.

Sue: It would seem so. I am Your work. Okay. Are You my work? God is my work? Sounds good. Not do God's work, but God is my work. Makes it easier. Hmmmm . . . God in all.

Sophia: The trouble starts when you categorize, Sue.

Sue: God is my work in my projects. God is my work. Why does that sound so different than doing God's work? God is the Work/ Word, what I do and be. Hmmmm . . . God is my project.

Sophia: When you have grown to love Me in all the places I am, then shall we be united.

St. Hildegard says, "Some people hold their work as equal to God's. They even call their work their God."[5] Sophia's message to me was opposite that of making work my god. "Because God is full Life without beginning and without end, so a person's work is also life in God."[6] Apparently the issue is not only a contemporary one. In my case the encouragement was to put God first, letting work be all about God.

Shortly after that dialogue, the gospel reading was John 15:1–11, about Jesus the vine and we the branches. It concludes, "So that My joy may be in you, and that your joy may be complete." I experienced bursts of joy, but I could not say it was "complete" or constant. I sometimes felt my branchiness and sometimes did not, like a faulty graft that periodically lost connection with the vine. "Constancy," as St. Hildegard says, "is the pillar and rampart of the virtues."[7] My only hope for constancy was to remain on the Vine. And, I knew it to be true that "the branch cannot bear fruit by itself" (John 15:4) and certainly not "fruit that will last" (John 15:16). How essential that I remain on the Vine! "The person of faith brings forth good sweet fruit."[8] What could I do but pray to remain?

I made it my prayer to live "God is my work" and to be continually on the Vine. I recollected more often during my day. I grew more perceptive of situations that threatened my remaining on the Vine, times when I felt pulled or tempted away. I recalled Sophia's counsel to "love Me in all the places I am." We "cannot escape God by running or fleeing."[9] *If God is my work*, I thought, *I stand for what God stands for.* I sought constancy in asserting service to patients in my pharmaceutical job even as other forces blew. "To the sight of Almighty God all roads are open that the living human mind can choose in the present state of its wisdom."[10]

Imagining the reign of God in a pharmaceutical company felt radical and bracing and closer to "God is my work." I journaled, "Cooperate with and support what God is doing, fidelity to that. Let God worry about the success. Let what I say be the product of prayer and reflection. I don't need any agendas of my own, for God is my work." God supported my every effort. "God is the weigher of spirits; God treats persons tenderly with sweet caresses and peace . . . that they may be conformed to the right measure."[11]

"The great clarity of God's visitation"

What is it like to be a branch on the Vine?

Now and then in prayer, through no effort of my own, I was drawn up into God as though God had simply soaked me up. The experience was more thorough than an embrace; it was more an assimilation. I found it wondrous, like I had great love both within and around me. Abundant strength and courage were imparted to me. "God Who rules every created being imparts the power and strength of this blessedness by the great clarity of God's visitation."[12] These experiences were brief. I journaled, "You live in me and I in You. How little I have understood. A deep sense of union that I can feel in every fiber of my being. Brief, but powerful and deeply pleasurable." I understood my inner ache for God as God's drawing me to God.

Afterward, I did not feel shaky or disoriented as I did in the stripping-away described earlier. Instead, I felt joyful and strong. I wrote, "This must surely be what a well-connected, sturdy branch on the Vine feels like." I felt ready for anything. "The Most Powerful Giver Whom no one can resist has given you wings to fly with. Therefore fly swiftly over all these obstacles! And I, comforted with great consolation, took wing,"[13] says St. Hildegard. My experiences fed my recollections and renewed my fervor in "God is my work." As it turned out, I would finish my scientific career in this way.

The company I worked for was purchased by a larger company. The labs in my area were closed, and we received severance packages. I went off to do the Spiritual Exercises of St. Ignatius in a thirty-day retreat. I planned to seek a new pharma job in my area upon my return. As the retreat unfolded, however, I grew less certain about continuing in pharma and more drawn to "God is my work" in a new, ever-fuller way. My desire grew to speak openly of God and to use spiritual language in complete freedom. My desire to write of spiritual matters bubbled up in greater force. I journaled, "It is pointless to try to hold back from the radical ways of God." St. Hildegard says, "The searchers, inquirers for good things, [leave] themselves behind and put aside their own wills."[14]

"In no way can a person grasp this Love with her senses"

Is there anything between you and God?

One afternoon during the thirty-day retreat, I sat in the choir loft of a big chapel. I dwelled in gratitude for the graces of the morning and rested with God before the afternoon exercises. By then I had been in silence for two weeks. With ease, I was still within.

With no effort on my part or sense that it was coming, I felt drawn upward, as though I was metal pulled toward a powerful magnet above me. Then there was nothing; no consciousness of what was happening. No sense of time. Nothing. Blank.

At some point I was released downward, as though that powerful electromagnet had been turned off. I did not know how long I'd been lost to the world and had no sensory information about the state I'd been in—just the initial drawing and the final release. "The abundance of Love is of so great an excellence in the flashing gleam of Her gifts, that She surpasses all human understanding and the faculty of knowledge . . . so much so that humans cannot in any way grasp Love with the senses,"[15] says St. Hildegard. She describes an experience in which "all my inner parts were shaken, and my bodily senses were wiped out. My knowledge was converted to something else, as if I did not know myself."[16] Surely St. Hildegard speaks of an experience similar to mine.

I did not believe I'd lost consciousness or fallen asleep. I was sitting exactly as I had been. I was aware of the beginning and end of the experience and had not felt sleepy or faint. I had not known such an experience was possible in prayer. What was this? "God . . . is so hidden in God's deep profundity that God surpasses all understanding of the human mind."[17]

Usually God and I had an interpersonal relationship: there was God and there was me. Had that changed momentarily? How difficult it is to describe the experience with no data from my senses. I knew I could neither create nor imagine such a state on my own. I concluded it was God's mysterious doing. "God is beyond the mind and understanding of all creatures."[18] I was mainly puzzled. I thought perhaps I was more open or susceptible to unusual experiences due to my retreat. I moved on to the afternoon exercises.

The next day, with my retreat director, I focused on graces specific to the exercises. Only in passing did I mention the unusual experience in the choir loft. My director simply said, "Such graces usually deepen," and we left it at that.

The retreat went on in grace-filled manner until at last I was heading home. The final exercise, "The Contemplation to Attain Love," continued at home. The idea was to review all the graces of the retreat and all I'd journaled so that "the true power and deeds and goal of the grace of God working in humans can be [more] fully known."[19] The exercise deepens love for God and willingness to follow Jesus. "Collect yourself in the sweetness of God's love,"[20] as

St. Hildegard says. I prayed the exercise over several weeks, and the fruits were many.

When I encountered my scant journal note about the choir-loft experience, I wondered anew. An incomprehensibly lofty event had occurred in an actual loft. I had no new understanding of it. I did not think it was part of the Spiritual Exercises, per se. It seemed somehow separate, except perhaps for the receptivity the exercises fostered. "Where no sound is heard, no meaning is used . . . no word will be understood."[21] I did not encounter it in books about the exercises, and later, when I wrote papers about my experience of the exercises, I left it out.

Then I had the opportunity to talk about St. Teresa of Ávila's *The Interior Castle* for a university class. As I created slides, I realized that I understood the material better than I had before due to my own experiences. "The Holy Spirit saw you as Her own habitation,"[22] as St. Hildegard says. During the class discussion, I responded to questions about union with God as though I knew what I was talking about. I explained that St. Teresa described a union that involved conscious, wondrous drawing into God, and also one with no consciousness of what happens. As I completed my sentence, I felt terribly exposed and shy. I could feel myself blushing—"aglow before God through a trellis of saints,"[23] as St. Hildegard says. I drove home thinking, *This is absurd. I am not the saint Teresa is. How could this be my experience, too?*

Since leaving pharma, I'd developed an active spiritual direction practice and begun writing a spiritual memoir. For the latter, I again confronted the strange choir-loft experience. I was on retreat again with the same director, so I brought it up. She remembered it. I described what had happened when I'd worked with St. Teresa's insights.

"Yes," my director said, "prayer of union."

"Yes, I now think so too," I said, "but what, exactly, is it?"

We agreed I'd pray about that. If God wanted me to know more, I was open. "God is God Who lives and Who is capable and Who knows."[24]

A short while later, during Mass, in the silence after communion, I posed my question to God and God said, clear as can be, "It is a moment when there is nothing between us." *Wow.* That made sense to me. Locutions always bring a succinct understanding beyond my own thinking. God affirmed the experience and explained it in one short sentence. I felt humbled, amazed, and grateful.

The next day, I repeated the locution to my director and we marveled together. I said, "It's bittersweet, really, because it is to say there are many more moments when there is in fact something between us. And yet maybe it is a taste of eternity. I have that sense of it." St. Hildegard says, "The Holy Spirit reveals eternity."[25] And she says, "What is eternity? It is God."[26] I felt grateful for humility and perspective, and to know that God desires such moments with us and reveals about them. My director encouraged me to savor the graces and to remain open to anything more God wished to reveal.

Years later, I discovered that God repeats Godself, just as I often repeat myself. I found the following report of God's words in the writing of St. Mechthild of Magdeburg: "Lady Soul, you are so utterly formed to My nature that not the slightest thing can be between you and Me."[27] Though the words were not the same, the description of union seemed analogous to me. St. Hildegard also says something similar: "O daughters of Jerusalem . . . no one can separate you from Him."[28] The saints inspired me to reflect on what the prayer of union had wrought in me. Was there a before and a more permanent after?

"*Your body's a chalice*"

Does union with God change a person?

St. Teresa says we cannot be fruitful with our faculties suspended as they are in the "nothing between us" state. St. Hildegard lauds our rationality as critical for discipleship: "Blessed is the person whom God made a tabernacle of wisdom, for she always ascends, with her five senses intact, from newness to newness, until the end of her life."[29] Ultimately, then, union with God involves our lasting inclination toward God, our being "formed to God's nature," as St. Mechthild said, and yet we are rational and aware. I returned to God's words to me, to Scripture, to my journals, and to prayer, seeking to more deeply comprehend the gifts and fruits of union with God in my day-to-day experience.

I have never forgotten the encouragement to live out "God is my work." Grace is always available to help me live that way. St. Hildegard quotes God's words, "Through Me you have in yourself all the means to work."[30] God's work is my work without distinction. I no longer feel that I shift between my own occupations and God's work. We are united in work. I once journaled, "A new era has been entered into of partnership and paying attention to God's agenda in everything. I learned I will sometimes bleed and have the pain of a heart filled with compassion." St. Hildegard says, "The Son of God directs a merciful gaze toward people."[31] May His gaze be our gaze as well, His hands our hands. Does union mean, as St. Hildegard says, "Your body's a chalice, its wine never drained"?[32]

Sophia told me, "When you have grown to love Me in all the places I am, then shall we be united." Ignatian spirituality also emphasizes "finding God in all things." My life is focused on God in all, including a rough cross or the bottom of a red-hot crucible. I do love God in all the places God is, even in the most paradoxical of them. I do not wonder if God is there; I know. I confidently help others to that discovery, leading the way to hope during great trials. I pray to love as God loves in all places and situations. St. Hildegard says, "Your true love binds all loves."[33] She prays, "May the Holy Spirit . . . make you at one with the sweetest and most loving Love, that Love that . . . produced the most harmonious music throughout all of heaven."[34]

One day I gave a talk in my parish on spirituality and humor. I boldly showed slides of cartoons I'd drawn that showed humorous exchanges I've had with God. Though funny, the cartoons were also intimate and revealing, and yet I felt at ease—felt no self-consciousness. St. Hildegard says, "You stand unashamed before the Living God."[35] I desired to encourage others to enjoy God and have greater intimacy with God. That was all that mattered.

Was my lack of self-consciousness rooted in my experience of "no consciousness" during union with God? That time of nothing between us? I think so. I journaled, "The new freedom in the relationship is in revealing that it exists." St. Hildegard says, "May the Holy Spirit so permeate you that you can maintain a humility that is resplendent in the . . . love of God, and, therefore be able to arrange all your affairs as with a faithful friend."[36] The cartoons reveal unabashed friendship with God, and I was unabashed in presenting them.

The vine-and-branches imagery of John 15:1–11 reappeared in my journal years after the choir-loft experience. I wrote, "I think I've become a more substantial branch on the vine. I always was a branch. Now I am a more substantial one, the flow between vine and branch more full bore, the fruit of the branch more certain. Less likelihood the branch will snap off in a high wind."

In a later journal entry, I wrote, "The relationship used to be quite interpersonal. Now it seems there's oneness. And yet I still pray interpersonally, rely on a transcendent and immanent God as I understand God to be, Jesus as a different person from me. My faith is so deep and personal. I love the God Who has drawn me into God, made me a branch on the vine. The vine-ness and branch-ness remain. The branch cleaves to the vine and is devoted to it." I comprehend the imagery, and yet God is ever beyond it. "Omnipotent God, incomprehensible in . . . majesty and inestimable in . . . mysteries, and the hope of all the faithful."[37]

In one of my journals, I recorded this exchange:

Jesus: Who do you think you are if not My word?

Sue: I am Your word, Jesus. Without You I do not exist.

Jesus: That should tell you that you are Mine. I am with you always.

Sue: And because of that, Jesus, I am with You always.

"Constancy . . . comes from true trust."[38] Constant awareness of Presence, of being with God always, whether felt or not, sustains and frees. "God has need of nothing, because God is perfect in Godself."[39] Therefore, to dwell in God and God in me is all I need. "Holy persons, in whom Love dwells, lack for nothing, because their hearts are surrounded with gentleness and peace, as by the flowing aroma of balsam."[40] I don't worry about feeling God, though I enjoy that experience. I know with certainty that we are joined at the deepest possible level in a union I cannot lose or escape, only disbelieve, ignore, or dishonor. The relationship has always existed and always will. Indeed, as I learned from the mystical experience I described earlier, I cannot step out of the light of Christ.

God asserted God's claim on me in the profound way we term *union*. I am God's own, God's friend. "God is that Fullness that no limit ever touched."[41] What flows from such a union is deep-down joy; absence of overpowering fear; peace; ease of remembering God's presence; mercy and love; delight in what delights God; concern for God's concerns; a capacity to fulfill what I am called to do; the ability to endure great difficulties with serenity; and a sense that "It is no longer I who live, but it is Christ Who lives in me" (Gal 2:20).

"Attending God"

Who guides the guides?

The saints "[g]uide us wayfarers on,"[42] as St. Hildegard says. Sts. Teresa of Ávila and John of the Cross are good sources for understanding prayer experiences. St. Hildegard describes and interprets her experiences in a sort of exegesis, but she does not offer explicit reflections on prayer per se. Many books on mysticism describe profound prayer experiences. Prayerful reflection on the before and after of our own encounters with God makes us more proficient in noticing God's activity in the life of another.

My own director's astute but simple comment on my experience—"Such graces usually deepen"—was perfect and true. It said, "Let this unfold in its own time." After all, as directors, we cannot do much with an experience for which the directee has no conscious information. "God is inconceivable and invisible. No one has the capacity to know or grasp God's hidden mysteries."[43]

When I myself pointed to union, my director affirmed that interpretation. She listened with understanding as I described the "nothing between us" locution. She subsequently affirmed the connection between union and my lack of self-consciousness in revealing. The value of a director who is well-read, savvy, wise, and spiritually experienced cannot be overstated. Such a one is truly God's gold and gift. "Spiritual people are God's eye."[44]

My director was familiar with the books I read to understand my experiences. I read the writings of those who "were touched from time to time with a gentle wind that came from the secret place of the Divinity . . . and [who] had brought forth good fruit."[45] We are wise, as directors of deeply prayerful directees, to note what they are reading or to make recommendations. Deeply prayerful people grow dissatisfied with superficial texts that do not address the rich, unfathomable caverns of their experience. Directees often do not know about the spiritual classics or works by and about more recent mystics, such as Jessica Powers, who was "also illuminated with the clearest and brightest light."[46, 47]

St. Teresa of Ávila described painful experiences with spiritual directors who had no insights about her mystical path. I have wounds of my own in this regard. Well-intended directors who do not know what they don't know are prone to do more harm than good. The inexpert director disappoints and upsets with unhelpful reactions to what directees report, and that makes it difficult for directees to continue revealing. However, St. Teresa advises that directors who are well educated on such matters as union with God can be very helpful even if they have not personally had such experiences. "One has no power over these things except what God allows one to have,"[48] as St. Hildegard says. A wise director reads and internalizes what well-vetted experts like St. Teresa teach.

If we have neither personal experience nor sufficient book knowledge to support a directee, we should refer her to a more experienced director. We might be alert to feeling threatened, defensive, disappointed God hasn't so gifted us, or a desire to shift focus to more comfortable topics. As St. Hildegard says, "These things are frequently servants."[49] These feelings serve as clues we may not be ready to direct the person.

In order to ascertain what is in a directee's best interests, we can discern and pray for the Holy Spirit's guidance. It is not easy for a mystic directee to open up to a new director, so she may resist what is actually best. Directors take some responsibility for the souls of their directees and therefore must constantly pray to serve them well.

Those who experience union have difficulty articulating it, so descriptions of union may vary. Moments of union are followed by life lived in greater unity with God. We may feel more comfortable helping directees appreciate how union unfolds into unity in day-to-day life. Their continued prayer is critical. St. Hildegard says, "Do not desert the devotion that God gave—and gives—to you in the embrace of God's love."[50]

At the end of *Book of Divine Works*, St. Hildegard describes Volmar, a monk who guided her and helped her with her writing. "In God's service, he listened . . . with great devotion and unceasing labor . . . [and] could never get enough of the words of these visions."[51] St. Hildegard wept and felt orphaned when Volmar died. She also describes Wezelin, her nephew and provost of St. Andreas in Cologne, who "listened to and noted down all the words of these visions with devoted care in the love of the Holy Spirit . . . and helped and comforted me in my deepest grief and despair . . . and . . . loved faithfully and tirelessly."[52] May we be spiritual directors in the service of God, listening faithfully and tirelessly in the love of the Holy Spirit, never able to be overfilled.

Reflection Questions

How do you understand "God is my work"?

What is your experience of or knowledge about prayer of union?

Have you grown to love God in all the places God is? What are examples?

How have your training, experience, and reading prepared you to direct deeply prayerful persons?

What is your prayer about living in unity with God?

chapter sixteen

———— ◆◆ ————

FRIEND OF GOD

"Be the special friend of God"

Where has this book taken us?

St. Hildegard says, "Be such that you become the friend of God."[1] What does this entail? We began our journey with the foundational question posed by St. Hildegard: "Is there a God or not?"[2] Early experiences of God made us seekers for more. St. Hildegard encouraged, "Be a faithful friend to your soul."[3] We reviewed spiritual practices that "contribute to the health of one's soul or lift one's spirit up to God."[4] We engaged Scripture to "understand that all these things pertain to us."[5] We "persevered in seeking God"[6] through prayer and discernment.

We gradually discovered God as the protagonist of our stories, including in our work. We saw that all of life must be spiritually integrated if we are to "be the special friend of God."[7] Yet work exposed our need for transformation and greater spiritual freedom. We could not "remain unaware of Who . . . God may be, wishing only to have God as our servant."[8] A relationship of friendship emerged in our life with God and became the focus of prayer.

"How do I deserve to share in the highest joys?"[9] In drawing closer to God, we found "that our faces were very dirty."[10] The prospect of greater intimacy with God stirred our fears. But "God mercifully drew us toward Godself."[11] We found ourselves "in the dark night of our experience"[12] and let go in loving trust, for "God alone and no one else is able to free us."[13] Through mystical stripping-away, "God . . . made us new persons, with a life in us different from what we had . . . before."[14] We attained a greater ability to "be mild and gentle in . . . spirit and heart."[15] We became more our true selves and better, deeper friends of God.

In our longing "to be with the sweetness of God"[16] was the seed of mysticism. God became for us One Who "is not silent."[17] We became people whose minds are touched by the grace of God, who thirst for the justice of God, who desire to be of the same mind as Christ. In the deep sincerity of prayer, the Holy Spirit touched us, that we may always "look to God Who has touched us."[18] We discovered that God sometimes takes over prayer such that our "seeing, hearing, and knowing are simultaneous."[19] In prayer, "things are shown to us" such that we must truthfully say, "I see as I saw, and I hear as I heard."[20]

At first we "showed to no one"[21] what is mystical, but God did not allow reticence to persist, for "God works . . . for the glory of God's name, not for the glory of any earthly person."[22] "Like the sparks of a fire,"[23] our experiences occurred "as God foresees the need."[24] Through mysticism, we were transformed into more passionate, freer disciples, convinced of God's presence and action in our lives. We now "burn with so great a desire in love for God, that we can never be satisfied."[25] God invites, "Hold Me earnestly . . . as your dearest Friend."[26]

We embraced the mystic's responsibilities for continual prayer, openness, and availability to God, for God desires to "make us burn yet more for love of God."[27] We assimilated our experiences "not in pride, but in humility, the joy of the soul."[28] We reflected on the Good News of our experiences and looked through the lens of our faith tradition, so as not to "merely to chew and gratify our own appetites."[29] We examined the authenticity of our prayer experiences and "acknowledged that we have no power except in God and through God."[30]

We sought a spiritually wise person to help in "watching over that garden which the Divine gift has planted"[31] and so that we "may be assured."[32] We now seek to be trustable to God in living the "for others" purpose of our gifts, for "God compels us to good"[33] with regularity. Our way is "not wanting anything else than what God wants."[34] Through much reintegration and change in who we understand ourselves to be, we are the friend and disciple God seeks for the long term. Our priority is the reign of God, "for God is like a head of a household Who entrusts His goods to a close friend."[35]

Mysticism helped us develop healthy, authentic self-esteem, that we might bear witness, seeking to "carry God's light diligently."[36] We are asked by God to "commit to fixed writing these things that you see with the inner eyes and perceive with the inner ears of the soul, to be useful for humankind."[37] God and God's revealing "must not be concealed, but made manifest."[38] In the breaks from mysticism, we "look sharply to the work in hand."[39]

Old wounds surfaced. We "endured tribulation and fear and grief in the tumult of life."[40] We asked where God was in our worst experiences. Our fundamental brokenness was unmasked, and the Spirit of God became "like a medicine."[41] We saw Love in our worst moments. We were anointed, raised up, and freed. Our wounds were transformed to the locus of the Good News of resurrection. Having received mercy, we "do not withhold it from those to whom it should be extended."[42] Everything we experienced belongs in our story, for all is "life in God."[43]

"Fly swiftly over . . . obstacles"

What is the nature of our freedom?

Gratitude abounds for all God has done to free us. We are freed to love and desire. Our memory is filled with God's goodness, mercy, and love. "A river from the Holy Spirit . . . waters all these things in us."[44] At times we are nevertheless a faulty graft on the vine, lacking constancy, "the pillar and rampart of the virtues."[45] Yet "all roads are open and the living human mind can choose."[46] So, more and more we choose God as our work.

God draws us and "imparts the power and strength"[47] to "fly swiftly over . . . obstacles . . . with great consolation."[48] We cannot resist God's radical ways—and it seems God cannot resist us. In "the abundance of Love," we are drawn into a union that "surpasses all human understanding."[49] It is "a moment when there is nothing between us," when "no one can separate us from God."[50]

We are now united with God in the same work. "Our body's a chalice, its wine never drained."[51] We love God in all the places God is: everywhere. God's true love binds all loves. "The Holy Spirit so permeates us"[52] that we are no longer self-conscious about God. We "lack for nothing because our hearts are surrounded with gentleness and peace."[53] We truly are friends of God, and ours is a deeply committed, mutual friendship. We see this as our eternal destiny.

"The terrible shipwreck . . . will not overwhelm you"

What must we do?

"God does not reject you, but keeps you as God's friend, and therefore, the terrible shipwreck of this world will not overwhelm you."[54] The "terrible shipwreck" torments and challenges and requires our continued effort to find God in all the places God is and to choose God as our work. We must be concerned about all that gives God concern. We are at work as disciples, branches on the vine, praying ceaselessly.

Because we dwell in hope, we bring hope to others. Because our wounds are transformed, we tend the wounds of others. Because we have known forgiveness, mercy, compassion, and love we extend these to others. Because we have learned, we teach and guide. Because God has listened to us, we listen generously to others. We have "the highest of all callings as Christ's representatives,"[55] and through us "the grace of God pours out God's dynamic good will."[56] This is now more reliably our way.

"Attending God"

How do we accompany the spiritually seasoned?

"Just as an experienced gardener gathers herbs that are wholesome and perfect for everyone's benefit, so the Son of God chose good and perfect persons who were like wholesome plants in fertile soil, for they listened to Him and willingly obeyed His precepts in faith and love."[57] And now such a person sits in the chair across from us. "Therefore, O humankind, rejoice . . . [for] a new song resounds among us."[58] We recognize that this directee has responded to great graces and "we embrace You in our hearts."[59]

We pray "so that, by Your aid, we do not fail, and that Your Name be not forgotten among us. And through Your own name, we ask: 'Please help us.'"[60] We pray to be the spiritual director God and the friend of God require. Yet, no doubt, we accompany a person whose direction regularly comes straight from God, a person who readily aligns with God. Is there nothing we need do for this person?

St. Hildegard reminds us to "avoid destroying the honor and

bliss of your happiness."[61] Everyone struggles. Everyone needs someone to talk to. Everyone discerns their path at key forks in the road. Everyone needs opportunities to process experiences of God. Everyone needs to come in off the road and say, "It's tough out there." Everyone needs help to notice what they do not see. Everyone needs affirmation. What threatens "the honor and bliss of . . . happiness" in this directee?

Nevertheless, the friend of God, sturdily connected to the Vine, is strong and retains deep-down joy even during an adverse wind. We might inquire how the directee is doing deep down inside, and help to renew this awareness. We are there to support and listen, with our repertoire of Scriptures that nourish and refresh, with our reminder that the Holy Spirit is "the breath of holiness" needed and the "anointment of hearts."[62] We are there to affirm that God "calls to you with the sweetest sound and prepares places of abode for you"[63] where you may rest and abide in God.

Friendship with God is eternal. At times we are the spiritual director for the dying directee seeking to trust that. We review the many moments of friendship with God that grew their trust. With our own hearts aching, our own confidence in God called forth, we accompany as far as we can, and we pray with them to the end, "Deign to gather humankind to Yourself."[64]

Where are we in our spiritual direction ministry? Have we learned and deepened such that we can contribute to the ministry in new ways? Perhaps we can share insights by writing papers or books or by training others. Many directors need supervisors—are we ready for that? Do we have directees who should be invited to discern becoming directors? Can we support new directors by referring direction requests to them?

How will we know when our service as spiritual directors is ending? Does it ever happen that "God is my work" ceases? Perhaps the work changes. Age and illness make trips to the vineyard impossible. The new vineyard is the life of prayer and humble acceptance of "many grave infirmities."[65] We remember "the younger life we can no longer have"[66] and ask for new graces. "I pray that You gather into the bosom of Your grace all those who zealously toil with me out of their pure faith in Your Name."[67]

REFLECTION QUESTIONS

What was it like for you to journey through this book?

Reflect on St. Hildegard's promise that "the terrible shipwreck of this world will not overwhelm you."

How would you name threats to "the honor and bliss of . . . happiness" in your directees? How do you proceed?

What is your experience with directees in end-of-life situations? How would you advise other directors in this situation for the first time?

How is God calling you now in your spiritual direction ministry?

What is your prayer about continued befriending of your soul, deepening of your friendship with God, and growing as a spiritual director?

afterword

———◦•◦———

"Carry God's Light Diligently"

W hat has it been like to write this book?
I feel exposed, having revealed much that once was private. I trust you to receive it all with goodwill and generous spirit. I have new freedom in this new trust. God has been present in all the narratives between the book's covers. God was writing the story all along.

I wrote in collaboration with St. Hildegard and God. I trusted them to bless, inspire, guide, and help me, and that trust became unwavering. My voice and theirs had to blend paragraph by paragraph. At times, my words were exactly what God hears in my prayer. Along the way, I journaled, "I am trying to share Your goodness with others. I am willing, Sophia, to expose what is in my heart that others may know the lengths to which You will go to help, to heal, and to love." As St. Hildegard says, "If a person works in accordance with the soul's desire, all her works become good."[1] May this be so.

While writing this book, I developed breast cancer, for which I had surgery and then chemotherapy. For a time, I was a much-weakened scribe. How wonderful to grow in wisdom, grace, and fruitfulness as a scribe even as I grew weak from chemo. At times I felt slow and unperceptive, yet I always felt joy in the work. I am fortunate I had a wonderful project to help me through my chemo retreat.

St. Hildegard wrote 30 percent of this text and provided the book's structure through her themes of befriending the soul and becoming the friend of God. She gave me new insights into my own experience and into spirituality and spiritual direction along the way. Every day I knew her encouragement, example, and witness. Her insight that God defends one's spirit is apparent to me. I often reflected on her courage and the intimacy of her writing about God. She became my friend, and I, hers. Friends of God are friends of one another, and this is true eternally. God seeks friendship with us, and that is our opportunity on the spiritual journey. The Communion of Saints is real, and friendship with the saints is also our opportunity.

I imagine St. Hildegard putting the last bits in the Riesencodex, stopping at thirty-three pounds. One stops at some point, leaving many things out. I have reached the end of this pilgrimage, and now new ones beckon. St. Hildegard's gems and pearls are one book more available. I hope this book preserves her timeless wisdom for other pilgrims like you.

I hope mysticism became less exotic and more credible and practical for you through this book. I hope St. Hildegard blessed the paragraphs of your life, too, and took you deeper. I hope your reflections brought you insights and joy, and that your prayers about each theme will be answered with abundance. St. Hildegard's words are not just lovely quotes; they become wisdom within us that we can offer to others. If you are engaged in the spiritual direction ministry, may you feel supported, helped, and cherished for your contributions to our world's spiritual health. Most of all, I hope you have befriended your beautiful soul and become a faithful friend of God.

"I hold you with joy in my heart, being confident in God that through God's grace, you will be made God's dear friend."[2]

Selected Bibliography

For those who wish to learn more about St. Hildegard,
I list some possibilities below.

Abbey of St. Hildegard in Germany. www.abtei-st-hildegard.de/
english.

Benedict XVI. *An Apostolic Letter Proclaiming Saint Hildegard of Bingen,
professed nun of the Order of Saint Benedict, a Doctor of the Universal
Church.* Rome, Italy. October 7, 2012.

Butcher, Carmen. *Hildegard of Bingen: A Spiritual Reader.* (second
edition) Brewster, MA: Paraclete Press, 2013.

Flanagan, Sabina. *Hildegard of Bingen: A Visionary Life.* London:
Routledge, 2001.

*Hildegard of Bingen, The Book of Divine Works (volume 18 of Fathers of
the Church: Mediaeval Continuation)* trans. Nathaniel M. Campbell.
Washington, D. C.: Catholic University of America Press, 2018.

*Hildegard of Bingen: The Book of the Rewards of Life (Liber Vitae
Meritorum),* trans. Bruce Hozeski. New York: Oxford University Press,
1994.

Hildegard of Bingen: Scivias, trans. Mother Columba Hart and Jane
Bishop. New York: Paulist Press, 1990.

Hildegard of Bingen: Homilies on the Gospels, trans. Beverly Kienzle.
Trappist, KY: Cistercian, 2011.

Hildegard of Bingen: Solutions to Thirty-Eight Questions, trans. Beverly Kienzle with Jenny Bledsoe and Stephen Behnke. Collegeville, MN: Liturgical Press, 2014.

International Society of Hildegard von Bingen Studies. www.hildegard-society.org/p/home.html.

King-Lenzmeier, Anne. *Hildegard of Bingen: An Integrated Vision.* Collegeville, MN: Liturgical Press, 2001.

Kujawa-Holbrook, Sheryl. *Hildegard of Bingen: Essential Writings and Chants of a Christian Mystic—Annotated and Explained.* Woodstock, Vermont: Skylight Paths Publishing, 2016.

Maddocks, Fiona. *Hildegard of Bingen: The Woman of Her Age.* (third edition) London: Faber and Faber Ltd., 2013.

Newman, Barbara. *Sister of Wisdom: St. Hildegard's Theology of the Feminine.* Los Angeles: University of California Press, 1987.

_____, ed. *Voices of the Living Light: Hildegard of Bingen and Her World.* Los Angeles: University of California Press, 1998.

Storch, Walburga. *Prayers of Hildegard of Bingen.* Cincinnati: Franciscan Media, 2003.

The Letters of Hildegard of Bingen, Vol. I, trans. Joseph Baird and Radd Ehrmann. New York: Oxford University Press, 1994.

The Letters of Hildegard of Bingen, Vol. II, trans. Joseph Baird and Radd Ehrmann. New York: Oxford University Press, 1998.

The Letters of Hildegard of Bingen, Vol. III, trans. Joseph Baird and Radd Ehrmann. New York: Oxford University Press, 2004.

The Wiesbaden ("Giant") Codex, Hochschule RheinMain, www.hs-rm.de/de/service/hochschul-und-landesbibliothek/suchen-finden/sondersammlungen/the-wiesbaden-giant-codex.

Saint Hildegard of Bingen, Symphonia: A Critical Edition of the Symphonia Armonie Celestium Revelationem, 2nd ed., trans. Barbara Newman. Ithaca, NY: Cornell University Press, 1998.

30-Day Journey with St. Hildegard of Bingen, compiled and ed. Sharon Sterringer. Minneapolis: Fortress Press, 2019.

Acknowledgments

The seed for this book was planted at Siena Retreat Center in Racine, Wisconsin. My thanks to Claire Anderson, the executive director, who invited me to lead a reflection day featuring St. Hildegard, which got me started sharing her wisdom. Sister Kathleen Bohn, OP, asked me to identify accessible books on St. Hildegard for the attendees of the reflection day, and I found that the options were few. I am so grateful to Sister Kathleen for her wisdom, insight, and affirmation as my spiritual direction supervisor, which included guiding me in my writing ministry. She listened to and commented on pieces of the book along the way and always expressed enthusiasm for the mission.

I greatly appreciate the reflection day and retreat attendees over the years who've shown me the appeal St. Hildegard's wisdom has to them. My lectio divina groups and one-on-one spiritual directees also shared their reactions to St. Hildegard's pearls and helped me see the potential of a book full of them. They also led me to see that including a spiritual direction theme was fitting. I am indebted to the brave directees whose stories (changed in details for privacy) I have included— thank you for this privilege.

I wrote the first material of this book while on retreat. I was reflecting on St. Hildegard's relationship with God when my spiritual director, Susan Bowers Baker, wisely invited me to respond to the same questions I was posing to St. Hildegard. With that invitation, the collaboration with St. Hildegard was born, and we went on to write the book together. I am deeply grateful to Susan for her amazing insights, steadfast support, spiritual direction, prayer, and loving blessings, and for commenting on an early draft.

Cathie Gauthier, a spiritual director friend, also commented on an early draft of the book. My thanks to Cathie for taking time out from her own writing to give insightful comments and encouragement. I so appreciate her honesty and willingness to share her reactions.

Much gratitude to Dr. Barbara Newman, who is John Evans Professor of Latin and Professor of English, Religious Studies, and Classics at Northwestern University near my home. She has written three books and numerous articles on St. Hildegard, all of which I've read. I visited Dr. Newman early in the writing of this book, and she generously answered my many questions, gave me copies of papers, and encouraged me to enter the neglected territory of St. Hildegard's spiritual wisdom. Dr. Newman continues her support despite her busy schedule. I am so thankful she is nearby and the kind of expert who unselfishly helps another St. Hildegard explorer.

I thank Dr. Martin Mayer at the state library in Wiesbaden, Germany, who is the professor in charge of St. Hildegard's Riesencodex and who took time during my visit there to tell me the story of the manuscript's history, care, and impact.

This book would not exist without English translations of St. Hildegard's texts. Translating Medieval Latin presents many challenges, including local and individual differences. The St. Hildegard translator deals with the fact that she wasn't trained in scholarly Latin. Her Latin tends to be ungrammatical, and she invents new words, makes awkward constructions, and above all is often expressing the ineffable. Every sentence of St. Hildegard's words in English is the product of intense intellectual work as well as an entering into the spirit of what she was conveying. Heartfelt thanks to Mother Columba Hart and Jane Bishop; Bruce Hozeski; Barbara Newman; Beverly Mayne Kienzle; Nathaniel Campbell; and Joseph Baird and Radd Ehrman.

My thanks to Kellie Hultgren of KMH Editing, who did a thorough pre-submission edit of the book. She is a joy to work with and helped put the book's best face forward to potential publishers. I am also grateful to David J. Shuck, who partnered with me to proofread late-stage text. He truly helped the cause of improving the book.

The entire team at She Writes Press is top-notch, and I am the grateful recipient of their expertise and hard work. I especially thank Lauren Wise, Associate Publisher and project manager extraordinaire, for guiding me through the publishing process with calm, good humor, and patience.

Notes

Epigraph

The Letters of Hildegard of Bingen, Vol. I, trans. Joseph Baird and Radd Ehrmann, (New York: Oxford University Press, 1994), 91; *The Letters of Hildegard of Bingen, Vol. III*, trans. Joseph Baird and Radd Ehrmann (New York: Oxford University Press, 2004), 44.

Preface

1. *The Letters of Hildegard of Bingen, Vol. I*, trans. Joseph Baird and Radd Ehrmann, (New York: Oxford University Press, 1994), 91. Hereafter cited as Lett. I.
2. *The Letters of Hildegard of Bingen, Vol. II*, trans. Joseph Baird and Radd Ehrmann, (New York: Oxford University Press, 1994), 77. Hereafter cited as Lett. II.
3. *The Letters of Hildegard of Bingen, Vol. III*, trans. Joseph Baird and Radd Ehrmann (New York: Oxford University Press, 2004), 107. Hereafter cited as Lett. III.

Introduction

1. The Wiesbaden ("Giant") Codex, Hochschule RheinMain, www.hs-rm.de/de/service/hochschul-und-landesbibliothek/suchen-finden/sondersammlungen/the-wiesbaden-giant-codex.
2. *Hildegard of Bingen: The Book of Divine Works (volume 18 of Fathers of the Church: Mediaeval Continuation)*, trans. Nathaniel Campbell (Washington, D. C.: Catholic University of America Press, 2018), 250. Hereafter cited as Bk.
3. *Hildegard of Bingen: The Book of the Rewards of Life (Liber Vitae Meritorum)*, trans. Bruce Hozeski (New York: Oxford University Press, 1994), 27. Hereafter cited as Liber.
4. Lett. I, 146.
5. *Hildegard of Bingen: Scivias*, trans. Mother Columba Hart and Jane Bishop (New York: Paulist Press, 1990), 453. Hereafter cited as Sc.
6. Bk., 425.

7. Lett. III, 44.
8. Sc., 141.
9. Lett. I, 91.
10. Lett. II, 77.
11. Lett. II, 195.
12. *Hildegard of Bingen: Homilies on the Gospels,* trans. Beverly Kienzle (Trappist, KY: Cistercian, 2011), 70. Hereafter cited as Hom.
13. Lett. III, 49; 62.
14. Lett. II, 150.
15. Hom., 177–78.
16. Bk., 115.
17. Liber., 95.
18. Bk., 114.
19. Bk., 99.
20. Sc., 480.
21. Bk., 102.
22. Liber., 89.
23. Liber., 285.
24. Lett. III, 51.
25. Lett. I, 196.
26. Sc., 479.
27. Hom., 194.
28. Hom., 142.
29. Lett. I, 146.
30. Lett. III, 53.
31. Sc., 60.
32. Sc., 61.
33. Liber., 290.
34. Benedict XVI. *An Apostolic Letter Proclaiming Saint Hildegard of Bingen, professed nun of the Order of Saint Benedict, a Doctor of the Universal Church.* Rome, Italy. October 7, 2012. Hereafter cited as Apostolic Letter.
35. Sc., 428.
36. Lett. I, 47.
37. Lett. I, 200.
38. Lett. I, 119.
39. Liber., 22.

40. Bk., 37.
41. Lett. III, 27.
42. Lett. III, 182.
43. Bk., 389.
44. *Saint Hildegard of Bingen, Symphonia: A Critical Edition of the Symphonia Armonie Celestium Revelationem,* 2nd ed., trans. Barbara Newman (Ithaca, NY: Cornell University Press, 1998), 149. Hereafter cited as Symph.
45. Lett. III, 123.
46. Bk., 29.
47. Lett. I, 28.
48. Lett. III, 58.
49. Lett. I, 200.
50. Lett. II, 49.
51. Liber., 125.
52. Sc., 475.
53. Lett. II, 175.
54. Lett. I, 107.
55. Lett. III, 36.
56. Bk., 81.
57. Bk., 170.
58. Sc., 416.
59. Lett. II, 71.
60. Bk., 250.
61. Lett. I, 199.
62. Bk., 92.
63. Sc., 448.
64. Lett. III, 131.
65. Sc., 485.
66. Sc., 61.
67. Lett. II, 163.
68. Liber., 276.
69. Bk., 481–482.
70. Lett. III, 61.
71. Lett. III, 162.
72. Lett. III, 185.
73. Lett. III, 185.

PART I: BECOMING A SEEKER

1. Sc., 141.

1. *Radiant Beauty*

1. Lett. II, 199.
2. Liber., 271.
3. Bk., 38.
4. Liber., 37.
5. Lett. III, 118.
6. Sc., 120.
7. Sc., 123.
8. Sc., 455–56.
9. Hom., 115.
10. Bk., 328.
11. Sc., 352.
12. Sc., 352.
13. Sc., 352.
14. Sc., 354.
15. Hom., 71.

2. *Recognition*

1. Sc., 193.
2. John Cheever, interview by John Hersey, "Talk with John Cheever," *New York Times Book Review,* March 6, 1977, New York edition, www.nytimes.com/1977/03/06/archives/talk-with-john-cheever-cheever.html.
3. Lett. I, 32; 53.
4. Lett. III, 123.
5. Sc., 317.
6. Sc., 466.

3. *The Embrace*

1. Sc., 477.
2. Bk., 444.

3. Lett. III, 138.
4. Sc., 126.
5. Bk., 37.
6. Sc., 486.
7. Lett. I, 160.
8. Sc., 335.
9. *Hildegard of Bingen: Solutions to Thirty-Eight Questions*, trans. Beverly Kienzle with Jenny Bledsoe and Stephen Behnke (Collegeville, MN: Liturgical Press, 2014), 45. Hereafter cited as Soln.
10. Sc., 117.
11. Sc., 162.
12. Bk., 413.
13. Bk., 389.
14. Lett. III, 123.
15. Hom., 64.
16. Hom., 66.
17. Lett. I, 27.
18. Liber., 25.
19. Sc., 68.
20. Sc., 260.
21. Sc., 124.
22. Bk., 189.
23. Bk., 198.
24. Sc., 113.
25. Sc., 120.
26. Sc., 417.
27. Liber., 22.
28. Liber., 101.
29. Bk., 38.
30. Hom., 196–97.
31. Liber., 290.
32. Hom., 125.
33. Hom., 184.
34. Sc., 427.
35. Symph., 149.
36. Lett. III, 202.

4. *Mom's Answer*

1. Sc., 447.
2. Sc., 352.
3. Lett. III, 36.
4. Lett. II, 109.
5. Sc., 337.
6. Sc., 295.
7. Sc., 428–29.
8. Sc., 256.
9. Sc., 448.
10. Bk., 320.
11. Lett. I, 111.
12. Sc., 429.
13. Sc., 448.
14. Sc., 141.

PART II: BECOMING THE FAITHFUL FRIEND OF YOUR SOUL

5. *St. Hildegard's Invitation*

1. Lett. I, 91.
2. Sc., 217.

6. *Journaling*

1. Sc., 476.
2. Liber., 94.
3. Lett. II, 96.
4. Lett. III, 125.
5. Lett. II, 88.
6. Lett. III, 49.
7. Sc., 60.
8. Bk., 121.
9. Hom., 54.
10. Sc., 329.

11. Lett. I, 103.
12. Lett. I, 195.
13. Soln., 86.
14. Bk., 234.
15. Lett. III, 62.
16. Lett. I, 113.
17. Lett. I, 201.
18. Lett. II, 199.
19. Lett. III, 189.
20. Liber., 125.

7. Scripture

1. Lett. II, 150.
2. Lett. II, 133.
3. Lett. I, 105.
4. Sc., 475.
5. Liber., 147.
6. Bk., 307.
7. Lett. I, 88.
8. Bk., 92.
9. Lett. I, 154.
10. Sc., 120.
11. Lett. III, 27.
12. Sc., 335.
13. Lett. II, 195.
14. Bk., 445.
15. Symph., 115; 131.
16. Symph., 137.
17. Hom., 172
18. Symph., 133; 135.
19. Symph., 123.
20. Lett. I, 143.
21. Lett. II, 22.
22. Hom., 34.
23. Sc., 135; 490.
24. Lett. III, 189.

25. Lett. III, 190.
26. Hom., 70.
27. Lett. I, 197.
28. Sc., 477.
29. Sc., 477.
30. Liber., 204.
31. Symph., 257.
32. Symph., 259.
33. Lett. III, 124.
34. Lett. I, 195.
35. Liber., 83.
36. Liber., 162.
37. Sc., 231.
38. Lett. II, 170.
39. Lett. II, 192.
40. Lett. II, 41.
41. Lett. II, 121.
42. Lett. II, 75.
43. Lett. III, 149.
44. Lett. I, 77.
45. Liber., 25.
46. Liber., 88.
47. Lett. I, 109; 119.
48. Liber., 88.
49. Liber., 82; 83.
50. Liber., 82.
51. Lett. III, 203.
52. Lett. II, 139.

8. *Spiritual Direction:* "*Attending God*"

1. Liber., 89.
2. Sc., 452.
3. Sc., 228.
4. Liber., 84.
5. Bk., 40.
6. Liber., 205.

7. Bk., 250.

8. Bk., 408–409.

9. Sc., 455–56.

10. Bk., 40.

11. Sc., 112.

12. Liber., 89.

13. Bk., 431.

14. Hom., 34.

15. Lett. III, 202.

16. Sc., 485.

17. Liber., 253.

18. Hom., 48.

19. Lett. III, 39.

20. Lett. III, 106.

21. Sc., 295.

22. Lett. I, 194.

23. Lett. II, 141.

24. Lett. II, 148.

25. Spiritual Directors International, www.sdiworld.org.

26. Sc., 395.

27. Sc., 469.

28. Lett. II, 144.

29. Soln., 82.

30. Lett. II, 158.

31. After Lett. II, 163.

32. Lett. III, 152.

33. Hom., 48.

34. Lett. II, 149.

35. Sc., 59.

36. Sc., 60.

37. Sc., 60.

38. Sc., 61.

39. Liber., 153.

40. Liber., 176.

41. Lett. II, 49.

42. Hom., 45.

43. Lett. III, 170.
44. Liber., 87.
45. Sc., 368.
46. Sc., 534.
47. Bk., 390–391.
48. Lett. II, 150.
49. Sc., 403.
50. Lett. I, 129.
51. Liber., 201.
52. Lett. III, 147.
53. Lett. III, 106.
54. Lett. II, 95.
55. Lett. I, 47.
56. Soln., 61.
57. Hom., 42.
58. Lett. II, 95.
59. Symph., 103.
60. Hom., 98.
61. Lett. II, 29. In this letter in St. Hildegard's compilation, the monk Guibert writes to her.
62. Soln., 58.
63. Bk., 420.
64. Nan Merrill, *Psalms for Praying*. (New York: Continuum, 2004), 147.
65. Liber., 231.
66. Liber., 186.
67. Liber., 187.
68. Hom., 43.
69. Hom., 187.
70. Lett. III, 119.
71. Sc., 347.
72. Bk., 57.
73. Lett. III, 33.
74. Liber., 21.
75. Lett. III, 152.
76. Bk., 54.
77. Bk., 55.

78. Sc., 94.
79. Lett. I, 111.
80. Lett. I, 195.
81. Bk., 61.
82. Bk., 176.
83. Hom., 183.
84. Lett. I, 72.
85. Liber., 37.
86. Lett. III, 9.
87. Hom., 53.
88. Bk., 206–207.
89. Sc., 465.
90. Soln., 81.
91. Bk., 423.
92. Bk., 96.
93. Lett. III, 83.
94. Liber., 185.
95. Example provided with permission of the directee. For additional examples see: Sue Garthwaite, "God's Research Partners: Scientists and Spiritual Direction," *Presence* 19, no. 3 (September 2013): 46–53. Hereafter cited as Research Partners.
96. Hom., 194.
97. Lett. III, 62.

9. Prayer

1. Hom., 177–78.
2. Bk., 189.
3. Bk., 115–116.
4. Sc., 115.
5. Sc., 150.
6. Bk., 198.
7. Sc., 244.
8. Sc., 432.
9. Lett. III, 131.
10. Sc., 476.
11. Hom., 66.

12. Lett. III, 150.
13. Bk., 66–67.
14. Bk., 36.
15. Sc., 127.
16. Bk., 454.
17. Sc., 68.
18. Liber., 147.
19. Liber., 25.
20. Liber., 260.
21. Bk., 173.
22. Liber., 117.
23. Liber., 190.
24. Liber., 200.
25. Liber., 187.
26. Lett. III, 173.
27. Lett. III, 175.
28. Bk., 372.
29. Sc., 256.
30. Sc., 126.
31. Sc., 435.
32. Sc., 442–43.
33. Sc., 497.
34. Lett I, 79.
35. Sc., 533.
36. Bk., 381.
37. Liber., 107.
38. Liber., 107.
39. Liber., 108.
40. Liber., 107–8.
41. Liber., 108.
42. Sc., 110.
43. Liber., 247.
44. For a more current version, see *Thomas à Kempis: The Imitation of Christ*, trans. Richard Challoner (Charlotte, NC: Tan Books, 2013).
45. Sc., 110.
46. Sc., 254.

47. Lett. III, 52.
48. Sc., 128.
49. Sc., 374.
50. Liber., 107.
51. Liber., 41.
52. Liber., 53.
53. Liber., 41.
54. Hom., 130–31.
55. Lett. I, 59.
56. Lett. I, 67.
57. Lett. II, 67.
58. Liber., 135.
59. Sc., 432.
60. Liber., 192.
61. Bk., 399.
62. Lett. III, 126.
63. Lett. III, 153.
64. Lett. III, 146.
65. Sc., 443.
66. Sc., 486.
67. Lett. II, 22.
68. Sc., 247.
69. Lett. III, 57.
70. Sc., 125.
71. Sc., 247.
72. Lett. II, 137.
73. Bk., 232.
74. Lett. I, 196.
75. Lett. II, 22.
76. Liber., 27.
77. Lett. I, 200.
78. Liber., 79.
79. Bk., 173.
80. Hom., 54.
81. Sc., 436.
82. Liber., 94.

83. Liber., 40–41.
84. Lett. I, 109.
85. Liber., 204.
86. Bk., 169.
87. Bk., 389.
88. Liber., 25.
89. Liber., 117.
90. Liber., 272.
91. Lett. III, 203.
92. Hom., 115.
93. Bk., 343.
94. Bk., 343.
95. Bk., 413.
96. Sc., 161.
97. Bk., 391.
98. Liber., 226.
99. Bk., 319.
100. Bk., 413.
101. Sc., 503.
102. Sc., 436.
103. Bk., 213.
104. Symph., 105.
105. Lett. III, 111.
106. Sc., 477.
107. Lett. III, 152.
108. Lett. III, 151.
109. Sc., 488.
110. Bk., 167.
111. Liber., 289.
112. Sc., 477.
113. Lett. III, 51.
114. Bk., 376.
115. Lett. III, 153.
116. Sc., 426–27.
117. Sc., 427.
118. Sc., 117.

119. Bk., 102.
120. Bk., 320.
121. Liber., 13.
122. Hom., 48.
123. Liber., 181.
124. Lett. II, 6.
125. Lett. II, 175.
126. Lett. II, 14.
127. Lett. II, 7.
128. Bk., 425.
129. Liber., 202.
130. Sc., 485.
131. Lett. III, 158.
132. Lett. I, 195.
133. Liber., 205.
134. Lett. I, 56.
135. Liber., 21.
136. Sc., 503.
137. Bk., 122.
138. Sc., 436.
139. Lett. II, 14.
140. Lett. III, 102.
141. Bk., 94.
142. Bk., 476.
143. Liber., 205.
144. Bk., 275.
145. Bk., 314.
146. Sc., 162.
147. Liber., 26.
148. Bk., 192.
149. Sc., 113.
150. Sc., 113.
151. Lett. I, 131.
152. Sc., 486.
153. Bk., 178.
154. Bk., 295.

155. Bk., 234.
156. Bk., 285.
157. Sc., 448.
158. Bk., 347.
159. Sc., 127.
160. Bk., 56.
161. Sc., 405.
162. Sc., 486.
163. Sc., 127.
164. Bk., 37.
165. Sc., 377.
166. Liber., 206.
167. Liber., 81.
168. Hom., 71.
169. Bk., 404.
170. Liber., 78.
171. Lett. II, 22.
172. Bk., 393.
173. Sc., 375.
174. Lett. II, 154.
175. Bk., 164.
176. Bk., 404.
177. Sc., 447.
178. Sc., 443.
179. Sc., 335.
180. Hom., 188.
181. Lett. I, 48.
182. Lett. I, 201.
183. Lett. III, 108.
184. Bk., 370.
185. Sc., 427.
186. Hom., 180.
187. Bk., 474.
188. Sc., 447–48.
189. Lett. II, 6.
190. Lett. I, 113.

191. Lett. III, 33.
192. Liber., 199.
193. Liber., 27.
194. Bk., 233.
195. Lett. I, 200.
196. Sc., 117.
197. Sc., 447.
198. Lett. III, 62–63.
199. Bk., 169.
200. Soln., 60.
201. *Francis de Sales, Jane de Chantal: Letters of Spiritual Direction*, trans. Peronne Marie Thibert, (New York: Paulist Press, 1988), 194. Hereafter cited as St. Jane.
202. Lett. II, 194.
203. St. Jane, 194.
204. Hom., 48.
205. Symph., 205.
206. Lett. III, 182.
207. Symph., 131; 113; 115; 135.
208. Lett. I, 200.
209. Lett. III, 155.
210. Symph., 119.
211. Lett. III, 106.
212. Bk., 421.
213. Sc., 488.
214. Symph., 189.
215. Sc., 477.
216. Bk., 391.
217. Liber., 204.
218. Hom., 183.
219. Bk., 313.
220. Lett. I, 112.
221. Symph., 101; 103; 143; 149; 151.
222. Bk., 173.
223. Lett. I, 199.
224. Bk., 37.

225. Sc., 417.
226. Hom., 178.
227. Liber., 94–95.

10. Discernment

1. Lett. I, 40.
2. Sc., 384.
3. Sc., 443.
4. Bk., 114.
5. Bk., 99.
6. Lett II, 196.
7. Bk., 318.
8. Bk., 40.
9. Lett. III, 64.
10. Lett III, 152.
11. Lett. II, 111.
12. Liber., 190.
13. Lett. III, 152.
14. Lett. I, 90.
15. Hom., 118.
16. Lett. I, 103.
17. Lett. I, 103.
18. Lett. I, 103.
19. Lett. III, 122.
20. Bk., 397.
21. Bk., 117.
22. Lett. I, 58.
23. Bk., 58.
24. Sc., 405.
25. Liber., 129.
26. Sc., 114.
27. Sc., 373.
28. Lett. II, 75.
29. Bk., 451.
30. Lett. I, 199.
31. Lett. II, 72.

32. Lett. III, 152.
33. Sc., 220.
34. Liber., 24.
35. Hom., 183.
36. Sc., 480.
37. Sc., 476.
38. Sc., 115.
39. Liber., 236.
40. Liber., 235.
41. Sc., 123–24.
42. Liber., 289.
43. Liber., 289.
44. Lett. I, 42.
45. Hom., 43.
46. Lett. II, 111.
47. Lett. I, 92.
48. Bk., 144.
49. Lett. III, 44.
50. Lett. I, 97.
51. Lett. II, 196.
52. Sc., 445.
53. Hom., 171.
54. Bk., 441–442.
55. Lett. I, 72.
56. Sc., 244.
57. Bk., 120.
58. Lett. II, 70.
59. Sc., 403.
60. Hom., 154.
61. Hom., 51.
62. Lett. I, 124.
63. Sc., 406.
64. Sc., 102.
65. Sc., 416.
66. Sc., 337.
67. Sc., 364.

68. Hom., 182.
69. Bk., 156.
70. Bk., 165.
71. Lett. I, 196.
72. Lett. III, 131.
73. Lett. II, 88.
74. Bk., 57.
75. Sc., 121.
76. Bk., 301.
77. Hom., 51.
78. Bk., 397.
79. Bk., 146.
80. Sc., 151.
81. Symph., 99.
82. Sc., 220.
83. Liber., 236.
84. Sc., 115.
85. Soln., 61.
86. Liber., 25.
87. Liber., 127.
88. Lett. III, 41.
89. Liber., 232.
90. Lett. III, 76.
91. Liber., 236.
92. Hom., 98.
93. Lett. III, 33.
94. Soln., 74.
95. Lett. III, 146.
96. Bk., 296.
97. Liber., 202.
98. Liber., 186–87.
99. Lett. II, 86.
100. Lett. I, 97.
101. Lett. III, 144.
102. Sc., 428–29.
103. Sc., 69.

104. Soln., 82.
105. Bk., 397.
106. Liber., 45.
107. Sc., 406.
108. Lett. I, 85–86.
109. Bk., 376.
110. Liber., 84.
111. Bk., 300.
112. Sc., 443.
113. Lett. III, 109.
114. Bk., 420.
115. Bk., 206.
116. Lett. II, 150.
117. Sc., 383–84.
118. Sc., 115.
119. Sc., 122.
120. Bk., 127.
121. Liber., 197.
122. Lett. II, 175.
123. Lett. II, 11.
124. Sc., 114–15.
125. Liber., 95.
126. Bk., 207.
127. Bk., 102.
128. Liber., 185.
129. Sc., 190.
130. Sc., 488.
131. Liber., 89.
132. Liber., 94.
133. Liber., 94–95.
134. Liber., 285.
135. Sc., 351–52.
136. Liber., 23.
137. Sc., 489.
138. Sc., 384.
139. Lett. III, 124.

PART III:

BECOMING THE FAITHFUL FRIEND OF GOD

11. *Integration*

22. Bk., 414.
23. Lett. I, 133.
24. Bk., 433.
25. Sc., 119.
26. Lett. I, 109.
27. Bk., 433.
28. Sc., 193.
29. Liber., 247.
30. Hom., 131.
31. Hom., 80.
32. Bk., 91.
33. Lett. II, 150.
34. Lett. II, 174.
35. Sc., 406.
36. Sc., 453.
37. Lett. III, 124.
38. Lett. I, 109.
39. Lett. II, 96.
40. Liber., 135.
41. Lett. III, 103.
42. Bk., 454.
43. Sc., 220.
44. Lett. II, 95.
45. Lett. II, 149.
46. Sc., 347.
47. Lett. II, 147.
48. Liber., 135.
49. Liber., 140.
50. Lett. I, 92.
51. Bk., 454.
52. Sc., 503.
53. Lett. III, 51.
54. Lett. I, 143.
55. Sc., 243.
56. Lett. II, 193.
57. Lett. II, 195.

58. Lett. III, 131.
59. Research Partners, 46–53.
60. Lett. III, 117.

12. Surrender to God in Prayer

1. Sc., 476.
2. Hom., 142.
3. Sc., 476.
4. Liber., 153.
5. Symph., 143.
6. Symph 191; 205.
7. Liber., 272.
8. Bk., 421–422.
9. Liber., 129.
10. Liber., 139.
11. Soln., 50.
12. Lett. II, 22.
13. Liber., 233.
14. Sc., 477.
15. Soln., 45–46.
16. Sc., 438.
17. Sc., 110.
18. Lett. III, 185.
19. Liber., 37.
20. Sc., 154.
21. Sc., 156.
22. Lett. II, 14.
23. Lett. III, 24.
24. Liber., 20.
25. Bk., 38.
26. Sc., 466.
27. Sc., 153.
28. Liber., 88.
29. Liber., 267.
30. Lett. I, 146.
31. Liber., 26.

32. Liber., 125.
33. Bk., 355.
34. Sc., 88.
35. Lett. I, 174.
36. Lett. I, 180.
37. Hom., 171.
38. Liber., 233.
39. Sc., 373.
40. Sc., 150.
41. Lett. II, 22.
42. Liber., 199.
43. Liber., 205.
44. Bk., 38.
45. Hom., 184.
46. Lett. I, 200.
47. Bk., 40.
48. Soln., 83.
49. Bk., 454.
50. Lett. II, 143.
51. Sc., 326.
52. Sc., 427.
53. Sc., 445.
54. Liber., 15.
55. Lett. I, 143.
56. Lett. I, 98.
57. Lett. I, 103.
58. Lett. I, 130.
59. Lett. II, 10.
60. Lett. II, 10.
61. Lett. III, 39.
62. Lett. I, 119.
63. Liber., 23.
64. Lett. II, 135.
65. Liber., 31.
66. Bk., 421.
67. Lett. III, 53.

68. Bk., 318.
69. Sc., 126.
70. Liber., 16.
71. Lett. II, 196.
72. Liber., 27.

13. *Mysticism*

1. Lett. I, 183.
2. Liber., 37.
3. Sc., 87.
4. Hom., 113.
5. Sc., 447.
6. Sc., 448.
7. Liber., 26.
8. Sc., 482.
9. Liber., 271.
10. Liber., 236.
11. Sc., 60.
12. Lett. I, 72.
13. Bk., 198.
14. Lett. III, 42.
15. Lett. III, 168.
16. Liber., 205.
17. Lett. I, 199.
18. Lett. III, 39.
19. Lett. III, 149.
20. Liber., 247.
21. Lett. III, 36.
22. Sc., 60.
23. Lett. III, 75.
24. Lett. III, 44.
25. Lett. I, 85–86.
26. Lett. II, 23.
27. Hom., 98.
28. Bk., 435.
29. Liber., 21.

30. Sc., 157.
31. Hom., 183.
32. Lett. I, 88.
33. Lett. II, 14.
34. Lett. I, 124.
35. Sc., 60.
36. Lett. III, 27.
37. Lett. II, 14.
38. Hom., 182.
39. Sc., 174.
40. Bk., 365.
41. Apostolic Letter.
42. Sc., 61.
43. Apostolic Letter.
44. Liber., 290.
45. Sc., 150.
46. Bk., 385.
47. Liber., 21.
48. Sc., 234.
49. Lett. I, 199.
50. Sc., 121.
51. Sc., 121.
52. Sc., 122.
53. Sc., 428.
54. Liber., 247.
55. Lett. III, 124.
56. Hom., 197.
57. Lett. III, 117.
58. Lett. I, 146.
59. Lett. II, 71.
60. Lett. I, 42.
61. Lett. I, 119.
62. Lett. I, 199.
63. Lett. I, 48.
64. Liber., 22.
65. Lett. I, 107.

66. Sc., 489.
67. Liber., 143.
68. Liber., 243.
69. Lett. II, 192.
70. Liber., 41.
71. Bk., 318.
72. Hom., 153.
73. Sc., 69.
74. Lett. II, 67.
75. Bk., 341–342.
76. Liber., 195.
77. Lett. III, 151.
78. Sc., 391.
79. Sc., 384.
80. Sc., 119.
81. Bk., 58.
82. Sc., 428.
83. Liber., 27.
84. Lett. I, 47.
85. Sc., 429.
86. Sc., 220.
87. Lett. I, 200.
88. Bk., 37.
89. Sc., 430.
90. Sc., 477.
91. Lett. II, 143.
92. Lett. III, 27.
93. Lett. III, 51.
94. Liber., 82.
95. Sc., 488.
96. Bk., 114.
97. Lett. I, 43.
98. Sc., 439.
99. Bk., 173.
100. Lett. III, 27.
101. Lett. II, 196.

102. Lett. III, 182.
103. Sc., 474.
104. Lett. III, 153.
105. Lett. III, 117.
106. Lett. III, 152.
107. Bk., 389.
108. Sc., 220.
109. Liber., 27.
110. Hom., 175.
111. Hom., 52.
112. Liber., 231.
113. Sc., 68.
114. Bk., 320.
115. Sc., 432.
116. Symph., 149.
117. Lett. III, 131.
118. Bk., 56.
119. Symph., 141.
120. Sc., 161.
121. Bk., 460.
122. Sc., 499.
123. Lett. III, 123.
124. Lett. III, 141.
125. Lett. III, 140.
126. Lett. III, 142.
127. Lett. II, 23.
128. Lett. II, 195.
129. Lett. II, 100.
130. Sc., 311.
131. Sc., 311.
132. Lett. III, 44.
133. Liber., 283.
134. Bk., 308.
135. Lett. I, 72.
136. Sc., 174.
137. Soln., 54.

138. Sc., 481.
139. Sc., 190.
140. Liber., 136.
141. Lett. I, 95.
142. Lett. I, 111.
143. Bk., 29.
144. Liber., 235.
145. Bk., 389.
146. Lett. III, 186.
147. Bk., 198.
148. Lett. II, 23.
149. Lett. I, 183.
150. Sc., 181.
151. Sc., 60.
152. Lett. II, 23.
153. Lett. II, 23–24.
154. Liber., 285.
155. Lett. III, 56.
156. Bk., 445.
157. Lett. III, 172–73.
158. Sc., 174.
159. Liber., 205.
160. Lett. II, 24.
161. Bk., 284.
162. Sc., 94.
163. Lett. II, 24.
164. Lett. I, 97.
165. Sc., 169.
166. Lett. II, 23.
167. Lett. III, 51.
168. Lett. II, 16.
169. Lett. II, 75.
170. Bk., 435.
171. Bk., 282.
172. Lett. II, 23.
173. Lett. III, 18.

174. Liber., 95.
175. Bk., 102.
176. Lett. I, 72.
177. Lett. I, 28.
178. Lett. I, 27.
179. Liber., 290.
180. Sc., 434.
181. Sc., 163.
182. Lett. I, 183.
183. Lett. III, 109.
184. Lett. III, 149.
185. Sc., 150.
186. Liber., 88.
187. Lett. I, 116.
188. Sc., 59.
189. Symph., 147.
190. Sc., 429–30.
191. Lett. I, 146.
192. Sc., 60.
193. Symph., 263.
194. Liber., 275.
195. Symph., 99.
196. Symph., 149.
197. Sc., 479.
198. Hom., 82.
199. Lett. III, 36.
200. Lett. III, 161.
201. Lett. III, 152.
202. Lett. III, 44.
203. Lett. III, 24.
204. Soln., 63.
205. Hom., 172.
206. Liber., 26.
207. Lett. II, 192.
208. Sc., 299.
209. Liber., 27.

210. Liber., 130.
211. Sc., 60.
212. Lett. III, 63.
213. Bk., 423.
214. I recommend *The Collected Works of St. Teresa of Avila, Vol. I, The Book of Her Life, Spiritual Testimonies, Soliloquies*, trans. Kieran Kavanaugh and Otilio Rodriguez (Washington, D C: ICS Publications, 1987).
215. Carol Flinders, *Enduring Grace: Living Portraits of Seven Women Mystics* (San Francisco: HarperSanFrancisco, 1993).
216. Symph., 191.
217. Liber., 288.
218. Lett. III, 169.
219. Lett. II, 16.
220. Sc., 59–60.
221. Lett. I, 76.
222. Bk., 399.
223. Liber., 290.
224. Liber., 19.
225. Bk., 318.
226. Lett. III, 77.
227. Sc., 439.
228. Sc., 438.
229. Lett. III, 150.
230. Hom., 48.
231. Lett. III, 150.
232. Lett. II, 23.
233. Bk., 423.
234. Lett. I, 200.
235. Bk., 122.
236. Lett. III, 58.
237. Lett. II, 143.
238. Lett. I, 27.
239. Sc., 68.
240. Liber., 21.
241. Bk., 389.
242. Bk., 376.

243. Lett. I, 200.
244. Hom., 82.
245. Lett. I, 200.
246. Liber., 288.
247. Lett. I, 27.
248. Lett. II, 49.
249. Lett. II, 49.
250. Lett. III, 109.
251. Lett. II, 22.
252. Lett. III, 181.
253. Symph., 101.
254. Lett. I, 200.
255. Sc., 150.
256. Bk., 34.
257. Sc., 110.
258. Sc., 80.
259. Lett. III, 149.
260. Sc., 61.
261. Lett. I, 183.
262. Bk., 477.
263. Liber., 37.
264. Sc., 244.
265. Sc., 60.
266. Liber., 271.
267. Lett. I, 97.
268. Lett. I, 199.
269. Liber., 288.
270. Liber., 125.
271. Lett. II, 22.
272. Lett. II, 24.
273. Bk., 434.
274. Soln., 71.
275. Lett. I, 200.
276. Liber., 88.
277. Sc., 430.
278. Hom., 184.

279. Lett. III, 126.
280. Liber., 129.
281. Hom., 171.
282. Liber., 271.
283. Lett. III, 146.
284. Sc., 126.
285. Bk., 250.
286. Sc., 438.
287. Sc., 438.
288. Lett. III, 36.
289. Hom., 133.
290. Lett. I, 199.
291. Lett. III, 93.
292. Lett. II, 24.
293. Liber., 236.
294. Liber., 225.
295. Lett. I, 146.
296. Lett. I, 200.
297. Lett. III, 168.
298. Hom., 196–97.
299. Liber., 135.
300. Liber., 251.
301. Bk., 37–38.
302. Sc., 116.
303. Liber., 235–36.
304. Sc., 503.
305. Sc., 481.
306. Bk., 365.
307. Bk., 385.
308. Lett. II, 70.
309. Lett. I, 86.
310. Sc., 126.
311. Lett. II, 22.
312. Liber., 225.
313. Bk., 78.
314. Sc., 427.

315. Sc., 412.
316. Liber., 223
317. Bk., 391.
318. Sc., 475.
319. Sc., 439.
320. Lett. II, 175.
321. Sc., 479.
322. Bk., 314.
323. Liber., 193.
324. Sc., 115.
325. Sc., 352.
326. Hom., 184.
327. Bk., 374.
328. Liber., 204.
329. Liber., 205.
330. Lett. I, 107.
331. Bk., 37.
332. Lett. I, 122.
333. Sc., 169.
334. Lett. II, 143.
335. Sc., 59–60.
336. Sc., 60.
337. Lett. I, 200.
338. Lett. I, 27.
339. Lett. I, 104.
340. Sc., 60.
341. Lett. I, 27–28.
342. Lett. I, 31.
343. Lett. I, 135.
344. Hom., 48.
345. Bk., 421–422.
346. Hom., 153.
347. Sc., 489.
348. Lett. II, 23.
349. Lett. I, 146.
350. Sc., 488.

351. Liber., 27.
352. Liber., 247.
353. Lett. III, 146.
354. Sc., 117.
355. Lett. I, 63.
356. Lett. III, 44.
357. Lett. III, 36.
358. Sc., 436.
359. Sc., 60.
360. Lett. III, 185.
361. Lett. III, 77.
362. Bk., 29–30.
363. Bk., 425.
364. Bk., 34.
365. Bk., 423.
366. Lett. I, 76.
367. Sc., 60.
368. Sc., 60.
369. Lett. I, 116.
370. Sc., 126.
371. Liber., 202.
372. Lett. I, 124.
373. Sc., 60.
374. Sc., 61.
375. Sc., 150.
376. Sc., 59.
377. Sc., 59.
378. Sc., 59.
379. Lett. II, 181.
380. Lett. II, 181.
381. Lett. III, 70–71.
382. Liber., 10.
383. Lett. II, 21.
384. Bk., 233.
385. Lett. III, 168.
386. Sc., 453.

387. Lett. III, 189.
388. Liber., 19.
389. Bk., 34–35.
390. Sc., 94.
391. Lett. I, 195.
392. Lett. II, 196.
393. Lett. III, 27.
394. Sc., 126.
395. Lett. III, 186.
396. Hom., 196–97.
397. Lett. I, 88.
398. Lett. III, 49.
399. Liber., 10.
400. Liber., 9.
401. Bk., 29.
402. Lett. II, 23.
403. Liber., 20.
404. Bk., 391.
405. Hom., 184.
406. Lett. III, 9.
407. Liber., 231.
408. Hom., 83.
409. Hom., 153.
410. Liber., 27.
411. Lett. I, 86.
412. Lett. I, 94.
413. Lett. II, 110.
414. Lett. II, 41.
415. Lett. II, 196.
416. Lett. II, 192.
417. Lett. II, 41.
418. Lett. III, 44.
419. Lett. II, 156.
420. Lett. II, 194.
421. Symph., 111.
422. Symph., 113; 115; 117; 119.

423. Symph., 119; 121.

424. Bk., 285.

14. Deep Healing

1. Lett. III, 36.
2. Liber., 95.
3. Sc., 417.
4. Liber., 95.
5. Liber., 233.
6. Liber., 23.
7. Bk., 102.
8. Bk., 178.
9. Sc., 124.
10. Sc., 90.
11. Sc., 438.
12. Bk., 178.
13. Bk., 176.
14. Bk., 170.
15. Lett. I, 199.
16. Hom., 92.
17. Sc., 535.
18. Lett. I, 43.
19. Hom., 202.
20. Lett. II, 67.
21. Lett. I, 48.
22. Bk., 145.
23. Sc., 436.
24. Lett. I, 43.
25. Lett. II, 171.
26. Liber., 25.
27. Lett. II, 192.
28. Liber., 202.
29. Hom., 54.
30. Sc., 416.
31. Sc., 436.
32. Liber., 23.

Saint Hildegard

33. Sc., 447.
34. Sc., 507.
35. Hom., 66.
36. Liber., 101.
37. Lett. I, 184.
38. Sc., 335.
39. Sc., 98.
40. Hom., 144.
41. Liber., 24.
42. Liber., 26.
43. Sc., 416.
44. Sc., 120.
45. Liber., 236.
46. Liber., 231.
47. Hom., 133.
48. Hom., 142.
49. Lett. III, 203.
50. Liber., 94.
51. Liber., 180–81.
52. Lett. III, 62.
53. Sc., 416.
54. Sc., 416.
55. Garthwaite, Sue, and Susan Bowers, "Post-traumatic Stress Disorder and Spiritual Direction: Examples and Stages," *Presence*, 16, no. 4 (December 2010): 6–13. See also Letters to the Editor, *Presence*, 17, no. 2 (June 2011): 58–59. Hereafter cited as PTSD.
56. Lett. III, 194.
57. Lett. II, 12.
58. Sc., 119.
59. Liber., 136.
60. Lett. III, 43.
61. Sc., 486.
62. Liber., 55.
63. Lett. III, 170.
64. Lett. I, 160.
65. Hom., 150.

66. Hom., 150.
67. Hom., 151.
68. Hom., 151.
69. Hom., 152.
70. Lett. II, 141.
71. Lett. III, 55.
72. Hom., 48.
73. Soln., 48.
74. Lett. III, 172–73.
75. Lett. I, 122.
76. Lett. I, 197.
77. Sc., 427.
78. Hom., 31.
79. Hom., 34.
80. Lett. III, 204.
81. Lett. II, 16.
82. Symph., 141.
83. Lett. II, 180.
84. Lett. I, 120.
85. Lett. I, 196.
86. Lett. II, 71.
87. Lett. III, 180.
88. Bk., 411.
89. Liber., 102.
90. Sc., 466.
91. Sc., 439.
92. Sc., 256.
93. Bk., 36.
94. Sc., 251.
95. Lett. III, 100.
96. Sc., 442.
97. Lett. II, 117.
98. Lett. II, 117.
99. Sc., 407.
100. Sc., 440.
101. Sc., 105.

102. Sc., 163.
103. Liber., 243.
104. Hom., 129.
105. Bk., 444.
106. Lett. I, 119.
107. Soln., 45.
108. Lett. II, 191.
109. Lett. III, 90.
110. Sc., 162.
111. Bk., 477–478.
112. Bk., 30.
113. Liber., 100.
114. Bk., 250.
115. Liber., 253.
116. Bk., 241.
117. Sc., 115.
118. Sc., 488.
119. Sc., 345.
120. Lett. III, 153.
121. Hom., 64.
122. Bk., 478.
123. Hom., 114–15.
124. Liber., 156.
125. Liber., 154.
126. Liber., 180.
127. Lett. III, 136.
128. Liber., 25.
129. Liber., 15.
130. Lett. III, 106.
131. Liber., 50.
132. Sc., 109.
133. Lett. II, 7.
134. Liber., 194.
135. Sc., 460.
136. Bk., 247.
137. Lett. I, 199.

138. Sc., 251.
139. Sc., 478.
140. Lett. I, 193.
141. Symph., 117.
142. Sc., 233.
143. Lett. III, 144.
144. Lett. III, 161.
145. Sc., 233.
146. Sc., 87.
147. Liber., 290.
148. Sc., 260.
149. Bk., 270.
150. Sc., 448.
151. Bk., 39.
152. Lett. III, 82.
153. Lett. II, 70.
154. Bk., 92.
155. Sc., 443.
156. Lett. II, 194.
157. Lett. III, 107.
158. Bk., 390.
159. Symph., 149.
160. Lett. III, 199.
161. Bk., 170.
162. Bk., 59.
163. PTSD.
164. Liber., 231.
165. Lett. III, 131.
166. Lett. I, 199.
167. Bk., 66.
168. Bk., 411.
169. Liber., 81.
170. Bk., 81.

15. *Union with God*

1.   Lett. III, 156.

2. Lett. II, 162.
3. Lett. III, 147.
4. Bk., 376.
5. Liber., 89.
6. Bk, 250.
7. Sc., 485.
8. Sc., 489.
9. Sc., 368.
10. Sc., 367.
11. Sc., 368.
12. Sc., 68.
13. Sc., 112.
14. Hom., 174.
15. Bk., 36.
16. *Three Lives and a Rule: Hildegard, Disibod, and Rupert along with Hildegard's Explanation of the Rule of St. Benedict,* trans. Priscilla Throop (Charlotte, Vermont: MedievalMS, 2010), 43.
17. Lett. III, 172.
18. Liber., 21.
19. Sc., 447.
20. Sc., 443.
21. Sc., 164.
22. Symph., 185.
23. Symph., 187.
24. Liber., 21.
25. Lett. I, 97.
26. Lett. I, 95.
27. *Saint Mechthild of Magdeburg: The Flowing Light of the Godhead,* trans. Frank Tobin (New York: Paulist Press, 1998), 62.
28. Lett. II, 163.
29. Lett. III, 160.
30. Sc., 475.
31. Sc., 483.
32. Symph., 195.
33. Liber., 30.
34. Lett. III, 155–56.

35. Symph., 189.
36. Lett. III, 63.
37. Sc., 94.
38. Bk., 76.
39. Lett. I, 63.
40. Lett. II, 109.
41. Sc., 150.
42. Symph., 169.
43. Lett. III, 174.
44. Lett. III, 144.
45. Liber., 276.
46. Regina Siegfried and Robert Morneau, eds. *The Selected Poetry of Jessica Powers,* (Kansas City, MO: Sheed and Ward, 1989); Marcianne Kappes, *Track of the Mystic: The Spirituality of Jessica Powers* (Kansas City, MO: Sheed and Ward, 1994).
47. Liber., 276.
48. Liber., 197.
49. Liber., 153.
50. Lett. III, 141.
51. Bk., 481.
52. Bk., 482.

16. Friend of God

1. Lett. II, 77.
2. Sc., 141.
3. Lett. I, 91.
4. Lett. III, 146.
5. Lett. II, 133.
6. Sc., 477.
7. Lett. III, 51.
8. Sc., 476.
9. Liber., 129.
10. Lett. II, 22.
11. Soln., 45.
12. Lett. III, 24.
13. Liber., 233.

14. Hom., 184.
15. Lett. III, 39.
16. Liber., 236.
17. Lett. III, 75.
18. Lett. III, 117.
19. Lett. II, 23.
20. Lett. III, 44.
21. Sc., 60.
22. Lett. II, 23.
23. Bk., 423.
24. Lett. I, 200.
25. Bk., 78.
26. Lett. I, 86.
27. Sc., 479.
28. Hom., 184.
29. Lett. I, 107.
30. Lett. I, 200.
31. Lett. I, 104.
32. Lett. I, 28.
33. Hom., 153.
34. Liber., 27.
35. Lett. I, 63.
36. Lett. III, 36.
37. Bk., 30.
38. Sc., 453.
39. Lett. III, 49.
40. Lett. III, 36.
41. Bk., 170.
42. Lett. II, 67.
43. Bk., 250.
44. Lett. III, 147.
45. Sc., 485.
46. Sc., 367.
47. Sc., 68.
48. Sc., 112.
49. Bk., 36.

50. Lett. II, 163.
51. Symph., 195.
52. Lett. III, 63.
53. Lett. II, 109.
54. Lett. III, 61.
55. Lett. I, 195.
56. Lett. I, 195.
57. Lett. III, 191.
58. Lett. III, 194.
59. Lett. III, 195.
60. Lett. III, 196–97.
61. Lett. III, 162.
62. Lett. III, 202.
63. Lett. III, 203.
64. Lett. III, 204.
65. Bk., 30.
66. Liber., 50.
67. Lett. III, 185.

Afterword

1. Bk., 146.
2. Lett. III, 107.

About the Author

Photo credit: LifeTouch

SUSAN GARTHWAITE is a spiritual director, spiritual writer, prayer group leader, and retreat facilitator in the Chicago area. For many years, she was a medical physiologist and project team leader working on new medicines for cardiovascular disease. Besides her numerous scientific papers, she has published on spiritual direction in *Presence* and on spirituality, especially the wisdom of women mystics, in *Spiritual Life*.